"THE KING"

THE
MARVELLOUS
COUNTRY.

THE ANCIENT CIBOLA.

THE MARVELLOUS COUNTRY,

OR,

THREE YEARS IN ARIZONA AND NEW MEXICO.

CONTAINING

AN AUTHENTIC HISTORY OF THIS WONDERFUL COUNTRY AND ITS ANCIENT CIVILIZATION, WITH A FULL DESCRIPTION OF ITS IMMENSE MINERAL WEALTH, ITS REMARKABLE URBAN ANTIQUITIES AND MAGNIFICENT MOUNTAIN SCENERY, TOGETHER WITH A FULL AND COMPLETE HISTORY OF THE APACHE TRIBE OF INDIANS;

THE WHOLE INTERSPERSED WITH

STRANGE EVENTS AND STARTLING ADVENTURES.

BY

SAMUEL WOODWORTH COZZENS.

Illustrated by more than One Hundred Engravings.

BOSTON:

LEE AND SHEPARD.

LONDON: SAMPSON LOW, MARSTON, LOW & SEARLE.

PARIS: GARNIER FRÈRES.

TO THE

PIONEERS OF ARIZONA,

AND ESPECIALLY

TO THOSE SONS OF NEW ENGLAND WHO HAVE SOUGHT, AND MAY SEEK, HOMES

BENEATH HER SUNNY SKIES,

THIS VOLUME IS RESPECTFULLY INSCRIBED BY

THE AUTHOR.

PREFACE.

This book will acquaint the reader with the strange and wonderful history of a most marvellous portion of our own country.

It is compiled from the journal of a traveller, and is without pretension to especial literary merit; but it is offered to the public with the belief that he who reads its pages will find many facts that are new to him, so interspersed with incident of travel and adventure that its perusal will prove both entertaining and instructive.

THE AUTHOR.

LIST OF ILLUSTRATIONS.

CONTENTS.

CHAPTER I.

CHAPTER II.

CHAPTER III.

CHAPTER IV.

CHAPTER V.

CHAPTER VI.

CHAPTER VII.

CHAPTER VIII.

CHAPTER IX.

CHAPTER X.

CHAPTER XI.

CHAPTER XII.

CHAPTER XIII.

CHAPTER XIV.

CHAPTER XV.

CHAPTER XVI.

CHAPTER XVII.

CHAPTER XVIII.

CHAPTER XIX.

CHAPTER XX.

CHAPTER XXI.

CHAPTER XXII.

CHAPTER XXIII.

CHAPTER XXIV.

CHAPTER XXV.

CHAPTER XXVI.

CHAPTER XXVII.

CHAPTER XXVIII.

CHAPTER XXIX.

CHAPTER XXX.

CHAPTER XXXI.

CHAPTER I.

FOURTEEN HUNDRED NINETY-TWO gave to the world the startling announcement that a new world had been discovered; since which time, this later revelation of God to man has unceasingly developed to the inquirer new marvels of beauty, new forms of grandeur, new mines of wealth; and of no section of our vast dominion can this be more truly said, than of the Territory of Arizona.

It is a well-known fact that when, twenty-two years later, Cortez achieved the conquest of Mexico, he found the Aztecs in possession of immense quantities of gold, silver, and precious stones. So wonderful was this amount of treasure, that the Spaniards fully believed they had at last discovered the "El Dorado" of their dreams, and every inducement was offered to Montezuma and his *caciques* to cause them to disclose the secret source from whence they derived so much of their wealth. The most brilliant promises, however, availed them nothing. Montezuma's answer was ever the same, "From the Northwest." Actuated by the spirit of daring, which had manifested itself in so many different ways, Cortez's next movement was a bold one indeed. He conceived a plan to obtain by stratagem the knowledge which he had failed to gain by fairer means. Inducing the Emperor to visit him in the old palace of Azayacatl—the former residence of Montezuma's father, which had been assigned to the Spaniards as barracks,—he seized and placed him in irons, detaining him in prison for nearly six months. But even this audacious act failed of its purpose; for to the oft-repeated inquiry, the answer was still the same, "From the Northwest," with only the additional information, that the treasure came from a country known as Cibola, far beyond the boundaries of Montezuma's empire. Neither promises nor threats could induce him to reveal more than this, and Cortez was at last reluctantly obliged to accept these statements as truths.

The Spanish Conqueror now busied himself in fitting out an expedition to visit this land of Cibola; and though he could ill afford to spare a man, yet twenty of the most trustworthy of his little band were selected to start upon the voyage of discovery, under the leadership of one Francisco de Lujo, accompanied by nearly a thousand Tlascalan Indians, whom he had secured as allies. This expedition, like the two which succeeded it, never returned, and their ultimate end is one of the many questions concerning the history of the Conquerors, which time has never solved.

The most reliable information to be obtained demonstrates pretty accurately that the present Territory of Arizona covered a large portion of the country then known as the kingdom of Cibola, which extended south far enough to include the Mexican States of Chihuahua and Sonora of the present day; and which was, in truth, the land from which came by far the greater portion of Montezuma's coveted wealth.

Of the races that originally peopled Mexico, we have no written history. We know that the Toltecs were succeeded, somewhere about 1070, by the Chichimecas, who in their turn were succeeded by the Mexicans, or Aztecs, about the year 1170.

The only information to be obtained concerning these remarkable nations, is to be found in the traditionary legends of their descendants; and from them we know that as early as 1325, the Aztecs founded upon the shores of Lake Tezcuco, the city of Tenochtitlan, now known as the city of Mexico.

These facts are found recorded in a copy of the *Cronica de la Neuva España*, published at Medina, in Spain, as early as 1553, and written by one Francisco Lopez de Gomara, who claimed to give an authentic history of the Aztec race, from the founding of the city of Mexico up to that time.

A few years later, one Bernal Diaz, a licentiate of the Cortez expedition, and its chief and only reliable historian, produced a volume covering the same ground gone over by Gomara. From these two authors we derive most of the knowledge we have concerning this wonderful nation, and its remarkable civilization.

It was through the Territory of Arizona that Marco de Niza made his explorations as early as 1535; and it was to ascertain the truth of the wonderful stories told by Niza concerning the wealth of the country, and its marvellous beauties, that Coronado's expedition was organized in 1540. It was not, however, until 1658, that any other expedition was organized of which we have any authentic account. There are now in the monastery of Dolores, in Zacatecas, old records and parchments, which show that in that year an old Jesuit priest, by name Eusebius Francis Kino, inspired solely by religious motives, set out, determined to visit and explore, in the name of the church, the country which had for so many years poured into the coffers of the Spaniards so much of its native wealth. Single and alone this brave old padre started forth from the mission Dolores to go, he knew not whither,— the cross his only protection, the wilderness through which he must pass his only purveyor. Persevering in the face of the most trying difficulties, he succeeded in reaching a river,— supposed to be the Santa Cruz, in what is now the province of Sonora. He followed the course of this river until he reached its junction with the Gila. He then descended the Gila, examining the country as well as he could on his way. Crossing the Gila near its mouth, he retraced his steps, and ascended the river on the north bank, passing through a country the most wonderful ever seen by the eye of man.

He found it inhabited by a people who were kind, generous, and hospitable in the extreme, the better class living in houses built of adobes, while the more common people built their houses of sticks set in the ground, and bound together at the top by ropes made from the fibrous leaf of the maguey, and thatched with bundles of long grass.

These houses, he declares, were well-constructed and comfortable. Their towns and villages he describes as situated upon the banks of the streams, and generally built upon mesas, and well adapted for defence. He represents the population as vast, the settled portion of the country extending from river to river; the inhabitants frugal, industrious and contented. They manufactured a kind of cotton cloth from the leaf of the maguey, which grew in great profusion all over the country. He found them very expert in making the most beautiful feather-work, which they colored with dyes, both mineral and vegetable, manufactured by themselves. They were also well versed in the art of picture-writing, which they practised to a great degree, upon the walls of their dwellings—as also upon the walls of their *estufas*, or public buildings, which were very smooth and well-finished, where a kind of record was kept of the remarkable events in their history.

They used a kind of paper made of the cotton cloth above-mentioned, prepared with a coating of gum; they also possessed nicely-dressed skins, or kind of Egyptian papyrus.

He found among them many beautiful specimens of pottery ware, as well as utensils and vessels made of gold and silver, of which they had great store. He says some of the articles manufactured were of fine design and elegant workmanship, made with tools fashioned from copper and tin amalgamated, which ores were found in great abundance in the surrounding mountains. They irrigated their ground,* and raised corn, beans, and cacao, from the berry of which they made a delicious beverage, called chocotatl. They also extracted from the stalk of the corn a saccharine matter, from which they manufactured a very good sugar. He tells of a kind of liquor made from the fermented juice of the maguey, or Mexican aloe, which was most singular in its effects. The uses of this plant were truly wonderful,

* Irrigation is still practised in the Territory.

furnishing the natives with pins, needles, paper, rope, cloth, thatch for their dwellings, meat, and drink.*

Father Kino describes their flocks and herds as immense, although they had no horses or draught cattle, and says they understood mining to some extent,—not mere surface labor, but extracting the ore from veins which they opened in the solid rock, unearthing vast quantities of gold and silver, which they seemed to value only as it contributed to their comfort when made into articles of use or ornament.

Of their religion, he says they worshipped the sun as God; and upon all their altars kept a flame burning, which was never permitted to become extinguished, the simple-hearted people believing that to this fact they were indebted for the comfort and happiness they enjoyed as a nation.

In short, he found them resembling, in personal appearance and general characteristics, the Aztecs described by Gomara and Diaz, only differing from them in their more peaceful pursuits and disinclination for warlike strife. In his travels Father Kino passed to the south of the Fire Mountain,† through a portion of the Black Forest, to the northeast, where, after many weary days of toil and travel, he struck the head waters of the Mimbres. This stream he

* To this day the native Mexicans in Arizona, as well as in Mexico, use this plant for nearly, if not quite, all the productions obtained from it by the Aztecs.

† Supposed to be the San Francisco Mountain.

followed until suddenly its waters were lost in the earth. After describing the astonishment with which he beheld the vast volume of water seemingly disappear before his very eyes, he says, "But I ought not to be astonished at anything I see, for it is a country full of all that is strange and wonderful, possessing more marvels than I could tell of, were I to write for a year."

After spending some months in this portion of the country, and trying in vain to instruct the people in the religion which he preached, he finally determined to retrace his steps. Commencing his weary journey homeward, he again passed through the same country that had so delighted him, only to become more determined than ever to plant the cross there, and teach the inhabitants the doctrines of the Catholic church. After an absence of more than four years, Father Kino found himself once more at the monastery from which he had set forth on his perilous undertaking, firmly resolved to enlist the aid and sympathy of the church to enable him to return, and, in the name of the cross, take possession of the country through which he had passed. This determination necessitated his making a journey to the city of Mexico, where he proposed to lay the matter before the head of the church. Fired with the thought of the beauties of the country, of its immense mineral wealth, of its industrious and peaceful inhabitants, his eloquence soon overcame any feeble opposition that he encountered, and he shortly received the authority necessary to enable him to return, and civilize and Christianize these civilized pagans of the sixteenth century. Unavoidable delays occurred, however, and it was not until seven years later, in 1665, that he finally succeeded in making the necessary and final arrangements to return, and spread the Gospel among the simple-minded natives of Cibola.

Late in the year 1670, he, in company with three other Jesuits, set out upon their mission through the wilderness. Of their long journey, the hardships which they endured, the trials and dangers which they passed through, or the difficulties which they encountered, we have no record; we only know that in the year 1672, they reached the Gila, and there commenced the establishment of a mission among the Yaquis. From this time until 1679, they established no less than five missions among the Yaquis, the Opotos, and the Papagoes, locating them in beautiful valleys, yielding rich treasures of precious stones, while the snow-clad peaks of the surrounding mountains furnished gold, silver, and copper in the greatest abundance.

The natives, simple and industrious as they were, were easily persuaded to labor upon the edifices there erected, and thus aided in forging the chains that afterwards helped so effectually to render them powerless to defend themselves from the attacks of foes beyond their boundaries, but upon whose territory the cupidity of the priests had led them to encroach.

Obedient to the wishes and commands of the Jesuits, the natives were induced to venture upon soil outside of their boundaries, and thus incurred the enmity of a large and powerful tribe of native Indians, who inhabited the country north of, and adjoining, their own.

The adventurous spirit of the Spaniards, as well as their avarice, manifested itself in so many ways, that the Apaches were roused to resistance, as well as to a desire to punish the invaders.

It was not, however, until the year 1680, that the Apaches made any open demonstrations of hostile intentions; but they then attacked the Spanish settlements in such overwhelming numbers, that resistance was useless, and the missionaries were obliged to flee for their lives. Gathering together such spoils as they could take with them, they abandoned their mission settlements, leaving the people to carry out the unequal contest alone, and bear the brunt of the burden which the cowardly Spaniards had, by their culpable avarice, incited. Again and again did they attempt to return, being extremely loth to yield the rich harvest of gold and silver annually received as tribute from the unsuspecting natives, who still remained friendly to, and allies with, the men who had told them of their God, and taught them that they might extinguish the sacred flame that for generations had been kept burning upon their altars, dedicated to the unknown God.

As often as the missionaries returned, and were attacked, the natives rallied to their defence; but the constant war waged by the Apaches soon destroyed many of their finest cities and towns, completely ravaging their most thriving settlements, massacring the people, and thus, ultimately, compelling the Jesuits to abandon their missions, and seek refuge far in the interior of Mexico, while the remnants of a once happy and prosperous people became victims to a horde of blood-thirsty savages, who thus commenced the extirpation of a civilization, the remains of which are to-day a source of wonder and admiration, the like of which may never again be seen on that portion of our continent. To-day Arizona presents a sad spectacle, one that cannot fail to impress the beholder with wonder and regret; for its mute sentinels silently point to a civilization centuries old, which has not even the poor consolation of a history to record its rise and fall.

CHAPTER II.

FROM the time of the abandonment of the Spanish missions in Arizona in 1680, but little attention appears to have been paid to instilling into the minds of the natives any desire to learn more of the mysteries of that religion of which old Father Kino was the true expounder and great practical teacher.

The Spanish government seems to have devoted itself entirely to developing the vast mineral wealth of the country so wonderfully portrayed by Cortez, Diaz, De Cardenas, Niza, Gomara, Juan Matio, and Mangi, who accompanied Father Kino upon his mission in 1670.

However else they may differ, all these writers agree in their statements regarding the almost fabulous mineral wealth of the country, describing its valleys as rich in precious stones, and its mountains as filled with silver, gold, and copper.

Baron Humboldt, Ward the English ambassador, and Wilson of later years, fully corroborate these statements; and their testimony is confirmed by the records of the Spanish crown, which acknowledge the receipt of dues paid on masses of virgin silver, weighing from twenty to as high as two hundred and eighty-four pounds.

If the reader is sufficiently curious to visit the old Custom House at Guaymas, in Sonora, these statements can be substantiated by reference to the records found there. Among the archives therein contained is rather a remarkable one, establishing the fact that, in 1683, the King's attorney brought suit to recover from the proprietor of the Real del Carmen mine, one Don Roderigo Gandera, a mass of virgin silver, taken by him from his mine, weighing twenty-eight hundred pounds, which the officer claimed as belonging to the King, because it was a curiosity; and all curiosities taken from the soil, of whatever kind or nature, belonged to His Most Gracious Majesty.

We are quite sure that the reader will agree with us in considering such a mass of virgin silver as a curiosity indeed, but no greater one, perhaps, than the doctrine laid down by the King's most eminent counsel in the case.

This was, without doubt, the largest mass of virgin silver

ever found in the world, and its actual existence seems to admit of no question; for so well-authenticated is its history, that the King himself gave to the country producing it the name of Arizuma, or silver-bearing, from which the Territory has derived its present name — Arizona.

Humboldt says that, "Up to the beginning of the present century, the quantity of silver taken from the American mines has exceeded that of gold in the ratio of forty-six to one." *

Other and more modern writers, in commenting upon the vast quantity of treasure taken from these mines with the rude implements of those early days, and the crude manner then in vogue of assaying the ore, declare that fully one half was lost or wasted in getting at the results there obtained,— statements that are verified by the richness of the refuse slag left by the miners, thousands of tons of which to-day are to be seen near all the old mines worked by the Spaniards. Notwithstanding all these obstacles, we are told that up to the beginning of the present century, more than twelve million ounces had been paid as tribute to Spain, the tribute being established at one *real* † in eight — no inconsiderable amount, if we calculate the loss, waste, and stealings — for the Spaniards are adepts in this latter accomplishment even to the present day — that necessarily followed the honest production of this amount of revenue to His Most

* Political Essays of New Spain, Vol. 3.

† 12½ cents.

Gracious Majesty, the King. One can scarcely conceive the amount of treasure these mines have yielded; and when we reflect that the value of the *peso d'oro*, or ounce of silver, in those days, was equal to eleven dollars and sixty-seven cents, the yield is simply enormous.

Certain it is that these mines have always been, and still are, the richest in the known world; they lack but one thing to make them the most valuable, and that is, protection to the miner. Do you ask me why, if these assertions are true, the Territory of Arizona is so little known? Why her mining wealth is, as yet, undeveloped by the present age? Let me tell you. The mines are mostly situated in the western and northern portions of the Territory, in the midst of the Apache country,— a country inhabited by the most cruel and barbarous race of Indians living on the American continent, and who to-day bear the same distinguishing traits which characterized them in the days of brave old Father Kino, more than two centuries ago.

Let us leave the subject of the silver mines, however, to be further discussed, with that of the Apache tribes, in other chapters; and I will ask the reader to accompany me for a few moments, and glance at the geographical position of Arizona, as located on the map.

We see at once its complete isolation from all the civilized possessions of "Uncle Sam." With no port of entry, nor communication with the Gulf of California; separated from the State of California by a desert, across which it requires a man of stout heart to venture, and then only when provided with a numerous escort, and no niggardly amount of ammunition and provisions; surrounded by ranges of almost impassable mountains; twelve hundred miles from Lavaca, the nearest seaport in Texas, six hundred of which are through a country almost destitute of water, and inhabited by a race of Indians second only to the Apaches in barbarity and cruelty.

Is it any wonder that Arizona, rich though it is in its mineral wealth, with its fertile valleys untilled, its uplands shorn of their flocks and herds, its settlers' homes ravished and desolated by bands of marauding savages, should fail to attract by its beauties, what it embraces but to destroy? That its mines are less known than those of Washoe, Idaho, Nevada, or Colorado?

Remember, too, that Arizona never yet possessed a population of more than two thousand Americans, and those the worst class of gamblers, renegades, and cut-throats that could, by any possibility, be gathered together from the four quarters of the globe, a very large portion of whom sought a home in Arizona, only when driven by the Vigilance Committees of Texas and California, to find some country where law was unknown, and justice recognized only so far as it suited the particular ideas of the party administering it, and who, under its sacred guise, assumed the right to gratify his worst passions, answerable only to the stronger, or most dexterous in the use of the bowie-knife, or pistol.

Do not these facts answer, in some measure, at least, the questions of the reader? We trust so, although we say, in truth, that the half has not been told.

If you will accompany us in our travels through the Territory, visit the ruins of its vast cities and towns centuries old, descend with us into its deep mines, admire its wonderful scenery, stand upon the brink of its vast cañons, gaze out upon its mighty rivers, enjoy the quiet of a camp in its beautiful valleys, or share the perils of an Apache fight, we shall soon be able to convince you that Arizona is the most marvellous portion of this wonderful country — America.

CHAPTER III.

AT the time when the western boundary of the southern portion of our Republic was declared by the treaty of Guadalupe Hidalgo, to be the Rio Grande, there lay south of the Territory of New Mexico, and west of that part of Texas known as the "Pan Handle," extending through to the Pacific coast, a strip of what was supposed to be an arid, worthless country, nearly, if not quite, destitute of water, intersected by a number of ranges of mountains and vast deserts, inhabited chiefly by Indians, and utterly useless for any practical purpose that could be imagined.

This tract of country was about four hundred and sixty miles in length, by one hundred and thirty in its widest part, and contained about forty thousand square miles, forming, at that time, a portion of the State of Sonora.

It was acquired by purchase from the Mexican government in 1853, and was then known as the "Gadsden Purchase," for which the United States paid the sum of ten million dollars.

The commissioners who made the treaty were greatly surprised and perplexed at the manifest reluctance of Mexico to part with this strip of apparently worthless land; and those few Americans who took any interest in the acts of the commissioners, were equally perplexed to know what the United States proposed to do with the purchase.

Not one of our people then realized or imagined that by this purchase the United States had acquired a large portion of the identical country for which Cortez imperilled the possession of an empire; for which Coronado's expedition, under the direction of the viceroy Mendoza, was fitted out; for which De Soto so long sought, but never found; the land of which Spanish poets had for centuries sung, and for which kings had so long sighed; the country that for three hundred years had yielded by far the greater portion of the immense treasury that filled the coffers of Spain.

The territory was but sparsely inhabited at the time of the purchase, there being only about sixty families in the celebrated "Mesilla Valley," who had settled there on the first of March, 1850, with Don Raphael Ruelas as their leader, under the auspices of the "Chihuahua Colonization

Society," of which Rt. Rev. Ramon Ortiz was commissioner, and a small Sonoranian settlement around the old Mexican fort of Tucson, near the centre of the purchase.

There were, also, some thirty Americans in the country, who had gone there to "spekelate" in "head rights" that had been issued by the State of Texas to such persons as had served in her wars.

These head rights were for six hundred and forty acres of land each, and entitled the possessor to select any unoccupied land in the State.

These claimants generally cared little where they located, and in many instances they seemed to regard a "head right" as a sort of nest-egg, locating their mile square of land, and claiming around it as far as the eye could reach in every direction. They frequently entered upon the cultivated lands, that had been in the quiet possession of the descendants of old Spanish families for centuries.

If one of the Mexicans dared to remonstrate in any way for the unwarrantable intrusion, he was answered by the dirk or revolver, an argument that always "settled it." The Mexican invariably "vamosed the ranche," leaving the "spekelator" in undisputed possession. It was the facility with which these "head rights" were located, that induced those Texans, who were found occupying the territory in '53, to "Go West," where they could enjoy the fascinating life of the Mexican frontier.

Here they were free and untrammelled, and away from those laws which, at that time, were rigidly enforced in the interest of those who had families in that State.

In all, there were about one thousand souls inhabiting the purchase, aside from the native Indian tribes.

During the next few years, there was little change in the Territory.

By an act of Congress, in 1854, it was attached to New Mexico, a commissioner appointed to survey the boundary line between Mexico and the United States; and it is from the report of this expedition, as well as from subsequent surveys, that we derive much valuable information concerning the country at that time.

Forty miles west of the Rio Grande, is the Mimbres River, one of those singular streams which are so common in that country. It sinks into the plain in places, reappearing miles below, and then flows on as peacefully as if its mad freaks had never astonished old Father Kino, or travellers of more modern date.

In 1858, the writer, in company with three other gentlemen, determined to visit the copper mines situated on the Rio Mimbres, and known as Santa Rita del Cobre. Procuring a guide, and the necessary mules and attendants, we set forth from the town of Mesilla, one bright morning in June. No lovelier day could have dawned.

Our party numbered seven persons, and, including our

7

pack mules, thirteen animals. Striking on to the high lands northwest from the town, we soon left the beautiful valley of La Mesilla behind us, although the grand and lofty peaks of "Los Organos," lying directly east of Mesilla, remained in sight during the whole day. We passed a few ruined ranches, but saw nothing worthy of note, save here and there a spot, pointed out by our guide, where travellers had been murdered by the Apaches.

Camping for the night near a small aroya, through which ran a little stream, we reached the next day the Mimbres River. Crossing its bed, we commenced the ascent of its west bank, which we followed for about ten miles, when our guide informed us that we were near the "Ojo Caliente," or hot spring. We determined to visit it, and encamp there for the night. It is among the most remarkable springs I have ever seen. It lies in the top of a mound nine hundred and sixty-two feet in circumference at its base, and forty-six feet in height, the whole mound being undoubtedly a deposit made by the water of the spring. We found the surface of the water, about five feet below the top of the mound, very clear and quite hot, showing a temperature of 135° Fahrenheit, while it discharged large quantities of carbonic acid gas. When cooled, it was quite palatable.

About seventy-five feet from the summit of the mound is a small opening, through which the water pours, in a little stream, into a pool at its base, evidently designed for bathing purposes. We tried it, and found, even then, as hot a bath as we cared to take. The medicinal properties of this water are said to be very wonderful; and, judging from cases which have come under our own observation, we think they have not been overrated. In scrofulous and syphilitic cases they are especially efficacious.

Leaving the "Ojo Caliente" early the next morning, we journeyed as far as the "Santa Rita del Cobre," where we arrived about night-fall. These mines are situated in a magnificent valley abounding in the most luxuriant vegetation, and surrounded by lofty mountains, whose peaks are crowned with ice and snow, while the country for leagues around is covered with exceedingly valuable timber. That these mines were worked as early as 1678, is undoubtedly true, although we have no authentic history of them until 1799, in which year they furnished employment for some six hundred persons who came there from Chihuahua, four hundred miles distant. Provisions were dispatched by mule and ox teams to the miners every month, and the wagons were freighted back with ore, which was delivered to the Mexican government at a cost of sixty-five cents per pound, the government extracting from it more than enough gold to pay for the ore, using the copper only for purposes of coinage, it being far superior to any other copper known to them. Masses of virgin copper have been taken from these mines weighing tons; and the ore itself, which is a red oxide, seems inexhaustible.

We spent several days in this vicinity, during which time we visited some remarkable sandstone formations near by. We found about forty columns, worn by the winds and rains into most singular shapes. One of them measured nearly sixty feet in height, and more closely resembled an inverted bottle than anything we could compare it to. At its greatest circumference it measured eighteen feet, while at its base it was scarcely three feet. Some looked like churches, towers, castles, or barracks, and others very like human beings of colossal proportions. So striking were these resemblances, that it was hard to believe the hand of man had nothing to do with their formation.

It was on the return from these mines that our party met with an adventure, which may not prove uninteresting in this connection.

Our attendants, with the pack mules, had gone on early in the morning to select a camping-ground, and give our burdened animals a chance to rest, while, later in the day, our party of three accompanied by the guide, started to overtake them.

As we rode along carelessly, laughing and jesting, I noticed that the mule ridden by Mr. Laws showed unmistakable signs that Indians were near. Calling attention to the fact, it was voted a false alarm, Dr. Steck remarking,

A NATURAL SANDSTONE FORMATION.

jocosely, that savages though they were, still they knew better than to attack their "Great Father," as he was called by nearly all the Indian tribes in the Territory; therefore no further attention was paid to the matter.

We had just entered a small cañon, or pass, through the hills to the prairies beyond. Rocks bare and sterile towered far above us on either side. The only vegetation visible was an occasional cactus, twenty or thirty feet in height, and three or four feet in circumference, fluted with the regularity of a Corinthian column, and covered with beautiful variegated blossoms; or, perchance, high up in a cleft of the rocks, a prickly-pear, with its bright green leaves, and magnificent scarlet flowers, looking like the gift of some good fairy, hung there to relieve the eye by contrast with the sombre background of the rock.

Suddenly the appalling war-whoop of the Apaches sounded on our ears like a death-knell, echoed from side to side by the massive walls. It resembled the incarnate shrieks of ten thousand devils holding high carnival over the agony of some lost soul.

Startled as we were, we yet had presence of mind enough to spur our mules forward towards the mouth of the cañon, which was only a short distance before us. It took but a moment to reach it; and as we escaped from between the gloomy walls out into the beautiful green prairie, we uttered an involuntary shout of triumph; but alas! it came too soon. One of the shower of arrows sent whizzing after us, struck poor Laws in the back, and he fell from his saddle dead, his riderless animal galloping frantically over the plain.

To reach the nearest knoll, out of range of the arrows of the Apaches, was but the work of an instant. Here we halted, determined to sell our lives as dearly as possible.

We waited an hour, revolvers in hand, for the appearance of the Indians, but they did not come. We then cautiously proceeded to remove the dead body of our companion, which still lay where it had fallen; and, taking it on our saddles before us, sadly rode to the highest eminence we could find in the vicinity, and there encamped. When night had veiled the earth in its shadows, by the soft light of the moon we hastily scooped a shallow grave with such implements as were at hand, and deposited within its narrow walls the body of our comrade.

Lest the fresh earth should disclose the location of the grave to those human hyenas, whose rapacity knows no bounds, we coralled our animals above the spot, that their uneasy footsteps through the night might obliterate all traces of our sad labor.

Regretfully we turned away from the lonely resting-place of our friend; and as we wrapped ourselves in our blankets, while Dr. Steck kept guard, I shall never forget the im-

BURIAL OF LAWS.

pression made upon my mind by his repeating, with a beauty and pathos indescribable, these touching lines,—

"No useless coffin enclosed his breast,
Nor in sheet, nor in shroud we wound him,
But he lay like a warrior taking his rest,
With his martial cloak around him."

Three months later I received from a heart-broken mother in Philadelphia, a few lines, acknowledging the receipt of a lock of hair, and some articles we had taken from the body, and thanking us in such language as only a mother could use, for the last sad offices performed towards her first-born and only son. God help her!

There are many mothers in our land, who, like her, mourn for their sons, whose bones lie bleaching on the plains of Arizona, denied even the poor consolation of the thought, that a few handsful of earth hide them from the rapacity of the Apache and the prairie wolf.

CHAPTER IV.

TWO days later, and we again reached the valley of the Mesilla; and here let me give the reader some idea of this really beautiful place and its inhabitants.

This valley is about one hundred miles in length, and from twenty to thirty miles in width, the whole surface being easily irrigated by the waters of the Rio Grande. The principal towns in the valley are Mesilla, Santa Barbara, Las Cruces, and Doña Ana, which together contain a population of about three thousand souls. The real boundary on the eastern side is the Sierra de los Organos, or Organ Mountains, a range running from north to south about one hundred miles in length. These mountains are about three thousand feet in height, and are composed chiefly of a light-gray granite.

They receive their name from the peculiar shape of their pinnacles and sides, which resemble very closely the pipes of an organ. In this range are to be found considerable quantities of live-oak and pine timber. Here, also, is the celebrated silver mine of "Hugh Stevenson," discovered by that gentleman in 1851, and which, since that year, when the Apaches would permit its being worked, has yielded large quantities of silver. The soil of the Mesilla Valley is very fertile, and susceptible of a high state of cultivation. On each side of the Rio Grande are to be found large acequias, or ditches, through which the waters of the river are conducted in such a manner that from them the entire surface of the valley can be irrigated or overflowed, and thus cultivated. Large crops of corn, wheat, rye, and barley are raised, while figs, peaches, pears, apricots, and grapes are produced in great abundance. The grapes are particularly fine, and are called the "El Paso" grape, from which place the vines were brought. They were introduced into El Paso in 1680 by the Jesuits, and came originally from Portugal. About one hundred thousand gallons of wine are made annually in this valley, almost equal in quality to fine port or Burgundy; it will not bear transportation, however.

Notwithstanding the fertility of the soil in this charming valley, the mildness of the climate, and the peculiar adaptation of the land to agricultural purposes, only enough is raised to supply the immediate wants of the people, as its great distance from any market precludes the possibility of exportation.

Could a person familiar with Bible history be suddenly transported and set down in the Mesilla Valley, he would certainly imagine himself among the Children of Israel, so primitive are the habits and customs of the people. They use as a plough a sharpened stick of wood fastened to a beam, which beam is tied to the horns of the cattle by thongs of rawhide, serving the purpose of a yoke. No iron ever enters into the construction of their carts; they are made entirely of wood and rawhide, the wheels being sections of the stump of a tree. It has often occurred to me, when I have heard one of these lumbering old carts creaking along the road, that the genius who invented the steam-whistle must have obtained his first idea from the noise made by their wheels.

The houses are built of sun-dried brick — adobes — or else after the style described by Father Kino, when they are called *jacals*. All the grain is threshed in the field, by driving oxen over it; "nor do they muzzle the ox that treadeth out the corn."

It is rarely that a chair or table is seen in a Mexican house. The people eat, sitting upon the floor, and fingers take the place of knives and forks. Their food generally consists of *tortillas* — unleavened bread, *chilli* — red pepper, *frejolies* — or beans, and garlic.

Tortillas are made of corn, which is first soaked in a weak lye, and then boiled until it is perfectly soft, when it is crushed at a *metatte*, consisting of two flat stones, and afterwards moulded by the hands into a kind of pancake, and baked on a heated iron or stone. It is a very palatable article of food, and is undoubtedly a specimen of the unleavened bread mentioned in Scripture.

Chilli and frejolies are as necessary to a Mexican as is bread tc an American; in fact, they are not unfrequently his diet for months. Meat is rarely eaten by them, and never unless cooked in *chilli colorado*, or garlic.

Give a Mexican a peck of beans and a string of red peppers, and he is thoroughly contented; nor will he work while a particle of either remains.

Having heard much of the ruins of an ancient city lying about one hundred and twenty miles northeast of Mesilla, said to be one of the celebrated "Seven cities of Cibola," I arranged to visit them.

Organizing a party of five, with eight Mexican servants, we started with two ambulances and six pack mules. Our first day's journey brought us to the foot of the Organ Mountains, where we camped for the night in a beautiful grove of live-oak.

The next morning we took an early start, and reached the summit of the pass about noon.

Here we paused for a while to gaze with wonder and admiration upon the vast plain spread out before us.

Far in the distance rose in majesty the lofty peaks of the Sacramento Mountains, near which we expected to find the ruins of Le Gran Quivera. These mountains were also the

LOS ORGANOS MOUNTAINS.

home of the Coytero and Mescallaro Apaches, two of the worst bands in the whole nation. It was with these Indians that Lieutenant Lazelle, of the United States Army, had a desperate fight at Dog Cañon the year before, and the question naturally arose, should we be permitted to quietly pursue our explorations, or should we have trouble with them?

Upon questioning our guide as to the probabilities of an encounter, he shrugged his shoulders, and ominously shaking his head, gave us the usual philosophical reply of the Mexican, "*Quien Sabe?*" or "Who knows?"

Half-way across this vast sandy plain two or three blue specks were visible, which, our guide informed us, were salt lakes; also, that it was from the shores of these lakes that the Spaniards formerly procured their salt, and even the present inhabitants of the Territory used it to a large extent. He said, that in close proximity to these lakes was a very peculiar sandstone formation, well worth seeing; and, as all were but a few miles distant from our direct route, we determined to visit them. Bringing our glasses to bear upon that portion of the plain pointed out by the guide, we saw what seemed to us to be a large city, with its spires and domes and towers glittering in the bright sunlight, and rivalling in splendor even the creations of the genii conjured by "Aladdin's wonderful lamp."

But we must not linger longer admiring the wonderful panorama spread out before us, or we shall fail to reach the wood and water level before night-fall. We therefore descend the mountain, and are once more upon the plain.

Upon reaching a beautiful little stream that comes trickling down the sides of a rocky cañon, we encamp for the night.

Sunrise finds us again on our journey, and after a hard day's jaunt over the same unchangeable plain, night brought us to the first of the lakes whose blue waters had so enchanted us the day previous.

Its shores were white with pure, crystallized salt, and we were told by our guide that *carettas'* full were carried away every year, in its natural state.

The next morning the guide called us to behold the wonderful effect of the rising sun upon the city of enchantment that we had seen from the mountain the day before. As we approached this marvellous architecture of the elements, we could not repress exclamations of wonder and delight. Streets were plainly visible; massive temples with their spires and domes; monuments of every conceivable shape; castles of huge proportions; towers and minarets, all formed of pure white silica, which glittered in the bright sunlight like walls of crystal. It was hard to persuade ourselves that art had had no part in forming these graceful testimonials to the wonders of nature.

"Surely," said Dr. Parker, "this must be a city."

"Yes," replied I, "a city, but not made with hands."

Around the whole was a massive wall ten feet in height, with arched gateways and entrances as perfect as it is possible for the imagination of man to conceive. Entering the confines of this magical spot, we were soon undeceived, for what in the distance our imagination had conceived to be enchanted ground, was, in reality, a mass of white sandstone, worn by the winds and waters into a wonderful similitude of a magnificent city.

Regretfully turning our backs upon this marvel of nature, we resumed our journey, camping at night on the banks of a little mountain stream called the Tularosa, said to abound in trout, and whose waters sunk quietly into the plain about two miles from where it left the rugged side of the mountains.

As we approached the camping-ground, I noticed on a little eminence to the left a herd of antelope feeding. Unstrapping the blanket from my saddle, I handed it, with my rifle, to an attendant; and informing the party that we should have antelope steak for supper, I started after the herd, thinking I could easily kill one with my revolver. As I approached, they trotted leisurely off, I following them, and paying no attention to the course they took, so intent was I on securing some fresh meat for supper. The chase became an exciting one, and before I was aware of it the sun had sunk to his rest, and night was rapidly approaching.

Reluctantly I gave up the chase and turned towards camp, when, to my surprise and mortification, I became convinced that I had no means of ascertaining its direction, — in short, I was lost; and as darkness was already shadowing the earth, there was no alternative but to encamp for the night alone on the prairie.

To unsaddle my mule, picket him, and then examine the condition of my revolver, was but the work of a few minutes. Then, with my saddle for a pillow, I laid myself down upon the grass, with no covering save the starry heavens; and, being quite fatigued with the day's journey, soon dropped into a profound slumber.

I must have been sleeping some hours, when I was suddenly awakened by the snorting of my mule. Apprehensive that all was not right, I immediately arose, and taking my pistol, approached the spot where he was fastened.

I found him with eyes fixed, nostrils distended, forefeet firmly braced, and endeavoring, by every means in his power, to break his lariat, which, fortunately, was made of hair, and successfully resisted his efforts.

The first glance convinced me that Indians were near, for a mule will detect an Indian a long distance off by the smell. After much coaxing, I finally succeeded in quieting him a little, though he still showed unmistakable signs of extreme terror, trembling in every limb like an aspen leaf. I then lay down, and supporting myself upon my elbows, to enable me to bring my eyes on a level with the top of the grass, endeavored to ascertain what it was that had so frightened the animal.

A CITY NOT MADE WITH HANDS.

I lay perfectly still for some time, straining my eyes in the direction I had found my mule looking, buc could discern no cause for alarm. Still, from the continued agitation of the animal, I was convinced that there was reason for apprehension. Not a sound could be heard save the beating of my own heart, and the long, unsteady breathing of the mule.

I remember that the short, quick yelp of a prairie wolf seemed to me to be the most grateful sound to which I had ever listened, so intense was the stillness. Not a breath of air stirred the light tops of the grass.

At last I saw, or fancied I saw, some distance from me, a small bush that I had not noticed before. I tried to remember having seen the bush when I lay down for the night, but all to no purpose. As I gazed, fascinated, as it were, by the appearance of the bush, it suddenly occurred to me that I could see it more distinctly than at first, and congratulating myself on the approaching daylight, was beginning to take courage, when I thought I saw the bush move.

As no air was stirring, this could hardly be; and yet, as I watched it, slowly and surely it came towards the spot where I lay.

Suddenly the thought flashed upon me that immediately after leaving the Organos Mountains we had noticed Indian smoke-signals, and also in the Sacramento Mountains as we approached thom the previous day. In an instant I clearly comprehended my situation,—I was surrounded by Apaches, who had seen me separate from my companions, and had followed me, determined to have my scalp. What should I do?

If I fired my revolver, I should at once disclose my position to my foes; if I lay still, I should certainly be shot or

THE FORTUNATE SHOT.

tomahawked. I already fancied I could feel the sharp flint points of the Apache arrows in my body, and thought if I should be killed in the position in which I was now lying, my friends, should they ever find my body, would have reason to presume that I was trying my best to escape when overtaken.

I rapidly revolved the chances in my mind, all the time conscious that the bush was coming nearer and nearer, and finally determined that I would have one shot, let the consequences be what they might. I waited as long as I dared, and then, placing the barrel of my pistol between the fore and middle fingers of my left hand, to enable me to sight properly, I aimed at the foot of the bush and fired.

A yell, and I saw the bush no longer.

Already, to my excited imagination, a dozen tomahawks were whizzing through the air. The hum of a bug carelessly flying over me was the zip of an arrow. The suspense of the remaining hours until daylight was terrible. One thing alone tended to assure me,— my mule was quietly feeding: this seemed to indicate that there was no longer any immediate danger. Still the thought that Apaches were rarely alone in their raids, kept me in a state of agonizing suspense.

And so the tedious hours wore on, till at last the first gray streak of daylight was just discernible in the east. I immediately saddled my mule, and taking him by the bit with one hand, and carrying my revolver cocked in the other, I slowly started for the bush, which was about fifty feet from the spot where I had lain.

I found a long, snake-like trail, showing that whoever

carried the bush had approached me on his belly, using his elbows with which to propel himself.

Following the trail about eighty yards, I saw in the bottom of a small aroya an Indian, to all appearance asleep. He lay on his side. One half of his face was painted a bright vermilion, the other half daubed with mud, showing him to be in disgrace for some offence with his tribe, the penalty for which he proposed to settle with my scalp and my mule.

I descended into the aroya, and taking his bow and arrows, with his scalp, made for the highest ground in the vicinity, where, after a few minutes' anxious watching, I was rewarded by seeing a "white man's smoke" far away to my left, for which I struck a "bee line."

An hour's smart riding brought me within sight of the camp, from which a party were just starting out for the purpose of helping me bring in the antelope steak I had so generously offered to provide the evening before. A hearty breakfast of bacon and corn bread, with a dish of coffee, in some measure atoned for the loss of the fresh meat; but I then and there declared I never would go marketing again in that country alone. *I haven't killed an antelope since!*

CHAPTER V.

IT was noon the next day before our little party was ready to start on the trail through the Sacramento Mountains. We decided to take the road to Fort Stanton, then located in that range, as being the best point from which to start for the ruins, of which we had heard so much, and that so few Americans had ever visited. A short journey up the beautiful valley of the Tularosa, and Dr. Parker met us with as fine a string of speckled trout as I ever saw caught, even in the streams of New England, or the wilds of Lake Superior. A few miles farther on, and our guide (pointing to an opening high up on the side of the mountain, which was sparsely covered with balsam and fir trees, over which a fire had passed some two or three years before killing the growth of the trees, but leaving them standing) remarked, "Yonder is the hole of a Cinnamon bear."

The information was electrical in its effect, all expressing themselves, as with one accord, eager to share the adventure of a bear-hunt — myself excepted — I having had quite enough of that kind of sport, for the present at least. Still I resolved to stay by and watch the fun, for fun I was sure there would be before Bruin yielded himself captive. Selecting a position some distance from the scene of action, where I could observe the movements of the party, I watched them, rifles in hand, slowly and laboriously ascending the steep side of the mountain, here catching hold of the charred limb of a balsam, which snapped like a pipe-stem at the touch; now balancing themselves on a stone, which failed to give a firm footing, as with difficulty they worked themselves up to the mouth of the cave, where his cinnamon-colored majesty was supposed to hibernate.

The guide, who acted as leader, took a position directly over the mouth of the cave, pointing out to the others the places they were to occupy, with directions that as soon as the bear should emerge from his den, each one should fire, aiming directly behind the shoulder-blade.

When all had announced themselves ready, the guide picked up a handful of large pebbles and commenced dropping them immediately in front of the mouth of the cave.

In a few moments his bearship, evidently annoyed at this unwarrantable intrusion, slowly poked his head out of the cave, and proceeded to take a calm survey,

> "Of such as, wandering near his secret bower,
> Molest his ancient, solitary reign."

Just at this juncture Rogers, who had been stationed the farthest off, fired. The bullet evidently struck the bear in his nose; for, putting his huge paw beside it for an instant, and uttering a terrific growl, he sprang forward in the direction of Dr. Parker.

The doctor, seeing the bear approach, threw down his rifle, and hastily betook himself to a dead fir close by, about as big at its base as his wrist. This he labored as hard to climb as I ever saw a man work in my life. The branches snapped at every touch; but the doctor was so intent on reaching a place of safety, that, as he afterwards remarked, he certainly thought he was making fine progress in ascending one of the giants of the forest.

Before the bear had made many steps towards the scene of the doctor's desperate exertions, two well-directed shots touched him in a vital spot, and, slowly rolling over, he fell on his side — dead. It was now the time to laugh; and as I had been an interested spectator in the affray, I rehearsed the scene as taken by a "special artist on the spot," amid peals of laughter from the rest of the party, who had been too busily engaged at the time to notice the ludicrous appearance of the doctor, and his amusing attempts to reach an ark of safety.

The bear furnished us a fine lot of fresh meat, and many were the sly remarks I was obliged to hear on *my* success as a "marketist." That night we had a delicious meal of bear meat, which we cooked on the end of a stick over the coals. Thus ended *my* first bear-hunt in Arizona.

Starting with the sun the next morning, we travelled all day through rocky cañons and narrow passes, toiling wearily along, till, just as the sun was setting, we reached Fort Stanton, where we received a cordial welcome from Major Ruff, of the Dragoons, who was at that time in command. We spent a couple of days very pleasantly at the Fort, and the major kindly volunteered to send for a friendly Indian, living near, to act as guide to the ruins, situated some fifty miles north of the Fort, an offer of which we gladly availed ourselves.

It was on the 18th of July, 1859, that we started to visit the ruins of Le Gran Quivera. A two days' journey, with no incident worthy of note, brought us to a place on the plain about ten miles distant from the mountain. Here we discovered the remains of a large acequia fully twelve feet in depth, with the usual supply of smaller ones running in all directions, showing that a large quantity of land had at some time been under cultivation. Near here we encamped

THE BEAR-HUNT.

for the night. Noon the next day found us among the ruins of what had once been a city of not less than sixty thousand inhabitants.

The ruins extended for miles in a northerly and southerly direction, and consisted of old adobe houses, some of the walls standing from four to six feet high, others showing a line only a few inches above the earth. We also found the ruins of massive churches. Over the main entrance of two of these were sculptured the coat-of-arms of old Spain, while the walls, still standing, measured sixty feet in height. We found the ruins of what seemed to have been a large cathedral or temple, corresponding in some degree to the ruins of the *Casas Grandes*, found upon the Gila in 1694, as described by Father Kino. Also the ruins of a stone aqueduct, of sufficient size to enable a person to easily pass through it. The stones appeared to be laid in a kind of cement, which had preserved its adhesive qualities wonderfully.

This aqueduct was undoubtedly used for bringing water from the mountains, for we traced it nearly fourteen miles towards a spot in the mountains that gave evidence of having once been a large spring. Near this place we found several old shafts or openings in the side of the mountains, plainly showing that at some early day they had been extensively worked as mines.

Of the town we have no authentic history, save that it

was one of the "Seven cities of Cibola," into which, without doubt, the Spaniards intruded themselves, gradually obtaining control of it through the influence which the Church exercised over the people. There is a tradition among the Indians to the effect that this was once a very large and wealthy Aztec city, with exceedingly rich mines, the product of which was carried twice a year to Montezuma, until the entrance into the city by the Spaniards, when it was shipped direct to old Spain.

At one season — supposed to be about 1680 — when the people were making extraordinary exertions for transporting the precious metals, the Apaches attacked them, whereupon the miners buried their treasure, worth fifty millions, and left the city together. They were all massacred, except two who succeeded in escaping to Mexico, where they gave the particulars of the affair, and solicited aid to return and recover the treasure. But the distance was so great, and the Indians so numerous, no one was found willing to run the risk of so perilous an undertaking. One of the two afterwards went to New Orleans, then under the dominion of old Spain, where he raised five hundred men, and started by way of the Sabine. This expedition was never afterwards heard from.

All attempts to visit these ruins in search of treasure are thwarted by the Apaches, who punish with death any intruders. Dr. Wislizenus, in his "Tour through Northern

Mexico," speaks of the ruins of the aqueduct, the churches, the sculptured coat-of-arms, the pits showing the location of the silver mines, and also relates the tradition of the Indians.

When the city was built, and by whom, are questions that every beholder must ask as he stands among these crumbling monuments of an extinct race. We spent two days among these ruins. We didn't expect to find the treasure, and we were not disappointed.

Notwithstanding our guide informed us that nearly all the warriors of the two bands which inhabit these mountains had gone to the Navajoe country on a stealing expedition, we were uncomfortably reminded by frequent Indian smokes round about us, that there was some life yet left in the vicinity; and on the morning of our departure it was discovered that two of our pack mules and Dr. Parker's horse had been stolen during the night. This evidence of the near proximity with an enemy we had much reason to dread, caused us to make a hurried and early start, regardless of Dr. Parker's urgent entreaties that we should make an effort to recover his horse, which, he assured us, with tears in his eyes, he still owed for!

Even this sad announcement failed to change our determination to go, and go at once; and go we did, in the direction of the Rio Grande, leaving, as we fondly hoped, not the ruins only, but the Indians also, behind us.

Striking a course nearly due west, we started on a trail which our guide thought would bring us to the Rio Grande, somewhere near the mouth of the Rio Puerco. After half a day's travel, our course seemed to lie more to the north; and just at night we came to the banks of a little creek, called by Major Emery, in his report, the Little Bonita.

Here we came upon the remains of a petrified forest, prostrate, and partially buried in a kind of red marl. Hundreds of trees lay here, and had been converted by some chemical process into specimens of variegated jasper. One tree that we saw measured ten feet in diameter, and was over a hundred feet in length. Some looked as if they had been charred by fire; their trunks were of a dark brown color, while the smaller branches and twigs were of a reddish hue. To me there was something impressively wonderful in this stupendous result of old Nature's labors in her secret laboratory. Who should divine the cause? Who tell the history of the prostrate forest? How long has it there existed, and how many more centuries will it lie there undisturbed?

We brought away some beautiful specimens, although, owing to the depredations of our Apache friends, we were somewhat short of means of transportation. We found the waters of the creek delightfully cool and pleasant to the taste; and notwithstanding the suggestion of one of the party, that it might have the same effect upon us that it had evidently had upon the giants of the forest lying around us, we all drank of it freely, and enjoyed its refreshing coolness. Dr. Parker feelingly alluded to the loss of his horse, and the miseries of a pedestrian life through such a rough country, and urged us, in case we should observe any appearance of petrifaction about him, not to leave him by the road-side, for the purpose of petrifying the traveller who came after us, but to give him Christian burial; and that for a head-stone we should use a piece of the rock on which he split, with this inscription thereon: "Horseless and homeless a wanderer passed."

Promising to comply with his desires, a gleam of genuine satisfaction illumined his countenance, and we resumed our journey. The next day we arrived in sight of the cotton-wood trees which line the banks of the Rio Grande; and a pleasant sight it was too, after a hard day's toil over the rough, pebbly soil of the plains, without water or the grateful shade of even a single tree to shield us from the rays of the burning sun. We were glad enough to encamp for the night at a little spot where there was a prospect of our poor animals obtaining a supply of grass.

Before the sun rose the next morning we were on our way to the Rio Grande. We reached it about noon, striking the river at a point near the ruins of Valverde. Here we found encamped a family of Missourians, named Pennington, who were on their way to the Calabasas country. The old man had with him seven daughters, ranging all the way from thirteen to thirty years of age, and was going out to make a home on the Calabasas, where he had a son living. He was a fine, athletic-looking person, and was thoroughly imbued with the idea that he had just as much right to live in this country as the cowardly Apaches.

"And," said the old man, as he straightened himself up, and significantly tapped his rifle, "I'm d—d if I don't do it!"

Some months later, when in Tucson, a woman named Paige was brought into the town, who had been found in the mountains by a party of soldiers under Captain Ewell, since a major-general in the Rebel service. I went to see her at the *fonda*, where she was carried, and such a pitiable sight I hope never to see again. Naturally a good-sized woman, she was now wasted to a mere skeleton. Such a picture of starvation can never be portrayed by language. The glaring, hungry eyes, the sunken temples, the lips drawn so tightly over the jaw that each tooth could be easily counted through them, the arms scarcely larger than a man's thumb, and the continuous cry for food, was a spectacle to fill one with horror. I saw her a few hours later, and to my surprise she recognized me, and spoke of our meeting on the Rio Grande, near Valverde. I then learned that she was one of old Pennington's daughters, and had married a man named Paige, living near Tubac.

It seems that Mrs. Paige was at her father's home, when a party of Indians made their appearance, and seizing Mrs. Paige and two sisters, made off with them to the mountains. On their way thither they encountered Paige and three other Americans, who instantly gave fight, but were finally overcome and massacred by the Indians. Mrs. Paige, who was sick at the time of her capture, was unable to keep up with the party, so they knocked her in the head with a club, and supposing her dead, threw her body over a precipice. When she recovered her consciousness, she found herself lodged in a tree which grew out from the side of the precipice. Disentangling herself from this position, she managed to get down the declivity and away from a trail which she there found. Here she remained for sixteen days, living on such roots and berries as she could find, and this, too, within sight of her father's house.

"It was terrible," she said, "to be dying of hunger and thirst, and too weak to summon aid or to get to it."

She still lives in Arizona, or did, two years later, when I saw her,— a stout, hearty woman. Her sisters were never heard from.

Mrs. Paige's experience is not dissimilar to that of many others in Arizona; and from it we can judge what the frontiermen and their families are often obliged to endure.

Leaving old Pennington and the remnant of his family on the Calabasas, let us return to our camp on the Rio

Grande, where we shall remain only long enough to give our overburdened animals time to recruit before we start down the river. The next day being a fine one, a portion of our party started on foot to visit a celebrated spring, known as the Ojo del Mertu, about five miles distant from our camping-ground; and on their return, more fortunate than I, they succeeded in killing an antelope, a portion of which they brought into camp.

The night passed without incident worthy of note, and the next day found us *en route* for Mesilla. We had hardly been two hours on our journey before we encountered "Jim" Davis. Now "Jim" Davis is a character, even in Arizona,— a small, wiry, hatchet-faced, red-haired Yankee from the State of Maine. "Jim" came to Arizona in '52, and has retained all the shrewdness and smartness that he possessed before he left the pine forests of his native State. Like most Maine men, he possessed the demon "swap" to a great degree. It had grown with his growth and strengthened with his strength, till finally it had earned for him the sobriquet of "The Emigrants' Friend." "Jim" believed in emigration as firmly as the old emigrant commissioners of Castle Garden believed in it when they made their thirty thousand dollar per annum fees. He thought with honest old Horace, that 'twas every man's duty to "Go West," and firmly believed in every man doing his duty. He took good care that no emigrant train should reach Arizona until he had met it, and talked with the "boss"; and if the "boss" had any foot-sore or weary cattle lagging behind, "Jim" immediately became their owner. He has been known to start from home with an old blind horse, a jack-knife, and a smooth quarter, his entire stock in trade, and in

"JIM" DAVIS, "THE EMIGRANTS' FRIEND."

two weeks return with a drove of twenty-five or thirty head of cattle, and likely as not the same horse he rode away, all honestly made by trade with the emigrants. "Jim" would ride until he met a train with three or four foot-sore oxen following it; these he would trade his horse for; then he would stop in his journey long enough to give the cattle a rest, and afterwards trade them for the next ones he met; and so on until he procured a good drove.

But "Jim," seeing we had nothing to trade, pushed on, and with considerable alacrity, when we told him of old Pennington's camp. Two days more brought us to the town of La Mesilla, where for the present, kind reader, I propose to leave you, after asking you to refresh yourself with a delicious draught of El Paso wine, which we will draw from a huge leathern bottle made of an untanned ox-skin, the hair side being, of course, the outside, and which the worthy Don Anastacio Berella, the alcalde of the town, assures us is the only proper way of preserving the flavor of wine and preventing its tasting of the cask. It was this same alcalde whom, a few days after our arrival, we invited to dine with us, and who returned an answer to the effect that "he had plenty to eat at home"; evidently considering our invitation an insinuation that we supposed him to be out of chilli and tortillas. In reply to which Dr. Parker remarked, that " 'twas ever thus" his motives had been impugned by every one, from the time he had attempted to climb a tree to avoid *making* entertainment for a bear, until he had voluntarily *offered* to entertain one.

CHAPTER VI.

THE Apache tribe, which for so many years has been the terror of northern Mexico, and the scourge of the white man in Arizona, is composed of eight bands: The Mescaleros, the Mimbres, the Mogolones, the Chiricahui, the Coyteros, the Pinals, the Cerro-Colorados, and the Tontos. These bands have now no fixed residence, but wander at will over the Territory, making raids into Sonora and Chihuahua, killing men, women, and children, or taking the latter captives; stealing horses, mules, and cattle; destroying *haciendas*, ranches, and villages; then, retreating into the mountain fastnesses, not only defy pursuit, but laugh at the futile efforts made to overtake them.

In character they resemble the prairie wolf,— sneaking, cowardly, and revengeful. They are always ready to assassinate women and children, and then to flee if possible.

Otherwise they fight bravely and desperately. In no portion of our country have the settlers upon the frontier suffered so severely as in Arizona. There is scarcely a mile on any road in the Territory where the traveller is not pointed out some spot which the Apaches have consecrated with the blood of a victim; nor is there a family that has not suffered in some manner from their depredations.

There were formerly three principal war-chiefs of the tribe, under whose directions all hostile parties were marshalled: Mangus Colorado, Cochise, and Delgadito. Of these three, the only one now living, who exercises any control over them, is Cochise, of the Pinal tribe, which a few years ago was the only recognized tribe, but which has since been divided into several bands.

For more than four centuries these pests of the country have scourged northern Mexico and Arizona, and nothing has been sacred from them. Nor can anything ever prosper in a country that they inhabit. They have desolated Sonora and Arizona, which latter place, in 1860, had a population of thirty-four thousand, while in 1870 it had less than ten thousand.

At the time of my residence in the Territory, in '58, '59, and '60, the Apaches were generally regarded as being at peace with the white man; and during these three years there were probably fewer outrages committed than during any one year before or since. An overland mail coach was occasionally attacked or an emigrant party massacred, and all the animals that could be stolen were driven off. Still, these years were regarded as quiet ones. And thus I was enabled to pursue my explorations in the Territory with

COCHISE.

but little annoyance during that time, especially as the since renowned Cochise was persuaded to act as my guide through portions of the Apache country rarely pressed by the foot of a white man. I first met Cochise at the "Apache Pass," a narrow gorge through the Chiricahui Mountains, and through which pass ran the only road connecting the settlements on the Rio Grande with Tucson and Fort Yuma.

It was a beautiful day in June that I first saw him, naked as he came into the world, with the exception of his breech-clout and moccasins. He was a tall, dignified-looking Indian, about forty-seven years of age, with face well daubed with vermilion and ochre. From his nose hung pendent a ring about five inches in circumference, made of heavy brass wire, while three of the same kind dangled from each ear. His body had been thoroughly anointed with some kind of rancid grease, which smelled very offensively. His stiff black hair was pushed back and gathered in a kind of knot on the top of his head, while behind it rested on his shoulders. One or two eagle feathers were fastened to his head in an upright position, and swayed with every breath of wind. As he came near me, he laid his bow and arrow down upon the grass, and extended an exceedingly dirty hand, with finger-nails fully an inch in length, saying, in pretty fair Spanish,—

"Me Cochise, white man's friend. Gim me bacca."

Turning to "Jimmy," my Irish servant, whose experience among the Indians had been very limited, I found him staring at Cochise with amazement depicted on every lineament of his face, and 't was fully three minutes before he recovered himself sufficiently to ask,—

"Bedad! and what kind of a crayther is that, to be shure?"

And when I replied,—

"A live Apache," with a yell and a bound he sprang towards the corral of the overland mail company, and no threats or inducements could bring him forth until Cochise had departed.

I gave Cochise a supply of tobacco and some whiskey, and he disappeared almost as suddenly as he came.

We had drawn our wagons a few rods below the corral, close by a little spring that bubbled out from between the rocks, where we intended to spend the night. No particular guard was kept, as we were so near the protection of the mail company that we apprehended no danger. Yet during the night two of our mules were stolen, and so adroitly, too, that the thieves left no traces behind them. I was strongly inclined to suspect Cochise, though he indignantly denied the charge, asserting that he was a brave, and not given to stealing. Nothing could have exceeded the ludicrous scene that ensued in the morning, when I charged the loss of the mules to Jimmy's carelessness, and announced that I should have to send him out to recover them.

"Howly Mother!" says Jimmy. "And what would they be doin' while I was gettin' 'em back?"

When informed they would probably be taking his scalp, he exclaimed,—

"Och, Captain, dear; shure if I was you I'd lit the mules go. We don't nade 'em at all, at all."

Still I was obdurate, and Jimmy was finally frightened into starting out after them, protesting all the while, however, that "whin he cum back he knew viry will he'd have no head on his shouldthers."

Five minutes later I discovered him lying under one of

JIMMY'S MEETING — "HOWLY MOTHER! IS THAT AN APACHE?"

the wagons; and upon questioning him he informed me that "he wus so sick and intirely unwill, that 'twould be impossible for him to go on the expedition I was afther sinding him on," and no persuasion could induce Jimmy to move for the whole day. Here we were obliged to remain until we could procure mules to take the place of those of which we had been robbed. The fourth day, towards night, three Indians came in, driving four of the sickliest-looking mules it had ever been my lot to see, which they offered us for five *fanagas* of corn each. We purchased them, and some time afterwards learned that they had been stolen from a station of the overland mail company, some hundred miles or more west of Tucson, about five months before.

During the time we were encamped here I had an excellent opportunity to examine and admire the wild and magnificent scenery of the Chiricahui Mountains, and also to become acquainted with the character of Cochise and some of the Apaches, who were spending the summer in this vicinity, as its convenient locality enabled them to attack and rob any weak band of emigrants that might be passing on their way to California.

After the experience of the first night, through the kindness of Major De Rythe, Assistant Superintendent of the overland mail, we were permitted to put our animals in the stone corral of the company, and thus secure them from the visits of our Apache friends.

While here, a man named Frazier, with his family, consisting of his wife and four children, passed through with two two-horse wagons, on their way to San Diego, where they intended to settle. The oldest child was a boy, seventeen or eighteen years of age, smart and energetic; the next a girl, about sixteen, who drove one of the wagons, while the mother drove the other. They expected to reach Tucson in about a week, where they intended to recruit their teams and wait for company, before going on to San Diego. Two days later the conductor on the stage from Tucson reported that just beyond the mouth of the cañon they had found the remnants of two wagons, with the dead and mutilated bodies of Frazier and his son tied to the wheels and partially burned. Everything of value had been carried off, even to the iron about the wagons. The fate of the mother and children was never known.

Major De Rythe sent out the next morning for the remains of the unfortunate men, but no effort was made to capture and punish the murderers or retake the captives. I have no doubt myself but that the same band of Indians who were visiting us each day, smoking our tobacco and drinking our whiskey, were the parties who committed the murder; and yet we were powerless to revenge the injury. This outrage, in some particulars, resembles that of the Oatman family, the facts of which I will give as I learned them from one familiar with the details of the atrocious transaction, merely for the purpose of showing the brutality and diabolical cruelty with which the Apaches always treat those who fall into their clutches.

On the 11th of March, 1851, Mr. Royse Oatman, with

his family, left the Pimo villages, bound for California. His outfit consisted of two yoke of cows and one of oxen, with three wagons. His stock were jaded and worn by the long and tedious journey across the plains, and he had pushed on as far as the Pimo villages, hoping to be able to replenish his exhausted supply of provisions, as well as find company to cross the almost desert country that for two hundred miles lies between the Pimos and Fort Yuma. But it had been a bad year for the Pimos, and they had nothing to spare; indeed, were fighting hard to keep the wolf away from their own doors. With starvation staring him and his family in the face if he remained with the Pimos, he determined to attempt to reach Fort Yuma, where he hoped to find plenty of provisions and an escort. He pushed on, therefore, out into the desert, his family half starved, and his jaded cattle scarcely able to drag the wagons through the deep sand that surrounded them on all sides.

For seven days they toiled on, their only comfort at night the thought that they were a little nearer their goal. After being obliged to unload their wagons at the foot of every little eminence, in order to induce the weary cattle to make the ascent, the afternoon of the eighth day found them at the foot of a rocky bluff. Here unloading the wagons once again, they wearily toiled along, till at last its summit was gained. Halting here, Mr. Oatman gave himself up to the most gloomy forebodings, and the terrible prospect before him was indeed overwhelming,— the desert on all sides, with starvation staring them in the face. What was to be done? Where should they turn for succor?

Just at this juncture a band of Indians were seen approaching. Telling his terrified family to keep quiet, and no one would harm them, he walked towards the Indians, and, addressing them in Spanish, welcomed them to his camp. Asking them to sit down, he gave them pipes and tobacco, with the assurance that he would give them food did he have a supply, and treated them with kindness and consideration in every way. The Indians were close observers of the enfeebled condition of the emigrants, and after conversing together for a few moments they suddenly gave one of their terrible war-whoops, and fell upon their victims.

Lorenzo, a boy of fifteen, was first struck on the head and knocked down. Next half a dozen of the savages rushed upon Mr. Oatman, and despatched him with their knives, while Mrs. Oatman and her infant daughter were beaten to death with clubs. Olive and Mary, the first sixteen, and the other eleven years of age, were securely held by two Indians, at a little distance, where they could witness the terrible scene. Lorenzo was then seized and thrown down the rocky side of the mesa, and must have fallen at least forty feet to the ground below. If any person could stand and look at the place from which he was thrown, and realize how it was possible for him to escape instant death, their experience would be different from mine. And yet, strange as it may appear, he was not killed.

He says that after consciousness returned, strange, discordant sounds grated upon his ear, which, gradually dying away, were succeeded by strains of such sweet music as completely ravished his senses. He finally managed to creep up the hill to the camp upon the mesa, where the dead bodies of his father, mother, and sister met his gaze, lying mutilated and bloody among the scattered remnants of the wagons and their contents. He instantly missed the bodies of Olive and Mary, and knew that they must have been carried away captives. Weary and faint, he succeeded in dragging himself down towards the river, which, after terrible suffering, he reached, almost famishing with thirst. Here he laid himself down, and slept for several hours. When he awoke, his first thought was to return to the Pimo villages; and starting out, he travelled for two days, walking as long as he was able, and then crawling on his hands and knees, resting himself whenever he could find the shade of a friendly bush, delirious part of the time, and constantly haunted by the fear that he should again fall into the hands of the Indians. Every moment he grew weaker and weaker from hunger and thirst. Death seemed inevitable. And at last, yielding to despair, he laid himself down, expecting every breath to be his last. How long he remained there he cannot tell, but he was aroused to consciousness by the discordant bark of a pack of hungry wolves. Weak as he was, he fought them off with sticks and stones. Next day two friendly Pimo Indians found him, nearer dead than alive, and carried him to their village, where, after weeks of terrible suffering, he finally recovered.

From the account given by him, it appears that as soon as the Apaches had finished their murders, they plundered the wagons, and taking Olive and Mary captives, fled across the river. The girls were without adequate clothing, bare-headed and bare-footed, yet they were dragged along over sharp stones and brambles, no heed being paid to their exhausted condition, the savages even using clubs to force them along. Their feet were torn and bleeding, and their flesh lacerated by the thorns of the thickets through which they had to pass. The younger sister, always a weak, sickly child, was repeatedly beaten by the savages, who threatened to kill her if she lagged behind. Late in the night they halted for a few hours. Sunrise, however, found them again on the move. Thus they travelled for four days, the girls enduring the most incredible suffering all the while. At the close of the fourth day they reached the Apache village, where they were welcomed by songs, shouts, and wild dances, which continued with little intermission for three days, the poor children being placed in the centre of the fiendish circle, and compelled to witness the most shocking and obscene sights. They were afterwards compelled to labor from morning until night, in a state of such filth and abject misery, that it is difficult to realize how, young as they were, they could endure the extreme hardships to which they were subjected, and live. They were often without food for two days at a time, save as they could steal a few roots or berries while at work.

About a year after their capture, the Apaches sold them to a band of Mojaves, for some corn and skins. Now came the time of Olive's severest trial. Mary, worn out by toil and suffering, weary with watching and waiting for some sign of relief from a life of brutality and privation, at last yielded to despair and prayed earnestly that her sufferings might be ended by death. And that night, singing the hymns she had learned in happier days, her soul was ushered into eternity, and the weary little body buried, by the loving hands of her sister, in a spot of earth that, during their servitude, they had cultivated together for these inhuman wretches.

Olive remained four years among the Mojaves, enduring great hardships. In 1856, she was purchased by a Mr. Grinnell, who took her to Fort Yuma, and a few weeks later she was sent to her brother, then living at Los Angeles, California.

Such is a true history of the Oatman family, as corroborated by both Lorenzo and Olive. A sad one indeed, yet not uncommon for Arizona. Not one in a hundred, however, of those taken captives by the Apaches, ever live to tell the story.

It has since been ascertained that the party who massacred the Oatmans were Tonto Apaches, under the leadership of Mangus Colorado, who styled himself "The white man's friend."

CHAPTER VII.

IT was while in camp at the Apache Pass, that I began to experience a strong desire to learn more of the Apache tribe.

I broached the matter to Cochise one day, after treating him liberally to whiskey, but he did not care to talk on the subject.

My friends all tried to dissuade me from the undertaking; but a bale of smoking tobacco, a five-gallon keg of whiskey, with a pair of bright red blankets, were too strong inducements for Cochise, and his consent once gained, I determined to start alone for the *rancheria* of the Pinal and Tonto Apaches, situated about one hundred and twenty miles west of north from the Chiricahui Mountains, near the Rio Gila.

He assured me that there was no danger to be apprehended

from stray bands of Indians; and, after his consenting to leave his brother in the hands of Major De Rythe, as hostage for our safe return, we started for a trip to the home of the Apaches, my object being, as much as anything else, to see the country which every American in Arizona was confident furnished the gold with which these Indians were so lavish when they came into the settlements.

Cochise and myself each had one riding mule, and in addition thereto I had three pack mules, one of which was loaded down with two huge leathern bottles, holding about six gallons each, filled with water.

It was a lovely morning in June, that we started.

The parting with "Jimmy" was affecting, he swearing "if he'd iver thought I was a goin' that way he would have kilt me intirely before I started."

After leaving the Chiricahui Mountains, Cochise, striking across the country in a northwesterly direction, soon came upon a trail; following this trail, we travelled all day over an alkali plain, which reflected the rays of the burning sun with an intensity that would have done credit to the most highly-polished mirror.

There was absolutely nothing to relieve the eye, but the distant outline of the Chiricahui Mountains behind us, or the rough line of the high country we were approaching, save that occasionally we saw the beautiful blue waters of a magnificent lake with its white-capped waves rolling towards the shore, which appeared to be covered with trees of every conceivable shape and height.

Having frequently witnessed this mirage on the plains, I understood its deception, though never had I seen it so perfect before. Indeed, I could hardly realize that it was

JIMMY.

the "Greenhorn's Lake," a mere phantom of the imagination, that had lured many an unwary traveller miles out of his course, in the vain hope that he might quench his thirst, and lave his burning limbs in its delicious coolness.

As we approached the high ground, Cochise gave me to

understand that we should be obliged to camp for the night on the plains, without grass for our mules; but that by rising early in the morning, we should in a few hours reach both water and grass.

Before noon of the next day we came to a little aroya, down which trickled a small stream.

Cochise soon made a little tank, by scooping out the sand with his hands; this quickly filled with water, from which our thirsty mules drank eagerly. Here we tarried for the remainder of the day.

Early the next morning we started. Another day over alkali plains, rocky mesas, and across aroyas and gullies, until just at night we came to a low, green spot, where a little spring gushed forth from the foot of the bluff, and here we halted for the night.

Cochise killed an antelope with his bow and arrows, which furnished us some juicy steaks, far preferable to the hard, dry meat we had provided for the trip.

The next morning we commenced the ascent of the bluff. And here let me disclaim the ability to give the reader anything but a faint idea of the scene that burst upon my view, or the experiences of that day's travel.

No tongue ever spoke, no pen ever wrote, that could adequately describe the grandeur and sublimity, as well as the utter desolation, that appalls, while it enchants, the traveller, through the perils that here beset him at every step.

Well did Cochise call it the "*Jornada del Muerte*," or Journey of Death.

Imagine, if you can, a valley or plain eighty miles in width, and extending for hundreds of miles on either side of you. It is a valley, only because you are surrounded by interminable ranges of mountains; it is a plain, only because there are mountains before you and mountains behind you. To your uneducated eye, it presents a smooth and unbroken surface, yet there is hardly a level spot upon its face. It is a mass of cañons, ravines, ridges, gullies, chasms, and mountains, piled one above another in inextricable confusion, in all conceivable shapes, towering above and around you on all sides.

Cathedrals of huge size, castles, rotundas, amphitheatres with domes and towers, are on every hand, while yonder, rising a thousand feet in the air, is a strange resemblance to a mighty organ, with its pipes consisting of huge columns of green, white, blue, brown, and pink sandstone towering high above you, with the tops worn by the winds and waters into points seemingly like needles. Count them: there are forty.

While we are wondering what mighty Mechanic constructed this huge instrument, and whose fingers press its wonderful key-board, our guide strikes once more into the path, scarce twelve inches in width, and we move forward again on the Apache trail. We commence to descend the banks of a deep ravine, our mules carefully picking their way along, the path constantly impeded by huge boulders of granite, blocks of sandstone, fissures and chasms worn into the earth by floods ages ago. Around you on all sides are to be seen mountain peaks, ranges, mesas, pinnacles, and crags, bald and gray. Yonder stands a castle, with its towers and spires hundreds of feet in height, its walls of blue gray limestone mixed with white and red granite, beautifully mottled with shales of every conceivable color. Seemingly but a few miles in front of us we readily imagine we are about approaching some enchanted castle, where we shall not fail to find the rest, as well as food, which we so much need, when we suddenly find ourselves upon the edge of a cañon, two thousand feet in depth.

As we gaze down into the depths of this vast abyss, a feeling of terror creeps over us, as we vainly strive to pierce the deep gloom that shrouds its rocky sides, and verges into total darkness far beneath us.

The walls are perpendicular, and of a blood-red color. No vegetation is anywhere to be seen; nothing but the stones around us, and the grayish white alkali on the surface of the plain on which we stand, with its surroundings of crags, pinnacles, towers, and mesas of rock rising far above us, until their summits pierce the clouds on the one side, and this black, yawning abyss just before us.

Cochise moves to the left, and there we find a narrow

shelf of rock jutting out from the perpendicular walls, just wide enough to stand upon.

We follow its course with our eye until it is lost in gloom; and yet this is the only way of crossing the cañon before us.

Cochise now dismounts, and from him I endeavor to learn something of this wonderful gorge which we are about to cross; but, Indian like, he is reticent, and reveals nothing.

He motions to me that we must leave our mules to follow us, and utters the single word *adelante*, or forward. As we descend into the gloom, we feel as if we were about to bid good-bye to the earth and the sunlight, and to enter the abode of the fiends. Our imagination peoples the chasm with myriads of imps and gnomes.

Just before us, the point of rock standing out so prominently resembles a huge giant ready to crush us in his terrible grasp for our audacity in presuming to venture within the realms guarded so sedulously by his misshapen form. On, on we go, now avoiding a rock in our path, here sending a pebble over the brink of the abyss at our side. The gloom becomes more intense as we descend. We cast our eyes upwards: a perpendicular wall on either side of us, and far above us a narrow band of light, against which the ragged and scarred edges of the gulf, seemingly almost meeting, stand out in bold relief, giving us the impression that we are about to be crushed between the teeth of two gigantic saws.

Not a sound is to be heard, save the hesitating footsteps of our mules; when suddenly Cochise, who is some distance in advance, utters an oath in Spanish.

The opposite side of the cañon echoes it, and it is carried from side to side, from point to point, from rock to rock, from crag to crag, with fearful distinctness, till it resembles, to our ears, the cries of the demons, who, we are sure, surround us, and inhabit this direct descent to the home of *Los Infernos.*

Still we go on, still continue to descend.

Soon we hear the faint murmur of water, as far below us it forces its way among the rocks and boulders that form the bed of the river, and we feel rejoiced that the poor animals so carefully following us are so soon to be refreshed with a draught of cool water, after their tedious journey over masses of rock, baked clay, and alkali powder.

Instinctively we look behind us, and we see that they too have heard the grateful sound, and are hurrying along, as though impatient to taste its refreshing coolness.

Then comes the thought, that frequently, when suffering from thirst, mules have been known to stampede at the smell of water. Suppose this should be the case with ours? What, then, would be our fate? We cast our eyes over the brink of the yawning chasm, and then back upon our mules, as if to measure distance and strength.

The sight of their erect ears, distended nostrils, and glaring eyes does not tend to reassure us, and we look in vain for some spot wide enough to enable them to pass us in safety.

Nothing but a solid perpendicular wall above us, and empty space for six hundred feet below.

We must go on. There is no turning back. The gloom increases with every step. The walls around assume in the darkness a thousand grotesque and misshapen forms. The obstacles in our pathway become more frequent and dangerous. The darkness becomes more and more intense. We can no longer see the path for more than four or five feet ahead of us.

Now, as it abruptly turns an angle, we lose sight of it altogether, and we feel as though the next step might precipitate us into—what?

And so we go on, hesitating, doubting, fearing, until, after hours of tedious toil, such as I hope never again to experience, we finally reach the bed of the river that has worn this mighty wrinkle in the face of Mother Earth.

After allowing our thirsty animals time to drink, and filling our canteens and leathern bottles with fresh water, we follow down the bed of the stream for a mile, cautiously feeling our way in the darkness as best we can, stumbling against boulders of granite, and over stones and masses of trap, that have been precipitated from the vast heights above us, until at length we reach the point where we are to begin the ascent.

Wearily toiling up the steep path, picking our way over rocks and fissures, gullies and stones, all the while gaining light, though losing strength, we at last reach the level of the plain that we left in the morning, to find ourselves in the twilight, only four miles below the point where we began the descent, having been more than ten hours in making the journey.

Here, upon the very brink of this fearful chasm, we throw ourselves upon the ground, declaring we can go no farther. Here we must camp for the night. No vegetation, no grass for our mules, no water, no food,—nothing but desolation.

We are no nearer the enchanted castle than we were before we made the passage of this frightful cañon. The pipes of that same grand old organ look down upon us. The same butes, mesas, pillars, towers, and needles of rock, with cañons, ravines, chasms, and fissures, surround us that surrounded us in the morning. Then, we saw them as the beams of the rising sun gilded their summits; now, we see them towering up in the twilight, and assuming a thousand fanciful and grotesque shapes that we had not dreamed they possessed before.

LOWER PORTION OF THE CAÑON.

Tired and exhausted, we wrap ourselves in our blankets, and throw ourselves upon the ground to sleep.

To sleep, did I say?

No; for again the scenes of the day pass in rapid succession before us. Our fears, our doubts, the descent of that perilous path, all a thousand times more fraught with danger than we had imagined at the outset.

While we are debating in our minds whether we shall be able to cross in safety an immense fissure that yawns frightfully before us, we hear the voice of Cochise saying "*ariva*," and we awake to a repetition of yesterday's toils.

I am fully aware, kind reader, that I have failed to give you but a faint idea of the perils that beset the traveller into the Apache wilds. I only wish I possessed the pencil of a Bierstadt, that I might portray upon canvas some of the features of the remarkable country which I visited during my two weeks' trip with Cochise.

Another day over a country presenting the same striking characteristics as those over which we had so recently passed. The same alkali powder, fissures, chasms, and turfless soil, relieved only by the misshapen rocks of brown and yellowish granite, that seemed to have been thrown together by some terrible convulsion of nature, the power of which no human creature could conceive.

Late in the afternoon, Cochise called my attention to four or five small black specks in the distance, apparently perched upon one of those mesas, or truncated mounds, which are so abundant in this country.

Cochise at once recognized them as Apaches, a fact that he communicated to me; but nothing would induce him to enlighten me further on the subject; and as I had literally

THE APACHES' HOME.

taken my "life in my hand," I felt there was no alternative but to abide the consequences.

Two hours' travel brought us to the top of a bare, rugged bluff, completely indented with fissures and gullies worn into its side by the winds and waters of a thousand years, when Cochise abruptly stopped, and pointing over the edge of the bluff, said, as I thought, with no small degree of pride, "Look! Apache home!"

I did look, and the sight which greeted my eyes made an indelible impression upon me.

A beautiful valley, carpeted with a rich green-sward, extending fully three miles in length, and nearly, if not quite, a mile in width, through which a stream, with water clear as crystal, meandered over its bed of pebbles,—its banks skirted with a kind of small willow, whose foliage of yellowish green contrasted strangely with the darker shade of the grass, and all surrounded by a range of bluffs, fully a hundred feet high, worn into representations of castellated forts, with bastions, scarps, lunettes, gorges, and curtains, till one could almost fancy the whole encompassed by an impregnable fortress.

Scattered up and down the valley were the Apache huts, looking, with their yellow thatch, like the inverted halves of so many huge melons.

Before nearly every door a little camp-fire was burning, from which the smoke was lazily ascending, until, losing its density, it was lost in air.

Far towards the upper end of the valley could be seen peacefully grazing a large herd of cattle, ponies, and mules; while near the lower end a few patches of squaw corn loomed up, as though proudly marking the only visible traces of civilization.

As I contemplated this really beautiful scene, I could not help contrasting the softness of the picture spread out before me, with the hard, sterile features of the country over which we had just journeyed, and I almost felt that I was about to descend into the "Happy Valley" of Rasselas, instead of into the home of the cruel and blood-thirsty Apaches, who were, in truth, the scourge of the land.

As we stood there motionless upon the top of the bluff, our presence was discovered by some of the Indians in the village, who at once signalled us by a yell; and in an instant, it seemed to me, the barking of a thousand dogs, mingled with the shouts of the warriors and the screaming of women and children, heralded our approach.

Cochise gave back an answering yell, and, as if by magic, every sound was hushed, save that the mule of Cochise gave a loud bray, which was instantly answered in a dozen directions by mules in the village.

We quietly descended the steep bluff by one of the paths that was worn into its face, and which seemed to form a complete net-work over it; and I soon found myself among a lot of the dirtiest, filthiest, most degraded-looking set of creatures that I ever saw in the guise of humanity.

The men were naked, except the breech clout and moccasins; the women had dirty old blankets tied around their waists, and the upper part of the body entirely exposed; while the expression on the faces of all was cruel and brutal, a look of cunning pervading each countenance.

The women were particularly ugly, fat, and dirty; and I looked in vain for some of the "beautiful squaws" that had been pictured so graphically by Cooper and Lossing. Not one was to be found.

Not a gleam of intelligence nor a line of beauty was to be seen either in the face or form of those around me. As I gazed at them, I almost wished, in the characteristic language of Jimmy, that I had "been kilt before I started."

There was but one course to pursue, however; to put a bold face on the matter, and be prepared for anything that might happen.

Cochise said a few words to the crowd, in a dialect I did not understand, and then motioned for me to dismount. This I did, and instantly the hands of a dozen warriors were extended to grasp mine, each one muttering his welcome in a low, guttural sound as he shook my hand.

I was shown to a hut which Cochise told me, in Spanish, I was to occupy while there; and the warriors at once commenced to unsaddle and unpack the animals, which were then turned out to graze upon the luxuriant herbage that surrounded us on all sides. I had a few moments' time to examine the hut in which I was thus domiciled, and found its framework to be poles set in the ground, and bent over until they reached a common centre, where they were tied together.

The sides were composed of skins, while the roof was formed of bundles of long rushes and *tulle*, firmly tied together, which had been bleached by the weather almost white. The place seemed to be clean, and Cochise at once proceeded to bring all the articles, even to the huge leathern bottles, into the hut, at the same time assuring me that his tribe were not thieves, like the Mojaves.

After partaking of a hearty supper of pemmican, I spread my blanket, glad of an opportunity to rest after the hardships of our tedious journey, quite content that Cochise should share my hut and guard it from intruders.

I was not permitted to enjoy the quiet long, however, for Cochise informed me that some of the braves proposed to have a dance in honor of my visit, and that I would be expected to be present on the festive occasion, and compensate the warriors with a piece of "bacca." Of course I was obliged to submit, which I did with a very poor grace indeed.

Upon going out, we found assembled about a dozen braves around a small fire, who arose upon our approach, and each extended a hand of welcome.

Seating ourselves, two Apaches commenced beating a drum, which was made by tightly drawing a skin of rawhide over the end of a hollow log about three feet in diameter. To the beat of this drum, the braves kept time with a kind of rattle, made of a short piece of wood, from which depended eight or ten thongs of rawhide, upon which were strung bears' claws, eagles' claws, deer's feet, bits of bone, and small stones.

These were furiously shaken together, while they kept their bodies swaying to the beating of the drum, and accompanying the motion by shouting in a high falsetto tone, "Hi yah, hi yah, hoo hoo."

Taken altogether, it was the most diabolical attempt at music to which I ever listened; and glad enough was I to give them their tobacco, and once more reach the shelter of my hut, where, crawling into my blankets, I was soon enjoying

> "Tired Nature's sweet restorer, balmy sleep,"

utterly oblivious to the fact that I was surrounded by as villanous a set of fellows as

> "Ever cut a throat."

I remained in this state of blissful unconsciousness till long after the sun had risen the next morning, and the whole village was astir.

CHAPTER VIII.

S I lay in my blanket the next morning, reflecting upon my situation, I was far from experiencing that sense of contentment and repose that had heretofore solaced me in my journey. I became painfully aware of the dangers which threatened me on every hand; and, on the principle, perhaps, that "misery likes company," most sincerely regretted that no one had accompanied me.

Enjoying anything but a contented mind, I arose from my lowly couch, and proceeded, towel in hand, to the little stream that meandered so quietly through the valley, to perform my morning ablutions. This, of course, attracted a crowd of women and children, to whom a piece of soap was as great a curiosity as would be the sight of a live Apache on Broadway. Its philosophy they could not understand. Why wetting it made the beautiful white foam, which they endeavored to catch in their hands as it floated down the stream, to vanish at their touch, was a mystery beyond their comprehension. Notwithstanding the soap-plant grew all around them in profusion, not one of them knew its value or use.

After satisfying their curiosity as well as I was able, at

SOAP AND WATER.

the expense of a large share of my soap, I returned to my quarters to prepare breakfast, Cochise having faithfully kept guard during my absence, declining the oft-repeated invitations to partake of the messes in their huge camp kettles, which were boiling over the fire before the huts.

While making a hasty meal of beef and atole, I became conscious that something of an extraordinary nature was going on in the village. Even Cochise seemed excited as he informed me that the scouts had signalled the approach of a large party of Indians, but whether friendly or otherwise could not as yet be ascertained, so great was their distance from the village. They were probably Apaches, though possibly they might be Mojaves, with which tribe the Apaches were then at war.

Here was a situation which I had not anticipated. To be killed in an Apache village as an Apache, was a fate of which I had never dreamed, even in the wildest surmises as to the probable termination of my earthly career. With as much indifference as I could assume, I asked Cochise his opinion of the advancing party. His reply, "*Quien Sabe?*" was anything but consoling to me in my present situation.

Regretting the temerity that had induced me to undertake such an expedition, I hastily finished my breakfast, and went out of my hut, to find the larger portion of the people assembled on the top of the bluff, gazing at the approaching band. A dozen or so of the braves had sprung on to their ponies and were riding across the plains as fast as their animals could carry them. All was confusion and excitement. Some of the warriors were examining their spear-heads, others their bows and arrows.

Cochise soon announced, much to my relief, that it was a portion of their own band, who had gone out under Mangus Colorado, for a raid into Sonora. They had been gone about "a moon"; and judging from the number of cattle and mules driven before them, the raid must have been a successful one.

As soon as it was known that Mangus Colorado was returning, the excitement at once subsided. The braves released the lower jaws of their horses from their lariats, and permitted them to stroll at will over the green sward, while they lazily reposed in the sun. The squaws went out to gather fuel and perform such labor as usually falls to the male portion of humanity.

Feeling some misgivings as to the reception I might receive at the hands of Mangus Colorado, I could not refrain from asking Cochise, in as *nonchalant* a manner as possible, what Mangus Colorado would say to see a white man so quietly domiciled in his village.

"Oh!" said Cochise, "I sent him word as soon as I knew it was he, and you know too, he is the 'white man's friend.' "

The barking of hundreds of curs, the shouting of braves, with the shrill voices of the women, now announced the appearance, on the top of the bluff, of about thirty warriors.

Under the circumstances, I thought it best to remain out of sight as much as possible until such time as Mangus should in some way evince a knowledge of my presence. This he shortly did by visiting my hut, and, extending his hand, said, in Spanish, "Good day! Gim me 'bacca!'"

After shaking hands with him, I presented him with some chewing tobacco, also a small bale of smoking tobacco,

MEETING OF MANGUS COLORADO, COCHISE, AND THE AUTHOR.

which latter present not only won his good-will, but secured his friendship.

It was with no small degree of curiosity that I regarded this great chief. He was, indeed, as noble a specimen of the Indian race as I had ever seen. More than six feet in height, straight as an arrow, his physique splendid; his long black hair hung loosely about his shoulders, and was profusely ornamented with eagle feathers; his face was painted with vermilion and ochre, while his sides were striped with green. Upon his feet were a pair of richly wrought moccasins. A heavy red Mackinaw blanket hung from his shoulders, and was fastened at the waist by a silk sash that evidently had once belonged to some officer of the army. His only weapon was a spear, the head made of obsidian, attached by deer sinews to a pole about eight feet long. Altogether, he presented a very picturesque appearance, and received the homage paid him by his people with much native dignity.

To the lance of one of the party was fastened what I at first supposed to be a flag of truce; but a closer examination revealed the fact that it was a little child's dress, elaborately embroidered, and of exquisite make and material. Extending it to me, all blood-stained as it was, he signified by signs that the little one who had worn this beautiful tribute of a mother's affection, had been ruthlessly murdered by the same barbarous weapon which he held in his hand, and its soul sent to the "Great Spirit."

The sight of this trophy was anything but an assuring one to me, and I at once resolved that, as soon as circumstances should permit, I would leave the Apaches and their home. Cochise informed me that the plunder of the expedition amounted to thirty head of cattle, fifty mules, sixteen ponies, and six scalps, which, he took particular pains to impress upon me, were Mexican scalps. He also told me that there was to be a grand feast and scalp-dance in honor of their recent successful raid, and that it would be advisable for me to be present at the ceremonies; that I was perfectly safe; that no one would harm me; that his tribe were not thieves, but Apaches.

Unsatisfactory as these assurances were, I consoled myself as best I could, and accepted his invitation with expressions of pleasure which I was far from experiencing.

I spent the greater portion of the day in strolling about the *rancheria*, visiting the huts, and conversing with those who understood Spanish. From them I gathered some information concerning the surrounding country. I ascertained that the village contained not far from seven hundred inhabitants, and that the home of Mangus Colorado was situated nearly a league to the westward, where he lived, surrounded by about one hundred of his braves and their families. That no white man had ever before visited the *rancheria.* That the country around abounded in game, and that large quantities of (*oro*) gold were to be found in the cañons and gulches about five leagues to the north of them.

Seeing that a crowd had gathered in the lower portion of the village, I walked towards it, and saw a number of the braves engaged in throwing a mule, which they had lassoed. Inquiry revealed the fact that they were about procuring the meat for their feast. After throwing the animal and securely tying his feet, two of these devils incarnate then advanced and commenced with knives to cut the meat from the thighs and fleshy parts of the animal in large chunks, while the poor creature uttered the most terrible cries. After cutting the meat clean to the bone, they proceeded to pierce the jugular vein, thus ending his misery, the squaws catching the blood in huge gourds.

I afterwards learned that this process was resorted to from the fact that the meat taken from a live animal was considered more tender.

The blood was fed to the children to make them brave, and was also considered an especial delicacy for seasoning their stews. After witnessing this scene, it may be superfluous to say that I fouud myself too demoralized to require any further sustenance of that kind, and sought the retirement of my hut, convinced that *fasting* is often more conducive to health than *feasting*, and that the events of one day in an Apache village rivalled, in all that was thrilling and sensational, the every-day occurrences of a civilized city like the great metropolis of our land.

My meditations were somewhat unceremoniously disturbed by the entrance of Cochise, who came to say to me that Mangus Colorado desired my presence at the festival.

Declaring my indisposition and utter inability to enjoy the ceremonies, and respectfully declining the invitation, I was informed by Cochise that it would give great offence should I fail to attend, though I was not expected to take any part in the festivities. Recognizing the force of his argument, I gave a reluctant consent, and prepared to accompany him, conscious all the while, however, that the wish nearest my heart was to be safe at home.

We soon came to a level spot in the lowei part of the valley, where we found Mangus Colorado in all the glory of eagle feathers, vermilion, and grease. He was seated on a blanket spread upon the ground. Motioning me to a seat beside him, he extended a huge hand with finger-nails like eagle's claws, saying, in a tone of voice that was intended to be winning and soft, "Gim me bacca." To which request I responded by placing in his hand my last piece of navy plug, which he at once conveyed to his dirty mouth with a most expressive grunt of satisfaction.

Accepting the position assigned me, I prepared to witness a scene which I was confident would fill me with aversion and disgust. Six braves now advanced, and with no small display of pride planted a lance near the camp-fire, which was burning in front of us, and over which hung a huge camp-kettle, steaming furiously, reminding me forcibly of the witch-scene in Macbeth. From the lance hung several objects, which, in the dim, uncertain light, I took to be tassels, but which proved to be trophies of the raid. Two of these scalps had attached to them long, flowing tresses, which clearly denominated the murdered ones to have been women. It was a horrid sight, and I wished myself well out of it.

By this time the moon was shining brightly, illuminating the valley around us and the bluffs beyond, giving to them a strange, phantom-like appearance, that was greatly enhanced by the faint flicker of a hundred camp-fires, which cast a sort of lurid glare over the dusky forms flitting about.

Occasionally a bright flame shot high into the air, and brought into bold relief the line of bluffs on the opposite side of the stream, giving to them the semblance of being covered with an army of misshapen giants.

Some twenty squaws now made their appearance, dressed *à la Apache*, their coarse black hair hanging unkempt about them. Forming a circle around the fire and lance, they commenced swaying their bodies to the sound of two drums that were beaten by some of the men, while others uttered a low, monotonous chant, keeping time with a kind of rattle made of gourds, containing small stones, bits of bone, etc. As the drums were beaten faster and faster, the noise of the rattles became more furious, which, mingling with the sharp, shrill tones of the squaws, made the most infernal din imaginable. Suddenly one of the old hags snatched from the boiling kettle a piece of mule meat, and holding it all steaming in her skinny hands towards the scalps, as though in derision, seized it between her teeth, and again joined in the dance, keeping time to the music.

This disgusting pantomime was repeated by each one of the repulsive old creatures, who, by this time, were whirling about in the most frenzied manner, thus celebrating the prowess of their husbands and sons, who had so recently returned from their cruel and cowardly raid into Sonora.

Continuing this demoniacal dance for more than an hour, their strength finally began to fail them. The warriors, by whose bravery these scalps had been taken, now advanced, and seating themselves in a circle around the camp-fire, began their share in the entertainment. The scalp-pole was handed round by the oldest of the squaws, and as it was presented to each brave, he signified his contempt for his enemies by spitting upon it, at the same time uttering a low grunt of satisfaction. Each was then helped to a bountiful supply of the boiling meat with which the kettle was filled.

During this time the music was kept up unceasingly, making an uproar that would have done credit to Pandemonium. Sick and tired, I signified to Cochise my desire to retire. He accompanied me back to my hut, where once again creeping into my blanket, I soon found repose from the exciting scenes of the day and evening. Need I say

THE SCALP DANCE.

that upon reflection I became satisfied that Charles Sprague was entirely wrong when he said in his beautiful poem on "Curiosity," that "it came from Heaven." I didn't believe it that night, and I doubt if I do now. Then, I should not have hesitated a moment to declare my conviction that it originated in a place supposed to be the antipodes of heaven.

The next morning, after partaking of a breakfast of pemmican,* I strolled out into the village, hoping that the season of dances was over.

Had I then known that not two years before, this same band of Apaches, in this very *rancheria,* had sacrificed a young Mexican girl, it would in no way have served to quiet my apprehensions. She was offered as a sacrifice to propitiate the Great Spirit, whose wrath had manifested itself by visiting upon them the small-pox.

After fattening her for several months, keeping her very quiet, and in ignorance of her fate, they brought her, on the morning when the sacrifice was to be made, to the place of torture. Here, placing her between two trees, they suspended her by ropes tied around her wrists, so that her feet, which were firmly fastened together, were about three

* The flesh of buffalo or deer, dried until it becomes hard and brittle, and then pounded fine, and put into bags made of buffalo hide or deer-skin, the tallow being melted and poured over it, and the whole mass pressed together, when it soon becomes as hard as a stone. This is a favorite and convenient method of carrying meat where game is scarce in the Apache Country.

feet from the ground. A fire was then kindled beneath her, and as the flames reached her flesh, scream after scream issued from the lips of the poor victim. One after another of these *brave* Apaches plucked a burning brand from the fire and applied it to the quivering flesh of the wretched girl, till finally death released her from her terrible sufferings. The body was then hacked to pieces with sharp stones, the pieces burned upon the fire, and the ashes scattered to the winds, in order to purify the air, and thus appease the wrath of the malign spirit.

I fully realized the truth of the old adage, "Where ignorance is bliss, 'tis folly to be wise," upon hearing a narration of the above facts, from an old Arizonian, more than a year after my return from the Apache *rancheria.*

CHAPTER IX.

AT the time I left the Apache Pass, I had some idea that a trip into the Navajoe country, at least as far as the seven Moquis cities, might, possibly, be a desirable one; and that it might be successfully made from the Apache *rancheria*, especially as Cochise had informed me that these Indians were at peace with the Apaches, and that he could easily act as guide through the country.

My visit to the *rancheria*, however, had completely extinguished every desire for further explorations; and, like John Phœnix, in the San Francisco Female Convention, my only desire was to "go home."

Still, curiosity prompted me to question Cochise concerning the country and its people; and he informed me that there were then residing at the *rancheria* two Navajoes, who could give me all the information I desired concerning them.

Requesting Cochise to bring them to me on the morrow, I composed myself to sleep, with as good a grace as possible, after the events of the day.

The sun was several hours high when I repaired to my dressing-room the next morning. There was quite a crowd of women and children present, who witnessed the spectacle of washing face and hands with great *gusto*. I was quite convinced that these children of nature were entirely unused to any such sight, as much from their own personal appearance, as from their looks of wonderment at seeing me perform my ablutions.

Untutored children of the Darwinian theory! They could gaze at the marvels of nature spread around them with such unsparing prodigality; could see a white woman fiendishly tortured, and made to suffer the most horrible indignities, or a white man brutally murdered, without a sign of emotion upon their faces; but the sight of a man washing his face and hands almost convulsed them with laughter.

After eating my breakfast, I spread my blanket beneath the shade of a pine-tree that grew near by, and, lighting my pipe, proposed to enjoy myself as well as possible under the circumstances.

Cochise soon made his appearance, bringing with him an

old man fully sixty years of age, and saying, abruptly, "Here's a Navajoe," turned away.

The old man squatted himself upon the grass, and drawing his knees almost up to his chin, seemed to await my pleasure.

Finding him able to speak Spanish pretty well, and posted on all matters pertaining to his people, I gleaned from him much interesting and valuable information, of which I will give the reader the benefit, hoping it may amuse and instruct him as much as it did me; for but little is known concerning this once formidable, but now nearly extinct, race of Indians.

He said that the Navajoe country extended from the Rio Grande to the Colorado of the West, and was about one hundred and twenty-five miles northwest of the Apache village. That the Moquis lived in the Navajoe country, and their houses were built of stone, and situated upon the tops of high mesas, but that the Navajoes knew little about them.

The Navajoes have no fixed residence, but wander at will over the country, stopping wherever night overtakes them. They number about twelve thousand souls, and of late years have not been much inclined to the war-path, as they are growing very rich.

They have large herds of cattle, also many fine horses and mules; but their sheep are by far the most valuable portion of their possessions. From the wool of these they manufacture a very superior blanket, which is famous on the frontier. So closely is it woven, that one may carry water in it all day with no fear of its leaking through. It takes a woman a year to weave one.

They dye their wool red, black, purple, brown, blue, yellow, and green, the dyes being made from flowers, roots, and the bark of trees. The red dye is made from the flower of the sumach, with a small root that grows near it. Yellow is made by boiling together certain flowers, and blue in the same way. Black is obtained from the bark of the maple and butternut trees. They get a kind of yellowish-brown color from the oxide of iron, which abounds in the mountains.

When in their wanderings they come across a fine range for pasturing their animals, they build little huts, and remain for months in the same location. Here they plant corn, beans, and sometimes wheat and pumpkins, of which latter they are very fond. A kind of wild potato grows all over the country. Many of the Indians have herds of five or six hundred horses, worth from sixty to eighty dollars apiece. They are expert horsemen, and spend much of their time on horseback.

The country is well-supplied with grass. Bears, black-tailed deer, antelope, wolves, prairie-dogs, wild-cats, and squirrels are very plentiful.

Horse-racing and gambling are the only amusements of the people.

They have a religion peculiar to themselves—worshipping the Great Spirit, who, according to their belief, made the Navajoes the first occupants of the earth;. and in moving their camp from place to place, they always carry with them a brand of fire, which singular custom the old man explained in this wise: In the beginning, the Great Spirit created twelve Navajoes—six men and six women. They were confined in the middle of a great mountain, with all the animals created. They emerged from the earth in the following manner:—

The locust and the badger aided them in boring through the ground. The locust bored the first hole, but finding it too small, called to his assistance the badger; and by their united efforts, they soon had an aperture sufficiently large for the Navajoes to come forth. The badger preceded them, and, springing out, he lighted upon the bottom of a lake in the Montezuma Valley, and his fore legs sinking into the mire, were covered with black mud, and remained black to this day.

No sooner were the Navajoes and all the animals out of the mountain, than fire and smoke began to issue from the hole whence they had emerged. This so frightened them that they went down into the valleys; but shortly after they discovered that they needed fire, and the coyote, or wolf, the bat, and the squirrel were sent out to procure it. They proceeded to the mountain, from which they had so recently issued, and the wolf, fastening some slivers of gummy wood to his tail, held it over the crater until the wood became ignited. The bat fanned the fire into a flame by darting hither and thither, and then the squirrel conveyed it to the Navajoes.

To this day not one of the Navajoes can be persuaded to taste the flesh of either wolf or squirrel, or to move their camp without taking with them a brand of fire.

Day and night were brought about by a difference in opinion among the animals. Those which preferred day are still permitted to wander by daylight, while those which chose "darkness rather than light," travel by night.

This account of the creation is fully believed by all the Navajoes. At this period in the old man's narration, Cochise came to inquire when I desired to return to the Pass.

I replied, without a moment's hesitation, "In the morning, of course."

His "*esta buenno*" was a most welcome sound to my ears, I can assure you; and requesting him to bring the animals for my inspection before we started, I wandered up to a spot near by, where a number of squaws were engaged in dressing deer-skins; as the Apaches are reputed to have the best method of tanning skins known among the Indians, I watched the process with no little curiosity.

HEAD-WATERS OF THE GILA.

The flesh was first carefully removed from the hide with a sharpened bone, and the hair shaved off with a sharp knife. It was then hung up to dry for a few hours, and afterwards thoroughly washed with ashes and water, to remove the grease, and then dipped in water containing the brains of a deer. Next it was boiled, and then stretched on poles to dry, after which it was again wet and scraped, and finally dried slowly by a fire.

This process is repeated three times, when, if the skin should prove hard, it is drawn swiftly over a piece of small rope, the squaw pulling it as hard as she can, which softens it nicely. It is then smoked for a couple of hours over a fire built of decayed wood, which is placed in a hole dug in the ground. Then it is ready for use.

It is not an uncommon occurrence for the Apaches to have the skins which are brought in in the morning, made into moccasins before night, and very good ones too.

Cochise now brought up the animals, and I was gratified to find them in as fine condition as could be desired. The trip had evidently been a beneficial one, to them at least.

Requesting Cochise to notify Mangus Colorado that I should leave in the morning, he at once dispatched an Indian with the message, which had the effect of bringing Mangus himself to visit me, arrayed, as usual, in all the glory of ochre, vermilion, and eagle feathers.

After a shake of the hand, and the usual request for

"bacca," he seated himself on a blanket, and began to plead his poverty in such a pathetic manner that I soon saw I should be obliged to submit to a forced loan. He shortly preferred the request that I should present him with my riding mule, as a token of the great esteem he entertained for me.

This honor I emphatically declined, assuring him that I could ride no other, and should fail to reach home should I accede to his request. Recognizing the force of my argument, he now proposed to compromise, by taking another of my animals.

I remonstrated, telling him I needed them all, and must have them, but that I would send him by Cochise, when he returned, red blankets, brass wire, and tobacco, with which promise he seemed so well satisfied that I began to think I had such a persuasive way with me, that my services would be invaluable to the government as a treaty-maker with the Indians, — a fact, however, that the government has not as yet seemed to appreciate.

After a few complimentary shakes of the hand, Mangus assured me that Cochise would see me to the Pass in safety, and that he would send five braves with him as a guard, an honor that I at once declined.

Reminding me not to forget the "big presents," Mangus bade me farewell, much to my delight and gratification, and I at once extended congratulations to a certain party on his success as a diplomat. Cochise departed with Mangus, and after an absence of a couple of hours, returned, saying, that he could have the animals on hand early in the morning, and advising me to retire very soon, so as to "sleep much," which advice I followed. Quieted by the thought of a speedy return to the Pass, I soon sank into a profound slumber, such as I had not experienced before since my advent into Apachedom.

I was aroused early by Cochise, with the pleasant information that one of my mules had mysteriously disappeared, nor could "hide or hair" of him be found anywhere.

I knew it was useless to attempt to recover him, and mentally promising myself, that if I once got safely away, Mangus should never receive the presents I had promised him, I determined to set out at once with my four remaining animals.

Declining firmly all offers of trade, I made a hasty breakfast, and fully an hour before sunrise found me toiling up one of the steep paths worn into the face of the bluff that environs the Apache *rancheria.*

Our journey lay over the same parched alkali country, the same arid desert waste, unrelieved by the sight of a green thing, which I had crossed when going to the village.

About the middle of the afternoon we reached the only camping-ground before we came to the cañon we were to cross. After a hearty supper of pemmican and *atole*, and watering the mules from the contents of one of the leathern bottles, I wrapped myself in my blanket, and enjoyed a comfortable night's rest.

In the morning, as I watched the rising sun gild the grand and lofty summits of the mountain ranges all around, I could not but wish that some one was near who could appreciate with me the soul-inspiring sight that met my gaze whichever way I turned.

I never before saw anything so truly grand and wonderful! It scarcely seemed possible that the magnificent old castles, looking so proudly down upon us, with their towers and spires and battlements lighted up with such splendid effect by the morning sun, were but a bleak and barren mass of rock, over which the foot of civilized man had never passed since its creation, or that the only notes breathed forth from the gigantic pipes of that mighty organ were those that woke in thunder-peals the solitude of the vast desert around us, responsive only to the touch of God's own hand upon its massive key-board.

I tried to imagine the convulsive throes of old Mother Earth at the creation of these stupendous marvels; and wondered how many centuries would elapse before the hand of man, and the providence of God combined, would cause "the desert to blossom as the rose,"— when my dreams were disturbed by two short words, calculated to force

JIMMY CAPTURED BY THE INDIANS.

me to leave the solution of these questions to old Time himself.

Cochise speaking, said, "Injun comin'."

I immediately sprang to my feet, and looking in the direction designated by him, discovered a camp some five miles away, apparently on the verge of the cañon we were to cross, and on our immediate course.

Cochise offered to reconnoitre, and I made not the slightest objection to his proposition.

He returned shortly after, with the information that there were four Indians and two white men in camp there.

This convinced me that it must be Dr. Parker, who had returned, and, finding me gone on the expedition, had induced Jimmy to join him, and the two had followed on my trail.

We immediately started on, and soon proved the truth of my surmises. It was Dr. Parker and Jimmy, accompanied by four friendly Apaches, who had started out to find me. We were delighted to meet, and I was especially pleased as soon as I ascertained that the doctor's larder was much better stocked with "creature comforts" than was mine.

Nothing could exceed Jimmy's joy at finding me. He capered and danced like the wild Irishman that he was, upsetting the coffee-pot in his enthusiastic demonstrations, and nearly putting out the fire, which he had been "a wake gatherin' the metherials for!" a statement that was not verified by the strength of the coffee.

While at breakfast, the doctor entertained me with an account of Jimmy's journey through the cañon, and a most amusing one it was, too, especially as his narrative was frequently interrupted by remarks from Jimmy, in explanation of some scene, which it would take the pencil of a Nast to properly portray.

The doctor said that Jimmy had protested most earnestly against "interin' that crack," as he termed the cañon, maintaining most stoutly that " 'twas jist a crack in the airth, and thet by walkin' a little way down he could aisy find a place where he could git acrost."

After much persuasion, however, Jimmy was induced to follow the guide.

Proceeding some distance down the trail, Jimmy noticed the increasing darkness, and chancing to cast his eyes upwards, the narrow band of light far above him, relieved only by the ragged edges of the cañon, gave him such a singular feeling, that he yelled loudly to the doctor, who was some distance in advance of him.

Of course the sides of the cañon echoed the cry, and as he heard the echo repeating "Docther, Docther," as it was carried from side to side, from point to point, from crag to crag, with a distinctness and fidelity that was truly wonderful, his excited imagination led him to suppose it to be the despairing wail of human souls, who, during some terrible convulsion of nature, had, like "proud Knorah's troop," mentioned in the old New England primer, been swallowed up, while he believed himself approaching a similar fate.

Rushing headlong towards the doctor, he besought him, in the most agonizing tones, to "presarve him from bein' carried among thim poor divils that was scraachin' at him so"; nor could anything the doctor said reassure him.

The constantly-increasing gloom, together with the terrific reverberations, but added to Jimmy's fear and confusion, and he started back, swearing that "all the divils in hell shouldn't carry him a stip further." The doctor's calls only accelerated Jimmy's footsteps, and finding that he was really determined upon returning, he was obliged to send two of the Indians after him, with instructions to bring him back at all hazards, while he proceeded, with the others, to the foot of the cañon, where, seating himself upon a huge granite boulder, he waited Jimmy's appearance.

Bethinking himself of some pitch-pine which was in his luggage, he proceeded to light a splinter, that he might see its effect upon the rocks and cliffs and fissures, which towered far above, and surrounded him on all sides.

The sight terrified even the doctor, who no longer wondered at Jimmy's frantic prayers to the Virgin, when he saw the lurid glare reflected upon the broken sides and ragged edges of this terrible abyss.

The sounds now indicated the near approach of the Indians, and Jimmy's voice was distinctly heard, at one moment uttering prayers for protection, and the next cursing roundly

JIMMY REFUSES TO "INTER" THE CRACK.

those who had him in charge; for, as he afterwards said, "I tho't shure that they wus a takin' me straight down to hell, without aither the absolution of the praste, or the satisfaction of dyin'."

The loud cries of Jimmy, as he was forced down the steep

and rugged path, were terrifying in the extreme; so much so, that even the usually quiet animals manifested symptoms of intense fear, so that it required all the attention of the doctor and his Indian allies to keep them from stampeding.

Jimmy finally made his appearance, escorted by the Indians, in a most pitiable condition, as much by reason of his exertions to escape from his captors, as from the terror which the strange and gloomy surroundings had inspired within him.

On reaching the bottom, the sight of Dr. Parker emerging from behind a huge rock, with a torch in his hand, so far reassured him, and he declared, "that the only satisfaction he filt in comin' to hell, wus in findin' the docthor there before him."

Resuming their journey, he grew much bolder, asserting, with real Irish bravado, that he had only been "tistin' the narves of thim bloody Injuns. An' by the powers, I think them intirely narvous, shure."

But I have no intention of giving you a detailed account of our journey back to the Apache Pass. Suffice it to say, we crossed the cañon safely, passed over the same desert waste, hemmed in by lofty mountains, and guarded by grotesque and misshapen forms, that stood like grim and silent sentinels keeping watch and ward in these solitudes.

It was not until the afternoon of the fifth day that we arrived at the Pass.

After a hearty supper, and a good night's rest, Cochise and his braves were dismissed, laden with many presents, not one of which, however, was intended for Mangus Colorado. Cochise received the lion's share, and left me with many assurances of his esteem and regard.

Of late years Cochise has taken to the war-path, and has proved a most formidable and dangerous enemy to the white man in Arizona, in avenging the treacherous manner in which the chief of the Apache tribe, Mangus Colorado, met his death at the hands of the white men in 1863.

Although quite conscious of the failure of my diplomatic interview with Mangus Colorado on the mule question, still I console myself with the thought, that it was entirely owing to the evident mulish disposition of the Apaches, rather than to any lack of talent on my part; and if afterwards I became convinced that Cochise stole my mule, I lay the flattering unction to my soul, that it was by the express order, and for the sole use and behoof of Mangus himself, and that the idea did not originate with my old guide, Cochise.

At the present time, I am more than satisfied with my trip and its results, when I reflect that, without doubt, I am the only white man who ever visited the *rancheria* of the Pinal and Tonto Apaches, near the head waters of the Gila, and escaped to tell the tale.

CHAPTER X.

Vase taken from Sacred spring at Zuni

A REST of two days at the Apache Pass, and we started on our trip to Tucson, and the silver mines in that vicinity. I do not propose to enter into the details of the journey, for had it not been enlivened by Jimmy's adventures, it would have been utterly devoid of incident or interest. No more dreary and uninteresting country can be found under the sun, than that lying between the Apache Pass and Tucson.

The principal features of the landscape have a marked similarity. The peaks of the Santa Rita and Cerro Colorado Mountains loomed up in all their gloomy majesty on our right, and the wonderful purple haze with which the distance clothed them, was a grateful relief to the brassy sky above our heads, and the gray alkali of the plains around us.

On our left the peaks of the Chiricahui and the Three Sisters lined the horizon, while far, far before us a faint line of blue, almost indistinguishable from the azure of the summer's sky, betrayed the location of the San Ignatio Mountains of Sonora.

The plains around us were covered with an abundance of cactus, wild sage, grease wood, and mesquit chaparral, at once the curse and blessing of the Arizona *rancheria;* for while it offers an almost impenetrable barrier to travellers over the plain, it furnishes them with the only fuel to be found. The wood-chopper of Arizona uses only a spade, or mattock, in laying in his winter supply of fire-wood, for the roots of the mesquit alone furnish it.

The second day of our trip gave the doctor and myself the most amusement, as well as the most vexation, of any day during the journey.

It was nearly noon. Jimmy had ridden on ahead of the doctor and myself, who were leisurely driving along, enjoying the shade afforded by the canvas covering of our Concord wagon, when the doctor called my attention to a horseman far away to our right, riding at breakneck speed, in a course which I knew was taking him directly into one of the worst alkali plains on the whole route.

Wondering who it was, and what the man's object could

be, for we knew by his manner of riding he must be either a Mexican or an American, the doctor and myself dreamily and vaguely speculated upon his probable fate, until, on arriving at the top of a slight eminence, we discovered, far beyond the solitary figure of the horseman, a mirage of the "Greenhorn's Lake."

There it was, sparkling and beautiful in the bright sunshine, with its white-capped waves lapping the shores, skirted by a light growth of forest trees, its deep, blue waters affording a refreshing relief from the dusty plain and glaring sunlight with which we were surrounded, when suddenly it occurred to us that it was Jimmy, who was thus galloping frantically over the plain in pursuit of the lake, which to all appearance was only a mile or so distant.

We immediately discharged our revolvers, hoping that the sound would attract his notice, and induce him to return. Thinking that he might see the wagon, and give up his fruitless chase, we waited for him some time. As he did not appear, we finally decided to drive on slowly, keeping a sharp lookout in the direction in which we had last seen him. It was not, however, until nearly five o'clock in the afternoon, that we discovered him slowly following us.

As he came up with us, his air of utter dejection told us more effectually than words could have done, that Jimmy was sadly disappointed and completely disheartened. After overtaking us, he rode beside our wagon for some distance.

before a word was spoken by either of us, when I remarked,

"Well, Jimmy, where have you been, and what did you go after?"

His reply was, "Shure, sir, I don't know."

"Who gave you permission to ride my mule as I saw you riding it this morning?"

"Shure, sir, I don't know."

"Where were you going?"

"Shure, sir, I don't know."

"How far did you ride?"

"Indade, sir, I don't know."

"Well, Jimmy, what is the matter, and what do you think?"

"Indade, sir, I don't know." Nor could other answer than this be obtained from him to any question we might ask.

In truth, Jimmy seemed so utterly dazed and bewildered, that I decided to say nothing more on the subject, well satisfied that erelong he would voluntarily unburden his pent-up feelings.

It was quite six o'clock in the afternoon when we came to the dry, sandy bed of an aroya, that seemed to come directly from the range of Picatchos, about three miles away to our left. As the grass was good, and the banks very high and steep, we concluded to encamp for the night, and not attempt to cross it before morning.

Our mules were soon enjoying the sweetness of the grass around us. Our supper had been eaten, and we were ready for our blankets, when I chanced to think that I had been annoyed all day by the rattling of the spokes in the wheels of our wagon. Knowing that the hot sun and excessively dry weather had caused the wood to shrink, I called Jimmy, and told him to go down into the bed of the aroya, and dig some holes in the sand, which would soon fill with water; and after watering the animals, to bring some up and wet the wheels thoroughly, and keep them wet for an hour or so, or until they were sufficiently swollen to become tight again. This he promised to do; and about half-past eight o'clock the doctor and myself "turned in," leaving Jimmy to attend to the wagon before retiring. I soon fell into a sound sleep, and must have slept some hours, when I was awakened by what seemed to be the roar of a mighty torrent.

Hastily rising, I proceeded to the bank of the aroya, where a sight met my gaze that for a moment astounded me. The aroya, which but a few hours before was parched and dry, was now filled nearly to the top of its banks with a torrent of dark, muddy water, rushing along at the rate of ten miles an hour, overturning immense rocks, and bearing upon its black and seething bosom trees, bushes, and stumps without number.

A moment's reflection convinced me that this aroya must

be the natural outlet from the mountains, and the rain which had undoubtedly fallen in them during the evening, had collected in the water-courses and gullies upon their sides, and finally found vent through this channel to the plains below.

I hastily awoke Dr. Parker and Jimmy, whose astonishment at the sight equalled my own.

The doctor understood the phenomenon at once. Not so Jimmy, however, who, the instant he heard the roar of the rushing waters, and saw the turbulent flood surging so madly by us, fell upon his knees, and with terrified countenance commenced a prayer to the Virgin, interrupted only by loud and frantic cries for a "praste."

Then he bewailed the sad fate that had induced him to enlist in the service of a man who travelled in such "God-forsaken counthries," and begged most piteously to "be sint right strate out of the divilish place."

The doctor and myself did our best to pacify him, telling him that no harm could possibly come of it; that it was simply the water from the mountains finding its way to the lake he had tried to reach the day before.

At this explanation, Jimmy regarded us with no small amount of suspicion, and merely remarking "that he should think there was a divil of a lake somewhere," he turned away; but the doctor, thinking it a good time to learn the history of Jimmy's expedition of the day before, questioned him respecting it, whereupon he gave us the following account:—

"Shure," said he, "I was a-ridin' along peaceably and quietly enough, till I looked up, and there, right before me, was a beautiful lake, with its blue waters a-dancin' in the sunshine like spangles on the driss of a play-actor, and I jist thought I'd ride down to it, and give the poor baste a sup of wather; and bedad, the farther I rode, the farther off I was from it, but I kept on ridin' and ridin', until by and by it jist sunk right into the ground, and disappeared intirely out of me sight; and when I got to the place where I saw it wid me own eyes, it wasn't there at all, and the ground under it was as dhry as the powther in me gun. Shure, Judge, it was the divil's own lake, and that's some of the wather of it down there. Sir, I'll die if I stay in this hathenish counthry another day; you must send me straight home."

Here noticing, for the first time, that the wagon was without wheels, I said,—

"Jimmy, where are the wheels?"

His reply, "I think they are gone to the divil, shure," did not in the least add to my amiability, and I again said,—

"Jimmy, where are the wheels of the wagon?"

"Indade, sir, I don't know," was the only answer I could obtain.

After much coaxing, Dr. Parker succeeded in eliciting the information, that after we had retired he had taken the wheels off, and carrying them down into the bed of the aroya, had put them to soak in the hole he had dug for the mules to drink from, intending to rise early enough to

THE WHEEL SCENE.

put them to the wagon before the doctor and myself should awake; and, added the doctor, "If we may judge from the ease with which the stones are rolled over by the force of the current, we shall probably find those wheels 'Rocked in the cradle of the deep,' sometime to-morrow."

Here was a fix; for a wagon without wheels on the plains is a somewhat useless encumbrance, and we had no other means of transporting our supplies for the trip.

I was thoroughly vexed at Jimmy's disobedience of orders, as well as at his carelessness, and am somewhat afraid that I then and there indulged in the use of language that would hardly have been deemed proper by members of Orthodox churches "in good and regular standing."

I reflected, however, that this loud talk would do no good, and that we must wait until the waters subsided, which they did, almost as suddenly as they had appeared.

About ten o'clock, the doctor and Jimmy started out to search along the bottom of the aroya for the wheels, while I remained in camp to look after our treasures there. It was three o'clock in the afternoon before they returned, bringing with them two of the wheels, which they had recovered about four miles below; the others they were unable to find. Another day must be spent in the search. About noon one more was found, nearly six miles from our camp; and on returning with it, the last was discovered, partially buried in the sand, with a ponderous stone resting upon it. Jimmy had the pleasure of digging it out; and upon recovering it, we were glad to find that, though somewhat damaged, it would still answer its purpose.

Jimmy, though rather reticent on the subject, was heard to say that, "If the Blissid Virgin would bring him safe to a civilized counthry once more, the divil shouldn't kape him from returnin' to ould Ireland by the first stamer," to which remark the doctor responded,—

"Well, Jimmy; if we lose the wheels again, you'll have to pack it, I'm afraid!"

The next morning found us once more on the road. We travelled all day without seeing any object worthy of note, and just at night came to a distilling camp, near which we pitched our own.

Here a party of Mexicans and Papago Indians were engaged in distilling mescal, the native whiskey of Arizona.

The maguey, or Mexican aloe, grows in great abundance here, and many come to this vicinity for the purpose of gathering it.

A large pit is first dug, and partially filled with stones; upon these a fire is built, and kept up until the stones are heated red-hot; then the roots of the maguey which have been gathered, each consisting of a bulb about as large as one's head, are placed upon the stones, and covered with blankets, where they are kept until perfectly soft. Next they are placed in large bags, made of rawhide, and stretched on poles, into which a man climbs, and by trampling upon them, presses out the juice, which runs through small holes in the bottom of the bag, and is caught in pails. This juice is then allowed to ferment, when a liquor is obtained, that, I believe, from Jimmy's appearance when he returned to camp that night, will make a person drunk clear through, in a very short space of time.

Jimmy's excuse that it was "pure mountain dew," was accepted; for in taste and smell it more strongly resembled Irish whiskey than any liquor I have ever seen.

An early start the next morning, and just after noon we entered the town of Tucson, nothing having occurred to relieve the monotony of the journey; for Jimmy manifested not the least desire to start on any more expeditions in search of either water or information, although he frequently complained that "thravellin' was very dhry wark."

Tucson, at this time, was the capital of the Territory, with a population of about six hundred inhabitants, nearly one-half of which were Mexicans, the balance consisting of a mixture of Apaches, Pimos, Papagoes, and cut-throats. Probably never before in the history of any country were gathered within the walls of a city such a complete assortment of horse-thieves, gamblers, murderers, vagrants, and villains, as were to be found in the city of Tucson.

The general appearance of the place gave one the impression that it had originally been a hill, which, owing to an unexpected but just visitation of Providence, had been struck with lightning; and the dilapidated mud walls, and dismantled *jacals*, that served as a shelter for the festering mass of corruption that breathed upon the site, were the residuum left in the shape of mud deposits, for not a white wall nor a green tree was to be seen there.

The only objects which met the eye were dilapidated bake ovens, old sheds, broken pottery, dead horses, tumble-down corrals, live dogs, drunken Indians, mules, pigs, and naked children. The sight was such an one as I had never before witnessed within the limits of civilization, and completely filled me with disgust.

There was no *fonda*, or other house of entertainment, and when one reached the apology that was called the *plaza*, he stopped, absolutely bewildered, not knowing where to go, or how to get there.

We soon found an unoccupied mud box, that served as a house, spread our blankets on the mud floor, and cooked our food in the mud fire-place; when night came, we brought everything, including wagon, harness, mules, and accompaniments, into the mud walls, and shut and barred the doors.

The miserable appearance of the city and its inhabitants determined us to get out of the town as soon as possible, and get out we did, early in the morning, Dr. Parker remarking that "there was little fear of our being *salted* for looking back, though if there ever was a place closely allied to old Sodom, it was Tucson."

We shortly entered the lovely valley of the Santa Cruz; and here, ten miles from Tucson, we came upon the beautiful mission of San Xavier del Bac, built by the

Jesuits in 1678, and the building would be an ornament to any city in the United States.

It is the most beautiful, as well as remarkable, specimen of the Saracenic style of architecture to be found in the country; nor have I ever seen a building in such perfect harmony with its proportions as is this. The moment the eye rests upon it, one experiences a feeling of entire satisfaction, so complete is it in every detail. Its front is richly ornamented with elaborate carving. Standing in niches, and grouped over and around the main entrance, are the remains of the figures of the twelve Apostles, evidently the work of a master's hand. From the front corners rise lofty and beautifully proportioned towers, one of which is surmounted with a most graceful spire. Over the main body of the church, which is cruciform in shape, rises a massive dome; while the walls, both inside and out, are capped by handsome cornices.

Nearly two hundred years have rolled over the walls of this magnificent structure, this splendid monument of the zeal, energy, and civilization of the ancient Jesuits.

It is now but a mere wreck, when compared with its former splendor. Eighty thousand dollars' worth of gold and silver ornamented its altar when the *Te Deum Laudamus* was chanted within its walls, and the mountain-tops around echoed the sound of the vesper bell, calling the poor Indian to prayer.

Alas! Time has blackened its frescoed walls, and sacrilegious hands have defaced its fine statuary and paintings; but the building itself will stand in its massive strength for a thousand years, and its graceful spire, silently pointing upwards, will not fail to remind the beholder that, hundreds of years ago, upon the deserts of Arizona, the example of the lowly Nazarene was held forth for the guidance of pagan Indians, in obedience to the Divine command, "Go ye into all the world, and preach the Gospel."

Does not this magnificent building, with its desert surroundings, teach the stay-at-home-and-take-your-ease Christians of the present day a lesson worthy of imitation?

'Twas an inexpressibly sad sight, this crumbling monument of man's faithfulness and devotion in extending the reign of our Lord Jesus Christ; and as I stood before its altar, my eye vainly striving to pierce the deep gloom of its shadowy aisles and recesses, the sight of a venerable-looking old Indian, devoutly kneeling with uncovered head before a little crucifix, carried my thoughts far back to the day and generation when the choir responded to the solemn mass, "Glory to God in the highest"; and I could almost hear the sweet tones of the priest, as they resounded through the arched and gloomy recesses of the old church, repeating, "And on earth peace, good-will toward men."

Desolation and decay, however, have left their ineffaceable marks upon the building; and as I left its portals it was

SAN XAVIER DEL BAÇ.

with the reflection that, after all, San Xavier was but a picture of life, drawn by a master's hand, whose outlines time never dims, and whose colors never fade.

The building is in charge of the Papago Indians, who still worship in it. There are about two hundred of these Indians, who reside in this vicinity, and cultivate the rich bottom-lands of the Santa Cruz, raising wheat, rye, corn, and vegetables in profusion. They also grow the most delicious pomegranates I ever tasted.

At the time of my visit, they were very much in need of stock, the Apaches having made a raid upon them only a few nights before, and driven off all their animals.

Old José was the chief of the tribe, and claimed a direct descent from royal blood. He informed us, in a peculiar jargon of Spanish, Papago, and English, that he was one hundred and four years of age, a statement that his appearance seemed to substantiate.

Let me attempt a description of him. Imagine, if you can, a short, thick-set person, weighing about two hundred and thirty pounds, clothed in an old-fashioned, snuff-colored dress-coat, the tails of which gracefully swept the ground. Upon one shoulder an old tarnished epaulet; upon his feet a pair of moccasins, richly wrought in silk, and ornamented with tiny bells of solid silver; his legs entirely destitute of clothing, and resembling very closely a pair of old-fashioned clothes-pins. His long, black hair, parted in the middle, was braided in a cue, the end ornamented with gaudy-colored ribbons, which, resting on the top of his high, stiff coat-collar, elevated it to an angle of forty-five degrees, giving his head a very singular and grotesque appearance. The parting of his hair was painted a bright green, while his cheeks were plentifully daubed with ochre and vermilion. In his hand he carried a high-crowned, narrow-rimmed hat, of so small a size that he could, by no possibility, get it on his head.

He informed me, with a smile that was intended to be "childlike and bland," and perfectly displaying his toothless gums, that he was habited in his best garments, for the express purpose of doing us great honor.

I could not avoid offering him a slight token of my appreciation of his politeness, in the shape of a silver coin, which he seized with an avidity that convinced me that this "venerable descendant of his ancestors" had the same overweening desire for filthy lucre that has ever shown itself in human nature, whether descended from royal blood, or born in the plebeian walks of every-day life.

Not wishing to be outdone in politeness, I complimented the old fellow upon his fine personal appearance, telling him that Jimmy had remarked, there was about him that majesty and dignity which could be found only among Ireland's most kingly kings, at which compliment the old fellow turned himself slowly around, to give me a better opportunity to appreciate and admire his elegant dress and majestic bearing; and taking from his capacious pocket a small piece of mirror, he proceeded to take a survey of his ugly features with evident delight and satisfaction, slowly repeating "*Si, señor, muy linda, muy linda;*" or, Yes, sir; very beautiful, very beautiful.

The old fellow's antics reminded me more of a fashionable dandy of the present day, than any animal I ever saw; and I came to the conclusion that one could study human nature quite as well in a Papago Indian, as in a Broadway exquisite.

Jimmy was really overpowered by the magnificent strut of Old José, and remarked to Dr. Parker, that "you could aluz tell a borned king whiniver yer seen him," a truism that neither Dr. Parker nor myself could contradict, as this was the first specimen of the kind we had ever met, and withal as *bare* a specimen of a monarch as ever swayed a sceptre.

That evening we attended vesper service in the old church, for the Papagoes still respect the religion of the Catholic Church, taught to their ancestors more than two centuries ago. I was surprised and delighted by the music; it was novel and charming.

When the priest reached a certain portion of the service, the air seemed suddenly filled by the warbling of ten thousand birds, whose melodious notes rose and fell and swelled and lingered through the arched passages of the church, now dying away as though in the far distance, and again approaching nearer and nearer, until the very air seemed resonant with the notes of the sweetest feathered songsters.

Again we heard it, but so exquisitely soft and low that its cadences more closely resembled the wailings of an Æolian harp, than music created by mortal agency. Once more it swelled into grand and lofty pæans of praise, until it seemed that such exquisite music must be created by a celestial choir. Even Jimmy, who was devoutly kneeling in prayer, stopped, and looking up, remarked, "What the divil is that now? I niver heard the likes er that, aven in ould Ireland."

As soon as we could withdraw from the service, the doctor and myself ascended to the gallery of the church, by means of a notched log of wood, that served for stairs.

Here we found, lying flat on their faces upon the floor, a dozen or more youths, before each one of whom stood a small cup of water, in which was inserted one end of split reeds of different sizes, the other end of the reed being held in their mouths, and blowing through it, they produced the sweet sounds which had so enchanted us.

It seemed impossible that such delicious music could be produced by such simple instruments. The vesper service, in the old mission of San Xavier del Bac, was one never to be forgotten.

We returned to camp that night well pleased with the experiences of the day, and quite delighted with our visit. Jimmy was highly elated, and frequently remarked that "he niver expicted to spend another day in the prisence ov a live king," as he persisted in calling Old José.

The next morning's sun found us *en route* for Tubac, from which point we intended to visit the silver mines of Arizona.

CHAPTER XI.

WENTY miles' drive through the rich bottom-lands of the Santa Cruz brought us to Bill May's ranche. Every one in Arizona knew Bill, — a whole-souled, generous-hearted, daring frontierman, who never turned a traveller away hungry from his door, or refused the shelter of his roof to the unfortunate. We had passed many ranches on our way, seen many fields of waving corn, but had ridden thus far because we wanted to see Bill May. We found him at home, and he bade us "Enter" in the loud, cheery tones of a man whose heart was in his words; and the warm, friendly shake of the hand with which he greeted us spoke a sincere welcome.

May was a fine, athletic fellow, fully six feet in height,

as brave as Julius Cæsar, and as cool as a cucumber, never losing his presence of mind under any circumstances. He was at war with the Apaches, and took every opportunity to "bag" some of them, as he expressed it. Only a few days before, he had followed a party who had stolen some of his cattle, and not only recovered the stock, but "bagged" two of the Indians, of which fact he felt justly proud.

A hearty supper of venison, with plenty of good coffee to enliven us during the evening, and help us swallow some of the Indian stories Bill entertained us with, together with a clean, sweet bed to sleep in, — the first we had occupied since we left Mesilla, — rested and refreshed us for our morrow's journey.

A delightful drive of some twenty miles through a most beautiful portion of the Territory, was the route for the day. We passed numerous traces of former cultivation, in the shape of unused and dry acequias, extending for miles in all directions, together with the remains of old ranches and adobe walls, which presented a sad contrast to the bright beauties of the day and the green bottom-lands of the Santa Cruz. It was late in the afternoon when we reached Tubac, which at that time was the head-quarters of the most refined and intelligent portion of the inhabitants of the Territory, — gentlemen from the East, in charge of the silver mines in this vicinity; scientific men, sent out to explore and report upon newly-discovered mines; German metallurgists; officers of the military fort situated near by, — in short, the *élite* of Arizona called Tubac their home. It was also the head-quarters of the Arizona Mining Company; and it was here that we met Mr. Poston, the agent and superintendent of the company.

The town itself was very attractive, with its beautiful groves of acacias, its peach-orchards and its pomegranates, situated, as it is, immediately on the banks of the Santa Cruz, and embowered in the most luxuriant foliage. In close proximity to this town are to be found the Santa Rita, the Heintzleman, and the Cerro Gordo mines, the richest yet discovered in the Territory. Game was very abundant, and our larder was well supplied with venison, wild turkey, fish, and many other creature comforts, much to the evident delight of Jimmy, who, in addition to the fact that he was cook, greatly loved "good aitin."

The population of Tubac consisted of about eight hundred souls, one-sixth of whom were Americans and Germans, the remainder being Sonoranians, with a few Yaqui Indians. This town, like Tucson, was originally an old Mexican fort, which, after the establishment of the boundary line, was deserted by the Mexicans, and the first settlement of Americans was made here in the year 1856. The only business transacted was that done by the mining company, if we except the trade in mescal, which was very extensive.

Four miles below Tubac, on a beautiful slope of the Santa

Cruz, is another old mission building erected by the Jesuits, known as the mission of San José de Tumaccari, which was built about the time of that of San Xavier del Bac, though it is far from being in as good a state of preservation, owing, no doubt, to the vandalism of the Americans and the depredations of the Apaches. In fact, the building is but little better than a mass of ruins. Like all these missions, Tumaccari was located in a fine agricultural country, as shown by the remains of old acequias, as well as the many cultivated fields that are plainly discernible for miles around; nor can there be any doubt that the Santa Cruz Valley was once the home of a vast population, though now, owing to the constant raids of the Apaches, 'tis but a barren waste.

Gravestones, or rather head-boards, stand by the road-side like sentinels, bearing the invariable inscription,—

"KILLED BY THE APACHES."

Ruined ranches, deserted *haciendas*, and untilled fields stare you in the face whichever way you turn, and tell a story that cannot fail to awaken in the mind of the beholder the most melancholy reflections.

A visit to Fort Buchanan, the next day, at the head of the charming Sonoita Valley, where we met with Captain R. S. Ewell and the officers of his command, was a most enjoyable one in every way. Upon Captain Ewell's expressing a desire to visit some of the silver mines in the vicinity, we urged him so strongly to accompany us that he finally consented; and, accepting the generous hospitality offered by him, we remained over night at the Fort, and the next morning, in company with the captain and an escort of ten mounted men, we left Fort Buchanan for a visit to the silver mines of Southern Arizona. We decided to first visit the Patagonia mine, then owned by Sylvester Mowrey, one of the first American settlers in the Territory. We found Mr. Mowrey at the mine, and received from him some important information concerning it, which may be of interest to the reader.

The mine is situated in the Santa Cruz Mountains, about six thousand feet above the level of the sea. It is nearly three hundred miles from Guaymas, on the Gulf of California, and about ten miles from the Sonora line. It was worked by the Spaniards as early as 1760, abandoned on account of Apache raids in 1820, and was rediscovered by Mr. Mowrey in 1856. At the time of our visit, the company were engaged in putting in a steam-engine, which had been hauled by mules from Lavaca, in Texas, a distance of fourteen hundred miles. A boiler weighing nearly six thousand pounds had also been brought in the same way, to the great terror of the Apaches, who not only kept a respectable distance from it, but could not be induced to approach it, believing it to be a huge cannon, brought into the country to accomplish their immediate and entire destruction at one discharge.

The necessary buildings for the machinery, the smelting-houses, reduction works, store-houses, and dwellings for the *peons* was a most pleasing sight in contrast to the signs of desolation to be seen in all other directions. The ore taken from this mine is an argentiferous galena, strongly impregnated with arsenic, and is easily mined and reduced. There are three veins, each large and well defined. The ore was yielding from sixty to seventy dollars per ton, which was considered a large paying yield. Since that time, a day's working, or twenty tons of ore, has yielded as high as sixteen hundred dollars, at an actual cost of about four hundred.

Notwithstanding these results, the proprietors have never been able to realize much profit from it, on account of the depredations of the Indians; and shortly after my visit, a band of Apaches drove off all of the company's stock, and murdered the superintendent and many of the miners: since then the mines have been unworked, the valuable machinery useless, many of the buildings destroyed, and desolation and decay have left their sad marks on all around.

That night we encamped near the foot of the Pintos Mountains, in a beautiful grove of cotton-wood, beside a spring whose clear, sparkling waters we found to be quite as cool as we cared to drink.

Rising early the next morning, I set out for a walk of

three or four miles, to visit a pass, or cañon, in the mountains, whose beauty I had often heard extolled by Captain Ewell. I had gone nearly two miles from camp, and was admiring the grandeur of the mountain scenery before me, whose peaks were fairly gleaming in the rays of the rising sun, when my ear caught the sound of unshod horses' feet resounding on the hard, pebbly soil, like the muffled gallop of a distant squad of cavalry. Failing to detect the sharp ring of the iron hoofs of our American horses, I at once decided that it was a party of Indians approaching. Hastily secreting myself behind a thick clump of hackberry, I breathlessly awaited further developments; nor had I long to wait, for I soon saw approaching a party of eight Apaches, each bestriding an animal gaudily caparisoned with eagles' feathers and brass ornaments.

They passed very near me, — so near, in fact, that I was enabled to note the face and peculiar ornaments of each one of the party. Not a sound was heard save the footsteps of their horses, nor was a word spoken as long as they remained in sight. Each one was naked, save the breech-clout, and carried in his hand the hated spear so well known and dreaded among the settlers in Arizona, while to the saddles of four of the party was tied an old Mississippi Yauger, of antiquated make and flint lock, yet quite effective in the hands of Apaches. Their faces and bodies were well striped with vermilion, ochre, and black, and as they passed, each brave sitting erect, and as firm as a rock upon the back of his horse, their eyes constantly turning to the right and left, as if scanning every bush and rock that might permit concealment for a foe, I could but admire their dignified and soldier-like

I RETURN TO CAMP WITHOUT MY HAT.

bearing, though I well knew that a discovery of my hiding-place would be certain and speedy death to me. I am bound to confess that during the time they were in sight I was more quiet than I had ever been before in my life.

As soon as the Indians were well out of sight, I started

for camp. I started in haste, too; not because I was hungry, as much as because I was lonesome and particularly anxious to see my friends.

In thinking the thing over, I am convinced that there is no white man living at the present time, who ever got over more ground in a shorter space of time, than did I in going from the clump of hackberry to our camp. When I reached the camp I was somewhat "blown," and found that I had very carelessly left my hat somewhere on the route. I needed that hat badly, still I decided not to go back after it, nor have I seen it to this day.

As soon as I could obtain a sufficient amount of breath to enable me to explain the circumstances of my hasty entry into camp, Captain Ewell started at once with eight of his men, in the hope of overtaking them. We remained here all day, and it was not until late in the evening that the captain and his party returned, without having been able to come up with the Indians, who managed to secrete themselves as soon as they reached the mountains.

The Apaches, when on a raid or on the war-path, are allowed to eat but one meal a day, and to rest but three hours out of the twenty-four. Their discipline when on their excursions is splendid, quite equal to that of any army of civilized soldiers, while their ability to endure the hardships and discomforts of a campaign is far superior to that of white men.

The Indians whom I encountered in my morning ramble were, undoubtedly, Coytero Apaches, and a part of Deligado's band. It is hardly necessary to say that I did not take any more lonely rambles, but confined myself strictly to camp, much to the delight of Jimmy, who remarked in my presence, that "such an escape ought to be a warnin' to any man that was in the habit of wanderin' over the counthry when honest men should be in bed and aslape."

CHAPTER XII.

WE broke camp early the following morning, in order to reach the Santa Rita mine, situated in the Santa Rita Mountains, the next day, the distance being about forty miles. We found at the mine a Mr. Grosvenor, who was the general manager of affairs there. He had but recently been appointed to the position, and was laboring hard to get things in order. He informed us that the Apaches, within the past twelve months, had killed his three predecessors in the management of the mines; and within six months from that time, Mr. Grosvenor suffered a similar fate.

Up to the time of our visit, several assays of the ore had been made, yielding from sixty to four hundred dollars to the ton. In less than a year afterwards, the Apaches had killed all the miners and stolen the stock, thus forcing the company to abandon the enterprise which had given such promise of great success. In close proximity to the Santa Rita mine, and in the same range, is the Salero mine. This mine is advantageously located as regards wood and water, and at the time of our visit was regarded as one of the most valuable mines in the Territory. Mr. Grosvenor informed us that more than a hundred and twenty years before it was worked under the superintendence of the Jesuits, then living at the mission of Tumaccari, and at that time yielded very large quantities of silver. The settlers about, call it the Salt-cellar mine, and tell the following story of the origin of the name.

At the time the Jesuits were working the mine, the bishop of Sonora, a very distinguished person in those days, took it into his head to visit the good fathers at Tumaccari. He arrived at the mission with a numerous retinue, and surrounded with much pomp and state. Now the bishop was but a man, after all, and a man somewhat noted for the same distinguishing characteristics that our friend Jimmy possessed, viz. he loved "good aitin." So when the holy fathers ascertained whom their guest really was, they hastily bestirred themselves, that they might give him a fitting reception, and an entertainment worthy of his Reverence. Everything was at length satisfactorily arranged. The capons were fat, the mutton fine, the wines delicious, the fruit luscious, — in short, everything that could tickle the palate and delight the taste abounded in lavish profusion. The good bishop, however, liked his food well seasoned, and in the midst of the sumptuous repast was confounded to discover a lack of salt, whereupon he called loudly for a salt-cellar.

Imagine the confusion and dismay of the holy fathers at being obliged to confess that within the walls of Tumaccari such an article as a salt-cellar could not be found.

"No salt-cellar!" cried the bishop. "Why, I would as soon think of keeping house without a house, as without a salt-cellar."

Humbly acknowledging their fault, the fathers could only promise that on the morrow the desired article should be procured.

"Well and good," said the bishop; "and for this once the omission shall be pardoned."

After the dinner was over, the good fathers consulted together as to how the missing salt-cellar could be supplied on so short a notice. At length a bright idea dawned upon them; and hastily summoning some *peons*, one of the fathers took them in charge, and started for the mine. The ore was dug, smelted, and, ere sunrise the next morning, made into a massive salt-cellar, so wonderful and valuable that the fame of it has descended even to this day and generation, and it is to be seen in the bishop's palace at Hermosillo, the wonder and delight of all beholders.

From this story the mine receives its name of Salero. This mine, together with the Fuller, Encarnation, Bustillo, Crystal, Cazador, and Tenaja, all in the same range, are mines that were worked many years ago by the Spaniards, and, although yielding largely, were abandoned on account of the Apaches.

There are hundreds of mines in the different ranges of mountains in this vicinity, all rich, and many, having yielded enormously when worked, now abandoned and desolate, as it has been proved impossible to work them so long as that common foe to industry and civilization, the Apache, remains unconquered.

Captain Ewell determined to start for Fort Buchanan at once; and we reached the fort about midnight, right glad to once more see around us signs of life and civilization. After refreshments, and a good whiskey toddy, mixed by the captain himself, we retired to our bed, and sought that rest and sleep we so much needed.

The next morning we returned to Tubac, where we remained for the day, to the evident satisfaction of Jimmy, who expressed himself heartily sick of "pokin' his nose into ivery hole in the ground that we come to, and Injuns all around us."

The next day, in company with Mr. Poston and Mr.

Cross, we started on a visit to the Cerro Colorado mine, better known as the Heintzleman mine, which derived its name from our brave old general of that name, who in early Arizona times was stationed in the Territory, and who, perhaps, did more to protect the citizens and develop the mineral resources of Arizona than any one man before or since.

The mine when we were there had passed into the hands of a company who have since taken the name of the Arizona Mining Company. The mine is situated in the Cerro Colorado Mountains, at once the richest and most barren range in the whole Territory. It is distant from Tubac about twenty-five miles, and at the time of our visit was in successful operation, employing about two hundred men, and paying a very handsome profit.

Mr. Poston very kindly placed at our command all the facilities in his power to enable us to explore the mine, besides giving us much valuable information concerning it. At that time the main shaft had reached a depth of one hundred and twenty feet, and the ore seemed to yield far better than it had yet done. The ore at a depth of thirty feet had yielded sixty dollars to the ton; at a depth of sixty feet it had yielded nearly two thousand dollars to the ton; and an assay had just been made in San Francisco of the ore at a depth of one hundred feet, and found to yield the enormous sum of nine thousand dollars to the ton.

Mr. Poston was satisfied that the ore would average as

high as six hundred dollars per ton, which, even when compared with the richest silver mines in Mexico and Nevada, is very large, their average being from sixty to eighty-five dollars to the ton.

The Heintzleman mine is, without doubt, the richest silver mine in the world; but in 1862, the Apaches made a descent upon it, murdering Mr. Poston and many of the miners, since which time the mine, like nearly all others in Arizona, remains unworked.

The same company of capitalists who own this mine, are also the owners of the celebrated Arrivacca ranche, a few miles distant, which is said to be the most valuable property in the Territory, containing some thirty thousand acres of fine agricultural land, together with many valuable silver leads, some of which have been worked, while others are yet virgin to the miner's hand.

While Dr. Parker, in company with Mr. Poston and myself, had been exploring the wonders of the Cerro Colorado, Jimmy had disappeared, and with him an old but highly-prized Sharp's carbine. Becoming somewhat alarmed for his safety, Mr. Poston kindly dispatched two *vaqueros* in search of him.

After an hour or so they struck his trail, and following it for some distance, at last found Jimmy sitting upon the carcass of a fine buck, that, much to his surprise, he had succeeded in shooting.

The Mexicans not being able to speak a word of English, and Jimmy not understanding a word of Spanish, they found much difficulty in forcing him to comprehend their object in coming after him, he resisting all their attempts to bring him back; for, as it was the first deer that Jimmy had ever killed, he had no idea of leaving it until it was brought into camp.

The *vaqueros*, finding their efforts unavailing, returned to Mr. Poston to report. After listening to the story, Dr. Parker volunteered to take a wagon and go with the men to bring the game into camp. Although quité late when the doctor reached the spot, he found Jimmy patiently waiting by the side of his prize for the arrival of some one to assist him to bring the game in.

In the mean while Mr. Poston and myself had quietly arranged a plan of action for our evening's amusement. The sound of wheels in the distance, together with voices, Jimmy's "rich Irish brogue" being easily distinguishable, announced the return of the party. Jimmy soon appeared, highly elated, and begging us to go at once and look at the game. We found it a very fine buck; and Mr. Poston, after examining it attentively for a few moments, gravely remarked to me,—

"Yes, that is the animal; I should have recognized it among a thousand." And then turning to Jimmy, requested him to relate his story, which he was nothing loath to do.

As soon as he reached the part where, in his own phraseology, "he fired at the deer shure," we all looked grave and incredulous, but said not a word, much to Jimmy's surprise and perplexity.

After he had finished his story, I turned to Mr. Poston,

JIMMY'S TRIAL.

and asked him if that was the deer which he had referred to. He replied in the affirmative; and in proof of his assertion brought forward the two *vaqueros*, whose testimony I gravely interpreted into English, to the effect that the deer had been lying in the spot where Jimmy had found it for more than a week; that they had repeatedly seen it there, and that was the cause of their going that way in search of Jimmy.

Requesting Dr. Parker to examine the wound, he did so, pronouncing it to be an old one, and assuring us that the deer must have been dead some time, and evidently had died from weakness occasioned by loss of blood.

Jimmy was confounded,— utterly nonplussed! In vain did he show the rifle, and declare "by the blissid Virgin" that he killed the deer. The more he protested, the stronger grew the evidence against him, until at last the poor fellow was made to believe that he had had no hand in the death of the animal, although he remarked, that "this was the most deciptive counthry that any mon iver lived in, and that he would like to lave it at onct for a place where a mon's eyesight didn't decave him in the outrageous manner it did here."

After convincing him beyond all doubt, by the most positive evidence, that he did not kill the deer, the *vaqueros* proceeded to dress it, and we feasted that night on the most delicious venison steak we had yet found in the country; nor did we give Jimmy the credit he so much deserved for killing the deer, until some days later.

One fact impressed us most forcibly during our visit to this portion of the Territory, viz. all the mountains are, to a greater or less extent, exceedingly rich, being filled with valuable deposits of silver and gold. Since our visit, the

Heintzleman mine, like all the others, has been deserted, in consequence of the depredations of the Apaches. Ruins alone mark the place which but a few years since was the home of thrift and industry. How long this state of affairs will continue, who can tell? There is no protection for life or property there, nor can I see how the government can adequately garrison such a vast extent of territory as would be necessary to protect the mining interests in this section of the country. With the experiences of the past, no capitalists can be found willing to invest their money in speculations of so uncertain a character as silver mining, without protection, in Arizona.

There are many other mines equal in value to those I have named, particularly in and around Arrivacca. The Cahuabia, Bahia, and, in fact, dozens of mines could be mentioned, all rich, and lacking but one thing to make them valuable,—protection. Give the silver mines of Arizona but this, and there can be no doubt but that they would rival the richest silver mines in the world in their productions.

Leaving the Heintzleman mine, we drove to Tubac, where we remained for the night, enjoying the hospitality of the Arizona Mining Company, and early the next morning were on the road once more for Tucson. It was a beautiful day, and as we drove along, enjoying the delicious breeze from the mountains, we could but exclaim at the prodigality with which nature had bestowed her fairest gifts upon a country, whose inhabitants, like Tantalus, were doomed to see, but not to enjoy.

We spent the night with our friend Bill May, who, after administering to the comforts of the inner man, entertained us until a late hour with a history of the wild and adventurous life he had led upon the Mexican frontier, he having been one of the few who escaped of the party that formed the Crabbe expedition into Sonora in 1851.

The next morning we again started, and long ere night reached the Papago village, nestled under the shadow of the spires of San Xavier. Here we remained for the night; for the sight of the green fields and waving grain were far preferable to the mud walls and filthy surroundings of Tucson. Jimmy was delighted to see the "king" once again, as he persistently called Old José.

That evening, while we were lying on the grass watching Jimmy prepare the venison steaks for our supper, Dr. Parker said to him,—

"Jimmy, that is the finest venison we have yet seen in the country, and we are really indebted to you for it, for you killed it."

"Did I shoot that deer mesilf?" asked Jimmy, with the utmost surprise depicted on his expressive features.

"Yes, Jimmy, you shot it yourself."

"An' the ividence agin me wuz a lie?"

"All a lie, Jimmy."

"Thin by the powers," said Jimmy, "don't I wish I had thim vicarus here now! To think of 'em thryin' to stael the honor from a stranger in the counthry — and they livin' in it too. Wouldn't I like to give 'em a bit of an ould Irish shillalah, tho'?

The only animosity Jimmy exhibited was towards the unfortunate *vaqueros*, whose testimony had been manufactured by me to suit the occasion; and I very much fear that could he have found them, he would have administered the sound drubbing he threatened, in spite of anything we could do to prevent it.

In the evening we attended vespers for the last time in the old church, and once more listened to the soul-entrancing music of the Papago choralists. After the service, we witnessed in the yard of the church a regular Spanish "cock-fight," at which silver ounces freely changed hands. Each cock was armed with the old-fashioned Spanish slasher, a long, thin, steel blade, shaped somewhat like a hook, and most effective in destroying the life of the bird in whose body it is once sheathed.

The priest who officiated at vespers was the owner of the winning cock, his opponent having been brought from Tucson. Of course we congratulated him upon his good fortune, and his hearty "*Mil gracias*," convinced us that his soul was quite as much with his bird, as it had been with his service.

CHAPTER XIII.

AFTER much deliberation, and many arguments *pro* and *con*, Dr. Parker and myself finally decided to leave our wagon and mules at Tucson, in charge of Jimmy, and take the overland mail-coach to the Pimo villages on the Gila,— or swift running water,— from which place we determined to start on our visit to the celebrated "*Casas Grandes*" situated near that stream, which for many years have engaged the attention of the scientific men and savans of the Pacific coast.

We were not surprised to receive from Jimmy a most earnest, but respectful protest against our leaving him in what he was pleased to term the "divil's own counthry, shure"; and it was a long time before he became reconciled to our making the trip without him.

It was at last decided, however, that he should remain at

the mission of San Xavier, in the Papago settlement; but for the safety of the animals, it was thought best to leave them with Colonel Robinson, at Tucson, who very kindly consented to look after them.

Arrangements having been concluded, we embarked about six o'clock in the morning, in one of Butterfield's coaches, for the Pimo villages, some ninety miles distant. Our ride thither was a most uninteresting one, beneath the scorching rays of the sun, over a hard, gravelly soil, covered with a thick growth of mesquit and cactus; in fact, the whole country was little better than a desert, the only water found upon the route being obtained from the wells which had been dug at the mail stations, for the convenience of watering their stock.

About daylight on the following morning, we arrived at the villages; and, after resting a little, and refreshing ourselves with a very comfortable sort of a breakfast, we started out sight-seeing.

The Pimos have lived upon and cultivated this spot for more than three hundred years. Marco de Niza found them here as far back as 1539. Father Kino also mentions them in his travels; and Savidra, who spent much of his life among the Indians of Sonora and Arizona, speaks of their being directly descended from the Montezuma Indians; and in proof of this assertion, cites the cutting of the hair square across the forehead, and permitting it to grow long behind.

a custom that prevails to some extent among fashionable young ladies of the present day, and which was, undoubtedly, derived from the Montezuma Indians, who have, for many hundred years, followed the practice, and indeed have regarded it as a distinguishing trait of their noble lineage.

As early as 1539, we have accounts of the Pimos living by cultivating the soil; and at the time we visited them, the United States government had just finished the surveys of a reservation embracing one hundred square leagues of land, nearly all of which was easily irrigated, consequently susceptible of cultivation. This reservation is about twenty-five miles long and seven miles wide, and is situated on both sides of the Gila.

Nearly the whole of the land thus set apart, has been cultivated by these Indians for more than three hundred years, and still, without dressing of any kind, yields full thirty-fold in crops. Golonel Grey, whom we met here, and who had surveyed the reservation, assured us that they had at least four hundred miles of acequias already constructed upon the reservation, and for many years had raised fine crops of wheat, corn, tobacco, and cotton. Wheat is sown in January, and harvested in May and June. Cotton and tobacco in February. Two crops are always raised on the same ground in a year.

There are ten of these villages, composed of about seventy-five or a hundred wigwams each. These wigwams are built of small poles, inserted in the ground, and bent at the top to a common centre, interwoven with corn-husks, straw, and rushes, so as to shed the rain, and protect the inmates from the intense heat of the sun. Many of them are also plastered over with mud. The doors are just large enough to enable a person to creep in on hands and knees. The cooking is all done in the open air, beneath a shed or roof.

Every family has a granary, or store-house, which is much larger and better constructed than their huts, and which, in fact, they use for sleeping purposes, as well as for shelter from inclement weather.

There are about six thousand of these Indians, and they have nearly a thousand separate enclosures, which are divided by very excellent fences, made of crooked sticks and mesquit. They have but few animals, and never use the plough, the hoe being the only agricultural implement they possess, except a few carts, which they have obtained from the emigrant trains passing through their villages; and yet, during the year of our visit, they had sold the mail company more than four hundred thousand pounds of wheat, besides large quantities of corn, beans, pumpkins, and melons.

When we reflect that this soil has been cultivated for nearly four hundred years that we have knowledge of, with only the hoe, and without dressing, we can form some idea of its fertility and productiveness.

The Pimos are not wanting in courage, and many a sound whipping have the Apaches received at their hands. Their only weapon is the bow and arrow, in the use of which they are very expert. They have always been very friendly to the whites, and have frequently aided them in recovering property stolen by the Apaches, and have also protected emigrant trains through the villages to Fort Yuma, when our government was powerless to do it.

These Indians manufacture certain kinds of pottery-ware, also beautiful baskets, blankets, and cotton-cloth. The work is nearly all done by the women. The men, as a general thing, go naked, excepting the breech-clout; the women wear about their loins a piece of cotton-cloth, falling to the knees, and fastened at the waist by a girdle, or belt; and usually possess fine, well-developed forms.

We spent the entire day in looking about the villages, and in organizing a party to visit the "*Casas Grandes*," which are situated near the River, about twenty-five miles above the Pimo villages. Colonel Buckley, the superintendent of the California division of the overland mail, very kindly furnished us with mules and an outfit for the trip, and our numbers were increased by the addition of two Pimos, who were to act as guides, and a Mr. St. John, who had been appointed by the government to superintend and instruct the Pimos in agricultural pursuits.

Our party, consisting of five persons, started early the

next morning on the trip. Keeping along the bank of the river, travelling through dense groves of mesquit and cotton-wood, we made during the day about eighteen miles, and camped at night in a beautiful grove on the banks of the Gila.

The next morning, after following the course of the river for several miles, we came upon the remains of a very large acequia, which we traced for a long distance, through a plain now overgrown by mesquit, but showing unmistakable evidences of having at some time been extensively cultivated.

All over the plain we found hundreds of branch acequias, together with marks of former habitations, broken pottery-ware, and stone *metattes*.

About noon we came in sight of three immense buildings, which our guide assured us were the "houses of Montezuma"; and we could but gaze upon them with wonder and awe, for never before had we seen anything so wonderful as these relics of an extinct race, of whom we have no reliable history, and no knowledge save traditionary legends.

The houses are situated on a slight eminence, and are about three or four hundred feet apart. They are built of a species of concrete, made of mud and gravel, while the timber, or rafters, used in their construction, are of cedar, and well preserved.

The largest of these was, undoubtedly, at the time it was built, four stories in height; and there are walls now stand ing, to the height of fifty feet.

Mr. Bartlett, who visited these ruins in '52, has given such a full and minute description of them, that I purpose giving it in these pages, well satisfied that the reader can gain a better idea of these remarkable structures than he could do from any description of mine. He says: "The *Casas Grandes*, or great houses, consist of three buildings, all included within a space of one hundred and fifty yards. The principal and largest one is in the best state of preservation; its four exterior walls, and most of the inner ones, are still standing. A considerable portion of the upper part of the walls have crumbled away and fallen inwards. Three stories now remain, and there was a fourth, which has nearly all crumbled away. The central portion, or tower, is about ten feet higher than the walls, which at their base are from four to five feet thick. The inside is perpendicular, while the exterior face tapers in a curved line towards the top.

"All the walls are laid with large, square blocks of mud, prepared for the purpose by pressing the material into large boxes about two feet in height and four feet long. When the mud becomes sufficiently hardened, the cases are moved along and again filled, and so on until the whole edifice is completed. The material for the buildings is the mud of

THE CASAS GRANDES IN 1859.

the valley mixed with gravel, which is very adhesive, and when dry, very durable.

"The outer surface of the walls appears to have been plastered roughly, but the inside is hard finished. This is done with a composition of adobe, and is still as smooth as when

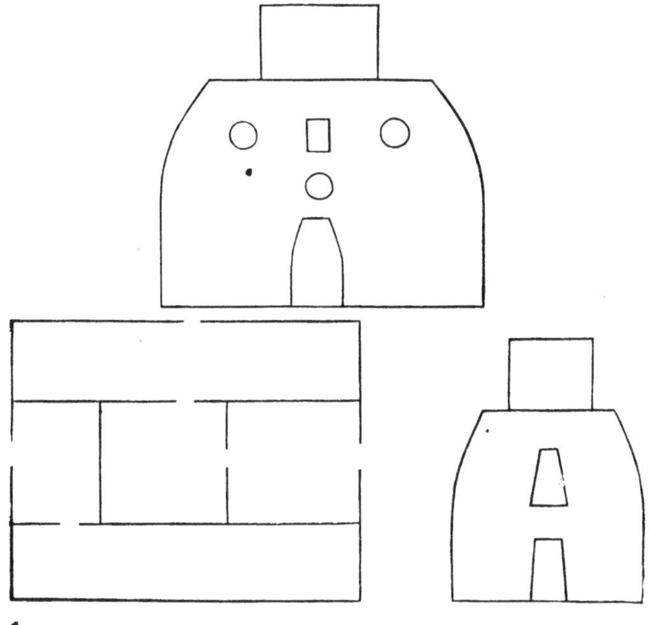

PLAN AND ELEVATION.

first made, and has quite a polish. On one of the walls are drawn rude figures, but no inscriptions. From the charred ends of the beams that remain in the walls, it is evident the buildings were destroyed by fire.

"Some of the lintels over the doors are formed of sticks of

wood stripped of their bark, but showing no signs of the use of any sharp instrument in their construction. The beams that supported the floors were about five inches in diameter, and placed about the same number of inches apart, and the ends inserted deep in the walls. Most of the apartments are connected by doors, beside which there are circular openings in the upper part of the chambers, to admit light and air."

The ground-plan of the buildings shows that all the apartments were long and narrow, and without windows.

The inner rooms were undoubtedly used for store-rooms. There were four entrances to each of the buildings. The door on the western side was but two feet wide and eight feet high; while all the others were three feet wide, and but five feet high, and all tapering towards the top, a peculiarity belonging to the ancient edifices of Central America and Yucatan. With the exception of these doors, there are no exterior openings, save on the western side where there are circular windows, like those before described. Over the doorway in the third story, there was a square window, and on either side of this two circular openings. The southern front has fallen in several places; the other three fronts are quite perfect.

The walls at the base, particularly at the corners, have crumbled away to the extent of twelve or fourteen inches, and are only held together by their great thickness.

The moisture in these portions causes disintegration to

take place more rapidly than in any other part of the buildings; and in a few years, as these walls become undermined, the whole structure must fall, and become a mere rounded heap, like those that are seen upon the plains around in all directions. A few days' labor spent in restoring the walls at the base with mud and gravel, would render this interesting monument as durable as brick, and enable it to stand for a long while. It is known to have existed in its present state for more than a century.

The exterior dimensions of the largest building are fifty feet from north to south, and forty feet from east to west. On the ground-floor are five apartments, those on the north and south sides measuring thirty-two feet by ten feet. All are open to the sky, nor is there any appearance of a stairway on any of the walls. The means of entrance to the upper apartments was undoubtedly from the outside.

A few hundred feet to the southwest is a second building, in a complete state of ruin, while to the northeast of the main building is a third one, which without doubt was a watch-tower. As far as the eye can reach in every direction, are seen heaps of ruined edifices, with but small portions of their walls standing.

To the northwest, about two hundred yards distant, is a circular embankment, from two hundred and forty to three hundred feet in circumference, supposed to be the remains of a corral, or enclosure for cattle.

25

The plains are everywhere strewn with broken pottery and *metattes*. The pottery is red, white, lead color, and black. The figures are geometrical, formed with taste, and are similar to those found on the Salinas, forty miles north of this place.

The texture of the pottery is very fine, and much of it is painted on the inside, a peculiarity found only here. The origin of these buildings is shrouded in mystery. When first discovered by the early explorers of the Territory, they were much the same as in their present condition; and the Indians affirmed that they had then been built five hundred years.

One thing is evident, viz. the entire valley of the Gila, as well as that of the Salinas, was at one time densely populated. The ruined buildings, the acequias, the quantities of pottery found, all prove this supposition. In fact, the whole country for hundreds of miles around shows traces of extinct civilization, and fills the mind of the traveller with the most perplexing questions.

What race of people dwelt here? By whom were these decaying walls erected? Who constructed the many thousand miles of acequias? How did they live, and where are they now? are questions that suggest themselves at every step; and as yet they have never been satisfactorily answered.

It seems to me that our government ought to take some

measures towards solving this great mystery, as well as preserving these monuments of an extinct people.

Father Pedro Font, who, in the years 1775 and 1776, made a journey from Sonora to Monterey in California, visited the ruins, and thus speaks of them in a manuscript copy of his journal, which is to be found in one of the old missions in Los Angeles:—

"The commandant determined that we should rest to-day, and examine the large buildings called Montezuma's Houses, situated one league from the Gila, and three leagues east-southeast from the Laguna.

"We were accompanied by the Governor Uturituc, who gave us the tradition of these houses, which I here give.

"The palace, or house of Montezuma, was built more than five hundred years ago. The buildings were erected by the Aztecs, when, during their transmigration, the devil led them through various countries, until they arrived at the promised land in Mexico; and in their long sojourn, they formed towns and built these edifices.

"The site on which the houses are built is level on all sides, and at a distance of a league from the Gila. They extend for leagues towards the cardinal points, and the land is partially covered with pieces of pots, jars, plates, etc., some common, and others painted in white, blue, and red colors, which is a sign that there has been a large town, inhabited by a distinct people from the Pimos of the River

Gila, who do not know how to manufacture such earthenware. We made a survey of one building, which we measured with a lance, and the measure I afterwards reduced to geometrical feet, which gave nearly the following results.

"The house forms an oblong square, facing exactly to the four cardinal points, east, west, north, and south. Around it there are ruins, indicating a fence or walls, which surrounded the buildings, particularly in the corners, where it appears there has been some edifice like an interior castle, or watch-tower; for in the angle which faces towards the southwest, there stands a ruin with its divisions and an upper story. The exterior wall extends from north to south four hundred and twenty feet, and from east to west two hundred and sixty feet. The interior of the house consists of five walls, the three middle ones being of one size, and the two extreme ones longer. The middle ones are ten feet in breadth from east to west, and twenty-six feet in length from north to south. The two extreme ones measure twelve feet from north to south, and thirty-eight from east to west."

Mangi, who, in company with Father Kino, visited the Territory in 1674, says of it: "There was one great edifice, in which our good Father Kino said mass. The principal room is in the middle of four stories, with the adjoining rooms on its four sides of three stories, with the walls two yards in thickness of strong mortar and clay, so smooth and shining that they appeared like burnished tables, and so polished that they shone like the earthenware of Puebla.

"At the distance of an arbequebus shot, twelve other houses are to be seen, half-fallen, having thick walls, and all the ceilings burnt, except in the lower room of one house, which is of round timbers, smooth and not thick, which appear to be of cedar or savin; and over these, sticks of very equal size, and a cake of mortar, or hard clay, making a roof or ceiling of great ingenuity.

"In the environs are to be seen many other ruins and heaps of broken earth, which circumscribe it two leagues, with much earthenware of plates and pots of fine clay, painted of many colors, and which resemble in form and texture the jars of Guadalajara, in Spain.

"It may be inferred that the population was very large; and that it was of one government, is shown by a canal which comes from the river by the plain, running around for the distance of three leagues, and inclosing the inhabitants in its area, being in breadth ten *varas*,* and about four *varas* in depth, through which was, perhaps, directed one-third the volume of the river, in such a manner that it might serve for a defensive moat, as well as to supply the wards with water, and irrigate the plantations in the adjacencies."

This was the condition in which Mangi and Father Kino

* Twenty-seven feet.

found these ruins in 1674. In 1775, more than a hundred years later, Father Font describes them. Bartlett describes them as he found them in 1851. The writer found them in about the same condition in 1859, with the exception of the south wall, no part of which was then standing; all the remaining walls have upon them the hieroglyphics of ambitious Americans, who have greatly defaced the smooth polished surface by inscribing their names or marks upon them.

We were rather desirous of visiting the ruins on the Salinas, about forty miles above those of the "*Casas Grandes*"; but after repeated assurances from Mr. St. John and our Pimo guides, that the visit with so small a party would be the height of imprudence, and not caring to risk an encounter with the Apaches, we reluctantly turned our backs upon the ruins, *en route* once more for the Pimo villages, which we reached on the evening of the next day, quite satisfied with our journey, and anxious to reach Tucson, where we hoped to find Jimmy with the mules all safe, and ready to start for the Mesilla.

We were obliged, however, to remain still longer in the villages, as no stage east was due until the following day; so making the best of it, we found comfortable bunks in the station of the mail company, and the next day we spent among the Pimos, learning what we could of their history and manner of living, and gathering much interesting information concerning them.

CHAPTER XIV.

HE Pimos, the Maricopas, the Cuchans, the Mojaves, and Papagoes, are without doubt all "Montezuma Indians," as they call themselves. They all speak a similar language, all cut their hair short in front, wearing it long behind, and all cultivate the soil to a greater or less extent,— thereby showing an affinity with the Moquis, Zunis, and other Pueblo Indians in Northern Arizona and New Mexico.

We met here an old Indian who had acted as guide to Mr. Bartlett in 1852. In conversing with him, we learned that on the Rio San Francisco, as well as on the Verde and Salinas, were found ruins quite similar in their general features to those upon the Gila; and that they are also to be found extending far into the Navajoe country. Indeed, there can be no question but that this whole country was once settled with a dense population far enough advanced in civilization to build houses four stories in height; to surround them with outworks for defence; to irrigate the land by building canals miles in length; to manufacture cotton-cloth, as well as fine earthenware, and ornaments of gold and silver. But who they were, whence they came, and whither they went, are queries yet to be solved. They have left behind them absolutely nothing from which we can derive any authentic information. A great many valuable relics have been found among the ruins, some of them extremely beautiful. Handsomely-carved pipes, bottles shaped like turtles, or made to represent animals, curiously painted and colored to the life, drinking cups, ladles, and many other utensils of household ware, are among the articles found.

We very much regretted that we were unable to visit the ruins upon the Salinas, which, we were informed, were more extensive than those of the *Casas Grandes;* but we found that those who knew the country best, thought it unsafe to attempt a visit with less than a party of thirty, so we reluctantly gave up the trip.

When I told the Pimos of my visit to the Apache *rancheria,* they seemed to be astounded; but when I afterwards informed them that Cochise was my guide, their astonishment subsided, as it was generally conceded by them that Cochise had quite as much influence with the Pinal and Tonto Apaches as Mangus Colorado himself; and that at no distant day he was destined to become their principal war-chief, a prediction which, I regret to say, has since been fulfilled.

Many questions were asked concerning their *rancheria;* and from the description I was enabled to give them of it, they came to the conclusion that it was situated in the very heart of the gold-bearing region of Arizona. Indeed, it was no uncommon thing for Apaches to come into Tucson with nuggets of gold weighing from ten pennyweights to half a pound, which they would freely barter for anything that happened to please their fancy, always, however, refusing to give any information as to the portion of country from whence they had obtained it.

One Felix Aubrey, who explored the country quite extensively in 1849 and '50, tells many marvellous stories of the quantities of gold which he found near the head-waters of the Gila, and also of the large amount then in possession of the Indians. He received nearly fifteen hundred dollars' worth of gold for some old clothing that he sold to them. He published a journal of his travels in 1853, in which he tells of Indians that used gold for bullets in killing their game, whenever they were unable to obtain lead, a story which has since been corroborated by others who have attempted to penetrate into the country. In 1856, Aubrey set about organizing an expedition to visit the gold bearing portion of Central Arizona; but, before completing the undertaking, he was killed in a broil at Santa Fé.

Numerous attempts have been made to penetrate this wonderful region since Aubrey's visit there, but not one of them has ever been successful. The explorers have either been obliged to return after enduring almost incredible hardships, or have perished by the hands of the Apaches.

I have myself seen pieces of gold in the possession of Apaches, weighing nearly half a pound, which they made but little account of, being ready to exchange it for any trifle that struck their fancy; and without doubt, if this portion of country could be explored, gold would be found to exist in as great abundance as it did in California in '49. The entire region north of the Gila, and east of the Rio Verde, must be full of silver and gold. We know that veins of silver have been found in the vicinity of Forts Yuma and Mojave that have yielded immensely, and that protection is the only thing needed to develop them into mines of great value. There are always adventurers in any new country ready to take their "lives in their hands," if they can have some show,— at least five or ten chances in a hundred; but with the condition of affairs that have existed in Arizona for the past ten years, their chances would scarcely be one in a hundred.

Gold was discovered on the Gila only the year before our visit there, and in less than a month Gila City was born, with a population of a thousand persons. It didn't pay, though. Water was scarce, and the dirt to be washed had to be carried down to the river, which in a few weeks dried up, and so did the diggings. One after another of the miners departed, the traders shut up their stores, the saloon-keepers drank their own whiskey, the Jews closed out their stock of goods for another exodus, the gamblers starved over their monte-tables; and so the bubble burst, and the city which came up like a mushroom was deserted, and all that was left to mark the spot where "pay dirt" had been found, was mud chimneys and rubbish.

About one o'clock the horn was heard, announcing the arrival of the San Francisco stage, and in an hour we were seated behind five mules, on our return to Tucson, where we arrived about noon of the next day. We found our animals all right, and only Jimmy was wanting to enable us to start at once on our return to La Mesilla. Colonel Robinson dispatched a Mexican to notify him of our arrival, and before night Jimmy was with us, quite as delighted to see us as we by any possibility could be to see him. We questioned him concerning his stay with "the king," but found him unusually reticent, and evidently not inclined to say much on the subject.

That night, however, while leaning over the mud wall of Colonel Robinson's corral, enjoying the light of an Arizona moon, Jimmy confidentially informed Dr. Parker and myself that "the king was an ould humbug; that he didn't know how to trate a gintlemin at all, at all, and had trated him like a *peon;* that he was a nasty baste, goin' round the house naked as he was borned. No king ivir did that in ould Ireland," said Jimmy; "and if the old haythin hadn't so many of thim sneakin' Injuns round, I should have bin jist timpted to have given him a touch of a raeal ould Irish shillalah."

Poor Jimmy! He had learned that a little brief authority will make itself felt wherever it can, and that Jimmy alone was a far different person in the eyes of old José than the Jimmy who accompanied Dr. Parker and myself on our visit to the old mission of San Xavier del Bac.

After debating the matter with Dr. Parker, we finally decided to spend the next day at Tucson, accepting the hospitality of Colonel Robinson, who very kindly offered to show us around the town, and introduce us to some of the celebrities of the city. During the day we met Phil Herbert, formerly a member of Congress from California, the man who, during his term of service, killed one of the waiters at Willard's Hotel, in Washington. He appeared genial and companionable, but those best acquainted with him said he was atoning for his "mistake of a life-time," by that bitter remorse which always follows in the wake of an action like that committed by Herbert. In any event, he was doing his utmost to drown the memory of the deed in the dissipation offered in a life on the Arizona frontier.

Ned McGowan was another Californian character. He

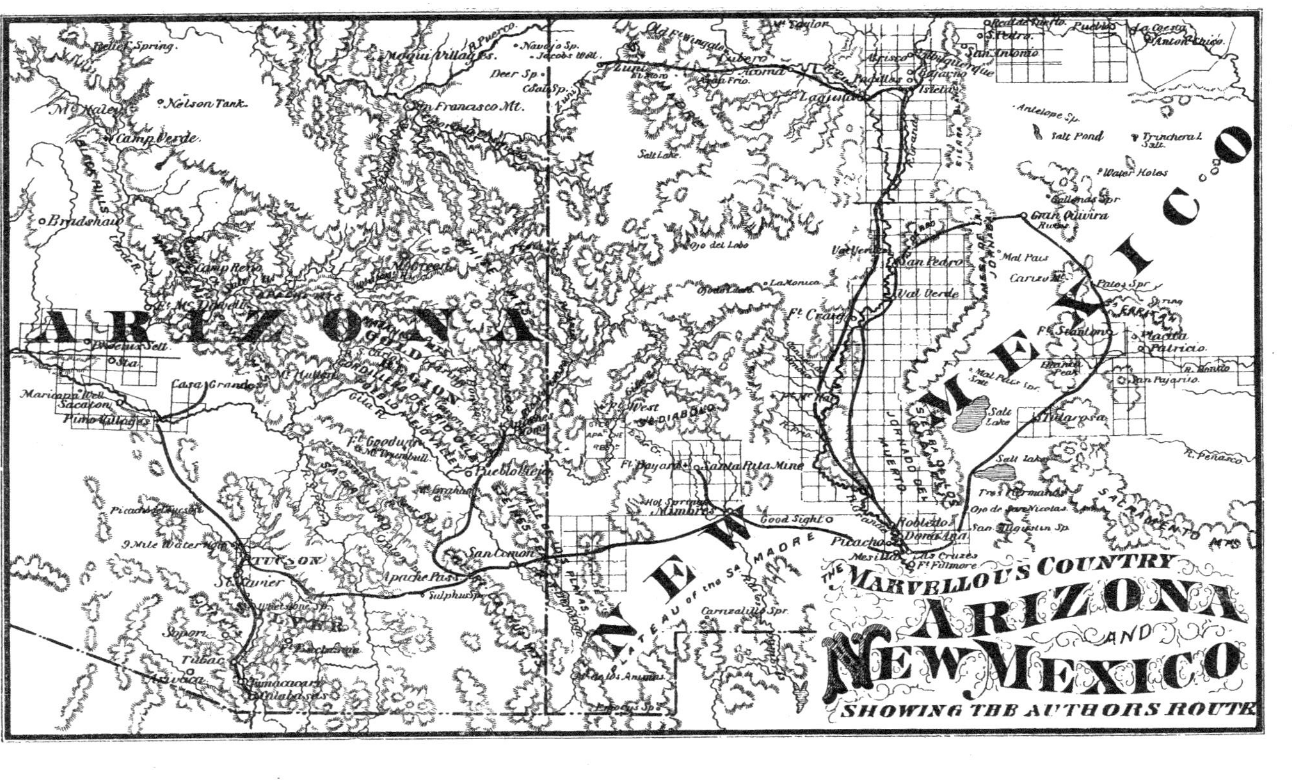
THE MARVELLOUS COUNTRY
ARIZONA AND NEW MEXICO
SHOWING THE AUTHORS ROUTE
ARIZONA
NEW MEXICO
Camp Verde
Nelson Tank
Bradshaw
San Francisco Mt.
Moqui Villages
Navajo Sp.
Deer Sp.
Zuni
Old Fort Wingate
Cubero
Acoma
Laguna
Albuquerque
Isleta
San Antonio
Antelope Sp.
Salt Pond
Water Holes
Gran Quivira Ruins
Mal Pais
Carizozo
Ft. Stanton
Patricio
Tularosa
Salt Lake
Salt Lake
Tres Hermanos
San Augustin Sp.
Ojo del Lobo
La Monica
Ft. Craig
San Pedro
Val Verde
Jornado del Muerto
Robledo
Dona Ana
Mesilla
Las Cruzes
Ft. Fillmore
Picacho
Good Sight
Mimbres
Ft. Bayard
Santa Rita Mine
Carrizalillo Spr.
Plateau of the Sa. Madre
Apache Pass
Sulphur Sp.
San Simon
Pueblo Viejo
Ft. Goodwin
Tucson
Tubac
Calabasas
Casa Grande
Maricopa Wells
Sacaton
Pima Villages
Ft. McDowell
Camp Reno
9 Mile Water Hole
Picacho del Tucson
Apache Pass

and Phil were firm friends and boon companions. After Ned had subsisted for months on roots and berries in the Californian mountains, enduring every hardship, and successfully evading the clutches of the Vigilance Committee, he finally managed to escape into Arizona, a place where the statutes never trouble, and the wicked are at rest. It was said, that though Ned had killed at least a dozen men in his life, he never killed one save in behalf of some friend's quarrel.

Here, too, was Lieutenant-Colonel Johnson, Kinney's lieutenant in his celebrated Nicaragua expedition, a few years before. He had sought an asylum in Arizona, where he was living, apparently happy and comfortable.

We also met Ex-Governor Gandera, the last governor of Sonora. He was an exile from home, anxiously waiting for the newly-appointed governor to send him a permit to return to his family.

But why particularize? Many there were, all distinguished for something,—all characters of some kind. One might write a book concerning them, but who would care to read it?

Within an hour after we left Colonel Johnson, a report reached us that he had been killed by our friend, Colonel Robinson, and so it proved.

As we stood beside the body, which, but an hour before, we had seen so full of life and activity, we could but feel that we had tarried at Tucson quite as long as we cared to, and were nothing loath to take our leave. We made no inquiries into the cause of the difficulty. The verdict of the people was, that Colonel Robinson was justified, and no further notice was taken of the affair. We had learned the lesson never to see nor hear in Arizona, and it had more than once served us a good turn.

In a conversation that night with Colonel Douglas, who resided on a beautiful ranche a few miles below Tucson, we learned that more than thirty persons had been killed there within the past year; and the colonel added, as an excuse for this wholesale slaughter, that "some of the fellers killed was awful provokin'!"

In addition to the other excitements of the day, we were told that a woman who had been carried off by the Apaches some time before had been retaken and brought into town in a starving condition. Of course we went to see her, and a most pitiable object she was. The sight of her emaciated form, and staring, hungry eyes, was enough to make any one who saw her, swear vengeance on the whole Apache race. I visited her again a few hours later, and much to my surprise she recognized me; and I found upon inquiry, that she was one of old Pennington's daughters, whose story I have related in a former chapter.

Notwithstanding the unpleasant scenes of the day, we passed a very pleasant evening, in company with Colonel

Douglas and Captain Ewell, he who had rescued Mrs. Paige, and brought her into Tucson. 'Twas not until long after midnight that the doctor and myself sought our blankets, quite satisfied that we had seen enough of Tucson, and thoroughly resolved to make an early start in the morning.

As we were preparing to leave town the next day, an orderly from Captain Ewell appeared, with that gentleman's compliments, and saying that the captain had determined upon going East as far as the Dragoon Springs, a station of the Overland Mail Company, situated upon our direct route, and, if agreeable, he should be happy to act as our escort. We joyfully accepted the proposition, and five o'clock found us on the road, our number having been augmented by thirty-two dragoons, which with our train, consisting of six wagons, made quite an imposing and formidable appearance.

Our journey was not without incident worthy of note. There was always something to relieve the monotony in the mountain scenery, which was as grand and beautiful as the most enthusiastic admirer could desire. The huge rough and jagged peaks that towered around us were toned and softened by the purple haze that enshrouded them into perfect models of architectural beauty. Here an apparently impregnable fortress, standing high in the air, with its frowning battlements, grand in their massive strength, would suddenly and almost imperceptibly assume the shape of a beautiful castle, or perchance a graceful Turkish mosque, with its towers and minarets, its domes and arches, so perfect that we could but gaze in wonder at the transformation, so enchanting, yet so instantaneous. Close by, barren hills of gravel and sandstone, serrated by floods, and worn by storms into perfect honeycombs, were to be seen; while here and there a magnificent *Cereus Grandes*, the sentinel of the desert, reared its head twenty, thirty, and even forty feet in the air, covered with beautifully variegated blossoms, and looking like some graceful shaft erected by nature herself, and decked with beautiful wreaths, that she might add a charm to the sterility of the soil, or perhaps the bright scarlet blossoms of a prickly-pear would be seen peeping out from behind the gray green of the mesquit, the whole, like the mountains, overhung by the rich purple tints of an Arizona atmosphere, relieved only by the clear blue smoke lazily ascending from the Indian camp-fires on the mountain-sides around us. Altogether, it was a picture both beautiful and pleasant to contemplate; and 'twas with no small degree of vexation that we heard one of the scouts inform Captain Ewell that he had sighted a party of Indians some distance ahead of us, notwithstanding we had all been wishing for an encounter with them, that we might see the "brave boys in blue," who were with us, astonish them with their new Spencer carbines.

Captain Ewell at once gave the order to start in pursuit,

and soon twenty-five gallant fellows were thundering along the hard, gravelly soil, with an earnestness that bespoke short work with the Apaches, if once overtaken.

We soon came to a slight elevation, where we could plainly see the Indians a long distance ahead, driving before

CAPTAIN EWELL'S PURSUIT OF THE APACHES.

them a small quantity of stock that they had doubtless captured from some poor *ranchero*, while as yet, far behind, our boys were fast lessening the distance between them.

The chase was a most exciting one, especially after we saw the Indians abandon their stock and strike for the mountains as fast as their plucky little ponies could carry them. We soon lost sight of them, though Captain Ewell and his boys continued the chase, not stopping even to collect the stock that now stood quietly on the plain.

We rode slowly along towards our camping-place, which we reached about five o'clock in the evening, right glad of the shelter afforded us by the rough stone walls and thatched roof of the mail company's corral, which had been kindly offered us by the agent.

It was not until nearly ten o'clock that we heard the bugle, announcing the return of the captain and his party. They had followed the Indians until they had reached the mountains, but had there lost track of them; and although they had thoroughly searched the cañon, no trace of them could be found. They brought in the stock, consisting of thirteen mules and nine oxen. The cattle were very lame and foot-sore, showing that they had been driven a long distance, probably from Sonora or Chihuahua, and were headed for the Apache country, a portion of which I have described in a former chapter.

Captain Ewell was much chagrined at his failure in finding the Indians, and said he,—

"I don't care for the Indians, but I'm going to find where the d—d cusses went to," assuring us that he should remain there another day, for the purpose of exploring the cañon, in which they had so mysteriously disappeared.

Dr. Parker and myself at once volunteered to accompany him, although we were well convinced that the search would be a fruitless one; still, we were quite anxious to see what the result of a day's explorations might bring forth.

Although we retired that night with the prospect of an adventure before us, we did not wake till the bugle sounded in the morning. We started early, our party consisting of twenty-four men, including Dr. Parker and myself. Our route lay for about six miles over a beautiful undulating prairie, rising gradually towards the mountains. The ground was covered with green grass and beautiful flowers, interspersed occasionally with small cedars, whose dark green contrasted splendidly with the lighter foliage of the spreading oaks, which dotted the landscape around us. Now and then a huge boulder would be seen, its dark-red brown presenting a curious contrast to its surroundings.

The whole scene was a charming one, as compared to the barren country over which we had so recently travelled,—one which we could but admire and gratefully acknowledge. We soon reached the mouth of the cañon in which the Indians had so mysteriously disappeared the day before. The stillness of death prevailed; not a sound could be heard save the tramp of our horses' feet, or the occasional ring of a trooper's sabre as it rattled in its scabbard. Massive rocks, hundreds of feet high, piled one upon another, towered far above and on all sides of us, while occasionally a small cedar or scrub oak was to be seen, firmly rooted in some gray cleft upon their sides. The ground over which we were travelling had once been the bed of a mountain stream, and our course was much impeded by the large quantities of stones and small boulders, that had been worn smooth and round by the action of the waters. On we went, endeavoring to follow the course of the Mexican guide, who was now some distance in advance, the soldiers, with their clumsy cavalry horses, finding it hard work to make much headway over the stones.

At this point we were approaching a very narrow part of the cañon, where the stream had formerly passed between two perpendicular walls from one to two hundred feet in height, and scarcely thirty in width.

As we drew near to it, so smooth were its sides, and so narrow the passage, it scarcely seemed possible that it was anything but a huge fissure in the rock, notwithstanding the guide assured us that the passage through it was feasible.

The cold, gray rocks, towering high above our heads, entirely bare of foliage, were covered with a dark brown moss, that gave to the surroundings a most gloomy and sombre aspect, in addition to which, the masses of sharp-cornered rock, round boulders, and smoothly-washed stones that covered the ground before and around us, seemed to offer an almost impassable barrier to the passage of this most forbidding little cañon.

The uncertain and suspicious aspect of the defile through which we were thus obliged to pass, caused Captain Ewell to halt before entering it. While he dispatched two scouts to examine the passage for signs indicating the presence of Indians, he ordered his men to prepare to proceed with the utmost care, keeping a sharp lookout for lurking savages.

In a short time the scouts returned, and reported no signs of Indians; and the order was given to advance cautiously. The scouts now started in the lead, followed by Captain Ewell at the head of his men. I had lingered behind with Dr. Parker and Jimmy, for the purpose of listening to a geological dissertation from the doctor upon a specimen of rock that he had discovered, which he pronounced to be the out-croppings of a very valuable lode of silver ore, when suddenly the most terrific yells filled the air, accompanied by sounds resembling the discharge of heavy artillery, above which the clear, clarion tones of Captain Ewell could be heard shouting to his men.

Springing upon our horses, we hastily started for the entrance to the defile, but before reaching it were met by two or three of the men, whose terrified manner and frightened faces plainly showed that they were endeavoring to escape as fast as the rough nature of the ground would permit them. We hurriedly questioned them, and from their incoherent answers gleaned the following information:—

They were proceeding cautiously through the pass; the stillness of death reigned around them; not a living creature was to be seen, save occasionally a chameleon, or great ground lizard, as, disturbed in its solitude by the tramp of horses' feet, or the sharp ring of their iron-clad hoofs upon the rocky way, it wound its noisome track over the stones beneath them, when suddenly, from far above them, the Apache war-whoop sounded in their ears. Looking up, they saw a dozen or more great pieces of rock descending from the heights above, evidently designed to crush them. Hastily turning their horses' heads, they urged them as fast as possible towards the mouth of the cañon.

Leaving our horses in charge of these men, we started for the cañon on foot. Upon entering it, a scene of dire confusion presented itself. Occasionally a piece of rock would be precipitated from the very top of the high wall, and striking the opposite side of the cañon, would rebound again and again, until it finally fell with a tremendous crash to the earth, causing the soldiers to huddle together at the foot of the wall, unmindful of their horses, or aught else save protection for themselves.

Captain Ewell, with perhaps a dozen of his men, had been separated from the remainder of his party by a mass of rock thrown from above, which, lying piled up at the bottom of the pass, completely blocked its passage. He seemed to be endeavoring to rally that portion of his command with him, in an attempt to scale the almost perpendicular walls, upon the top of which were the Apaches, whose demoniacal yells resounded through the narrow defile, rendering confusion worse confounded. Several of the men were endeavoring to release two of their companions, who with their horses had been struck to the earth by the terrible missiles hurled from above.

As yet not an Indian had been seen. The doctor caught a glimpse of a head peering over the edge of rock far above us, and raising his rifle, fired without even pausing to take aim. Down came the naked body of an Apache, his bow still tightly grasped in his hand. As he tumbled over and over, rebounding from against the steep walls, he struck the ground but a short distance in advance of us. Jimmy, rushing forward, commenced kicking the body in the most valiant manner, exclaiming at the same time, "There, ye dhirty, naked divil, git behind another rock, will yez, and thry to kill honest min that's passin' thro' th' counthry a sight-sain'; take that, will yez?" and he bestowed kick after kick upon the mangled body, after which he grasped the bow, and wrenching it from the grip of death with which it was held, again joined us, completely exhausted by his frantic efforts for revenge. For months afterwards this bow proved to be Jimmy's best card; for he related the story of his "capturin' it from an Apache, shure, wid these two hands, miself,'' many times, always forgetting to state, however, that the Apache was a dead one.

For a few moments we stood and watched the captain and his men toiling up the steep ascent, and then went forward to assist in extricating the poor fellows, whose lives had been so suddenly and unexpectedly crushed out. After working for a couple of hours, we succeeded in recovering the mangled and lifeless bodies from under the mass of rock; then slowly and with tender care we placed them upon a litter made of their comrades' rifles, on which they were borne to the mouth of the Pass, and there laid upon the green grass, to await the arrival of the rest of the command, who, with their captain, were scouring the rocks in the vain hope of overtaking and punishing the lurking foe who had attacked them in such a cowardly manner.

After many and repeated attempts, the men succeeded in removing a sufficient portion of the rocks that blocked the passage of the cañon, to enable them to get out their horses from behind the mass; and some hours later, Captain Ewell and his men returned from their fruitless pursuit, quite worn out with fatigue.

Upon reaching the top of the wall where the Apaches had stood, they found tons of rocks piled up, ready to be precipitated into the depths below; and close by the spot a wounded Apache, which one of the men hastily dispatched with his sabre. The rest of the band had disappeared as completely as if the earth had opened and swallowed them.

After a short rest we again took up the line of march for camp, the men carefully bearing with them the dead bodies of their two comrades. It was quite dark ere we reached camp. The captain immediately detailed four men to dig a grave upon a little eminence near by, and the bodies of Wilbur Carver and Charles Tucker were wrapped in their blankets and deposited within its narrow walls.

We stood by with uncovered heads, while Captain Ewell touchingly repeated a portion of the beautiful burial service of the Episcopal Church; and as the solemn words, "I am the resurrection and the life," fell upon my ears for the first time in many months, they awakened a host of long-forgotten memories, which came trooping up and crowding one upon the other in such quick succession that I quite forgot the sad scene which I was there to witness, as well as the circumstances that had caused it; nor did I wake from my reverie until the last sad duties were finished, and the men had returned to camp. Then the doctor touched me upon the shoulder, and we silently turned from the sad scene, and wended our way to the station.

It was late that night before we retired, right glad of the prospect of a rest after the fatigue and excitement of the day, and well-satisfied of the fallacy of pursuing Apaches in their native fastnesses with regular cavalry.

We were soon wrapped in our blankets and enjoying a refreshing sleep, only to be awakened by yells as of ten thousand devils. In an instant we realized that the Apaches were attempting a stampede, for their whoops were accompanied by the ringing of old cow-bells, the neighing of horses,

THE STAMPEDE.

braying of mules, and terrified lowing of cattle, intermingled with the discharge of fire-arms and the shouting of men, all combining to render the scene as near Pandemonium as 'tis possible to imagine. Of course we could do nothing but wait, and wait we did, until every sound had died away.

In a short time Captain Ewell's voice was heard at the gate of the corral, and he informed us that the Apaches had stampeded his stock, and he wanted some animals from the corral to mount his men to start in pursuit. He obtained five, and started back to camp, while we once more retired, waiting for daylight before we ventured out of the gates that had afforded us such perfect protection.

CHAPTER XV.

BEFORE it was light enough to see plainly, Mr. Twilly, the station-agent, called our attention to a peculiar roaring sound, which seemed to come from the mountains near by, at the same time informing us that it was raining up there very hard, and if the Apaches had succeeded in getting any start with the stock, the storm would delay Captain Ewell, so that it would be impossible for him to prevent their escape, as the water from the sides of the mountain would create such torrents that it would be useless to attempt to cross them.

As soon as it was light enough for us to see, we proceeded to the camp to ascertain the situation there. We found that the Indians had succeeded in stampeding all of Captain Ewell's animals, except ten, together with the stock captured the day before, making in all nearly fifty head, and that Captain Ewell had gone in pursuit with fifteen men.

Of course there were many stories told as to the strength of the Apaches, some setting their number as high as fifty, and others declaring that there were not more than ten.

After listening to the many conflicting reports, I made up my mind that undoubtedly it was the same band that Captain Ewell had been in pursuit of for the past two days, and that they had secreted themselves in the mountains, where they could observe the situation of his camp, and had taken advantage of the knowledge thus gained to repay the captain for his efforts to punish them.

These Apaches are certainly most adroit thieves, and manage to spirit off horses and cattle before the very eyes of their owners in the most unaccountable manner, and without detection. To do this, however, they are sometimes obliged to crawl for a mile upon their bellies through the tall grass. After reaching the animal which they desire, they quietly unfasten his picket-pin and stealthily draw themselves up upon his side, clinging to his neck with their arms, thus effectually interposing his body, so as to act as a shield between them and his owner. While in this position they gradually and surely succeed in getting out of rifle range; then urging their prize into a gallop, they are soon out of sight, leaving the owner to wonder where his animal could have strayed to so suddenly.

When a general stampede is intended, they first capture the leader of the herd, then with shouts and noises so terrify and confuse the other animals, that they all unhesitatingly follow this one, which bears upon his back the most daring and expert thief of the party.

It was evident that the rain which had fallen early in the morning had been very severe indeed; upon the tops and far down the sides of the mountains the heavy clouds still lowered, completely enshrouding their rocky sides, and effectually concealing the trees which grew near their base, nor did it require a very attentive listener to distinguish the sound of the rushing waters as they swept in an unresisting torrent down the rocky precipices and narrow gorges to the plains below.

It was nearly ten o'clock that night ere Captain Ewell and his party returned from their unsuccessful pursuit. They had been forced to wait several hours for the waters to abate at one of the "dry runs," which delay had enabled the Apaches to successfully elude their pursuers, although they were obliged to leave the cattle behind them, which three of the soldiers were driving into camp, as they could not keep up with the rest of the herd.

It was quite late when we returned to the station, having said good-bye to Captain Ewell, and echoing the wish which he so earnestly expressed, "That he might have just one brush with the devils before he returned to the fort."

The next morning as we started from the station, the captain came to bid us farewell, and to ask us to urge Major

De Rythe to send him some mules from the Apache Pass, to enable him to return to Fort Buchanan.

This we did on our arrival, and the major at once sent him a dozen. We afterwards learned that he reached the fort safely; and ere many weeks had elapsed he had the opportunity of administering to the Apaches a severe whipping, at the Puerta del Curcuco, near the Buseni ranche, in the Santa Rita Mountains, where no less than sixteen of the thieving rascals were left dead upon the field.

Our journey from the Dragoon Springs to the Apache Pass was without incident worthy of note; and it was not until noon of the next day that we entered this rocky cañon which enabled us to pass through the Chiricahui Mountains.

After travelling for miles along a road so narrow that there was barely room for one wagon between the steep and overhanging rocks, we finally reached the station. We found all well, and Cochise on hand to receive us. We learned upon inquiry, that Cochise and his five braves had only returned that morning, after an absence of three days; and from this circumstance, as well as from his peculiar looks when questioned about the Indians who had stampeded the stock, I was led to the belief that he and his party were among the band who had visited the camp at the Dragoon Springs. Of course we could only conjecture this, as we had no proof other than the very unsatisfactory replies to our questions concerning their whereabouts during their absence. But then, who ever received from an Apache a satisfactory reply to any question?

We tarried over night at the Pass, intending the next day to reach the San Cimon, where we expected to encamp.

After leaving the mountains, we rode for eighteen miles over one of the best natural roads I ever saw, until we reached the mail-station, on the San Cimon. Here we made our camp, the agent giving our animals stalls in the corral of the company.

The valley of the San Cimon is about twenty-five miles in width, and contains much fine grazing land, as well as some good agricultural districts. It is covered with a species of grass called *grama*, which for its nutritious qualities is rivalled only by the celebrated mesquit grass of Texas. In the region where it grows, the settler requires no grain for his mules or horses, as they are able to endure quite as much fatigue when feeding upon this grass as upon grain; and the stock-raiser who has fed his cattle upon *grama* during the entire winter, finds them in quite as good condition in the spring as does the Eastern farmer his stall-fed animals.

While here we learned that only two days before a small party of Apaches had made an attack upon the herders belonging to the station, and had stolen two of the company's mules, much to the disgust of the station-keeper and his assistants, who were powerless to overtake them, having driven them in the direction of Stein's Peak, which lay immediately on our route. Indian signals had been observed in its vicinity during the day, therefore we were reluctantly persuaded to remain for a time at the station, as well for our own safety as to give our animals a generous feed of *grama*, of which they were very fond.

Early in the morning, the overland coach from the East arrived, bringing papers only twenty-days old; and as they contained the first news we had received for nearly two months, we were quite overjoyed to get them. While the coach tarried here, the passengers, four in number, partook of refreshments, which the station-agent had kindly provided, after which they set out for Tucson at a rattling pace.

The following morning was a beautiful one, and just as the day was breaking, I heard the keeper opening the gates of the corral before sending the animals out for their morning meal. Further sleep being out of the question, I arose, and seating myself upon the green grass, watched the antics of the mules as they one by one came from the corral, and for the first time experienced a sense of their freedom.

The sun came up grandly, his rays gilding the snow-clad summit of Stein's Peak — an elevation nine thousand feet above the level of the sea — with crimson beauty, almost unearthly in its seeming scintillant light; and I watched it for hours, until its pure crystal covering no longer reflected a sheen of silvery light, but stood white and solitary in its bold relief against the clear blue sky, like the huge sentinel of the desert that it is, ever watchful and ever at its post.

As the sun rose higher in the heavens, the gray, precipitous sides of this stately peak afforded a most pleasing contrast to the dark, rich green of its base, while the purple haze toned down its angular points, until, half concealed and half revealed, I could almost fancy that I was gazing through "Timothy Titbottom's spectacles," and beheld my castles in Spain rising before me in all their beauty and grandeur.

The question which I had put to Dr. Parker, as to what our employment or amusement should be during the day, was speedily answered by seeing the herders frantically endeavoring to collect their stock, urging it as fast as possible towards the corral. For some time we could not perceive the cause of this alarm. The station-keeper, however, soon discovered a party of five Apaches, riding as fast as their ponies could carry them, towards the two herders, who by this time were well on their way to the station, which they soon reached. The stock safely housed, we all retreated to the building, and awaited coming events.

It soon became evident that the Apaches had no intention of making an attack, but that their design was simply to obtain possession of some of the stock, for they halted at a distance of nearly half a mile from the station, seemingly engaged in holding a council of war, sitting upon their ponies in the mean time.

Having in my hand one of Sharp's carbines, I brought it to bear, and elevating the sight, took deliberate aim at the five Indians, who were closely huddled together, and fired. I had not the slightest expectation of hitting one of them, but to my utter surprise I saw one of their number fall from his saddle, while the men around me uttered a shout at the success of my shot, which must have sounded to the ears of the red-skins like a yell of defiance.

A clap of Arizona thunder resounding through the clear, beautiful sky would not have more terribly astounded the Apaches than did the result of my chance shot. They had evidently thought themselves far out of rifle range, and as secure as though miles away. In an instant after their comrade bit the dust, they scattered in every direction; but as they witnessed no further attempt to reach them, they soon rallied, and two of their number rode hurriedly to the spot where lay the dead Indian. Stooping in their saddles they seized his body, and throwing it before them on their ponies, galloped madly away.

As for me, my unlooked-for success in bringing down this Apache gained me a most enviable reputation as a marksman along the line of the overland mail route, a reputation which I was exceedingly careful not to injure by attempting another shot.

The Indians soon disappeared from view, nor were we troubled by them for the remainder of the day. The station-keeper expressed some fears lest they should return during the night for the purpose of revenge, therefore we kept a close watch, but experienced no cause for alarm, however.

As our next day's journey lay through the "Doubtful Pass,"— a portion of our route considered quite dangerous,— we discussed the propriety of waiting another day, or proceeding in the morning. We came to no decision, however, until the overland mail-coach from the East arrived, and reported that they had been attacked by a party of Apaches in the "Doubtful Pass," and that the conductor, who was seated with the driver, had been badly wounded. The plan had evidently been to kill both conductor and driver, but owing to the darkness they had failed in their attempt.

As it was, Mashon, the conductor, received a severe arrow wound in his side, which we dressed as well as we were able with the few appliances at hand, and having our mules put to our wagon, we determined to set out at once, knowing that the Apaches would, for a day or two, or as long as they feared any pursuit, leave the vicinity of the pass, and seek other haunts.

A drive of eight miles brought us to "*La Puerta Grande*," as it is called, or "The Great Door," which is

THE BEST SHOT I EVER MADE.

the entrance to the "Doubtful Pass." It is, in fact, a cañon of the dividing ridge between the waters of the Atlantic and the Pacific; or in other words, the door of entrance to the Pacific slope.

Through this cañon our road for a couple of miles lay between two high walls of massive rock, barely wide enough to allow a wagon to pass. A solid wall of rock towered far above us on either side, and the road itself, which in the rainy season became a mere water-course, was washed and gullied by recent rains, until it was almost impassable for any wheeled vehicle. In addition to this, we were constantly ascending a very steep grade, which made our progress slow and laborious. Our patient mules, however, acquitted themselves nobly, and for the next six hours we toiled up the steep ascent, every step bringing us nearer to safety and a resting-place.

The scenery at this point was grand, gloomy, and peculiar. Immense gravel-hills, barren as the rocks which surrounded them; huge granite boulders and masses of sandstone flung out of the earth at random, met our gaze; strange jagged mountain-peaks rose on all sides, while towering high above all was the snow-clad summit of Stein's Peak looking down upon us, cold and silent, keeping its solitary "watch and ward," as it lifted itself far above the desolate wastes around.

At last we see the low thatched roof of Stein's Peak

Station, scarcely distinguishable from the gray rocks which overhang it. This welcome sight brings a feeling of relief to our anxious hearts, and we once more breathe freely, for we feel well assured that our principal danger is past.

Standing upon the dividing ridge, the backbone of the Continent, or what is now known as the Peloncillo Mountains, a portion of the Sierra Madre range, we turn our eyes to the west, and look at the wonderful country over which we have been travelling since we left Tucson. The magnificent panorama here spread out before us almost compensated for the trials and perils which we had encountered on our journey; even practical, matter-of-fact Jimmy seeemd lost in wonder and admiration, and enthusiastically exclaimed,—"Bedad, but it's a foine sight!"

And so it was, in very truth. Stretching for sixty miles beneath us lay what seemed to be a vast plain, bounded in the far distance by a faint line of blue, and half shrouded by the rich purple haze, so peculiar to an Arizonia landscape, softening its hard features, toning down its angularities, and lending an indescribable charm to the patches of forest, the gray alkali plains, and the white wavy sand-fields which lay stretched out like a gorgeous carpet at our very feet.

We had made the "Doubtful Pass" in safety. The only living thing that we had seen was an occasional mountain sheep, as, standing upon the point of some projecting rock far above us, he watched our movements with curious eyes, ready at the first sign of a hostile demonstration to seek safety by precipitating himself upon the jagged rocks below, or by leaping to some neighboring crag, where he might find a friendly retreat at a safe distance from his pursuers, leaving only the tip of his huge horns to guide the daring hunter to his place of concealment.

After admiring the beautiful view that met our gaze on every hand, we renewed our journey, and in a short time were knocking loudly at the gates of the overland mail-station for admittance. The keeper warmly welcomed us, and our tired, jaded mules soon found themselves feeding upon the rich *grama*, which grew so luxuriantly in the open space around the station.

The corral is built beside a huge granite boulder, a hollow portion of which forms a part of the station itself, and is nearly, if not quite, six thousand feet above the level of the sea, and with its high stone walls and formidable wooden gates it resembles a fortress far more strongly than it does a dwelling-house.

The hospitable occupants of the station set before us a most palatable dinner of *frejolies* and pancakes, and in the keen satisfaction derived therefrom we forgot the tedious and dangerous ride of twenty miles, which we had just made from the San Cimon. Dinner dispatched, we accompanied the station-keeper to a little pond or lake called Stein's Peak Lake, about three miles from the station, on the very top of the divide.

This little lake was scarcely a hundred and fifty feet in breadth, and was fed by several large springs, while from its sides ran two little streams, neither of them larger than my arm, but clear, cool, and sparkling. One of these streams fell over a steep precipice, now pushing its way through a rocky defile, or narrow gorge, and again flowing gently and quietly through a small patch of forest, gaining strength and power as it descended to the plain below, only to sink into the earth and reappear, after flowing through its subterranean channel for many miles; to again sink, and once more appear; until at last it lost itself in the bed of the Gila, to finally make its way into the blue waters of the mighty Pacific. Its companion stream toiled on and on, until it too found an outlet, and thousands of miles away it contributed its strength to swell the green waters of the great Atlantic. Flowing from the same common source, thus were they finally separated by a vast continent.

It would be exceedingly difficult to find words in which to describe the peculiar characteristics of the scenery around this miniature lake of Stein's Peak. It lay immediately at the foot of a huge pile of cold, gray sandstone and granite, promiscuously mixed with large quantities of volcanic rock, covered with a coating of bright and shining lava-form of every color, from light purple to deep red and sombre black. The edges of these rocks were sharply defined, and of the most fantastic shapes which the imagination could conceive. Scattered here and there, growing apparently without any soil, rose to the height of forty or fifty feet grooved columns of the *Cereus grandes*, or monumental cactus, as it is sometimes called. Interspersed with these were the brilliant green leaves of the prickly-pear, or the occasional gaudy blossom of the maguey, or the Spanish bayonet, with its bristling points, all of which, together with the clear blue sky above us, and the cold white summit of the Peak at our left, were most faithfully reflected in the waters of the little lake which lay so

CEREUS GRANDES.

quietly in the midst of this scene of desolation, like a beautiful mirror, spread out at our feet by the Almighty's own hand, to convince us how feeble is the creative genius of man, when compared with the most simple effort of nature. That mirror and its framing I shall never forget.

It was not until after the sun had sunk behind the Peak, and the stars had appeared in the heavens, that we could make up our minds to turn away from the contemplation of this grand picture, and return to the station. Upon arriving there, we learned that we were far from being out of danger, for only the week before the Apaches had attacked "Barney Station," a few miles below us, and killed one of the herders, besides driving off several mules which belonged to the company.

We at length decided to incur what risk there might be, in an endeavor to reach, on the following evening, the second station from the Peak, known as the "Soldier's Farewell," a distance of thirty-two miles. In order to do this, a very early start was necessary. We therefore "turned in" in good season, nor were we disturbed save on the arrival of the coach from San Francisco, about one o'clock in the morning.

CHAPTER XVI.

THE next morning at daylight we were ready to start upon our journey, expecting to reach the station of the Overland Mail Company, called the Soldier's Farewell, before night overtook us.

As we rode out of the corral into the beautiful bright sunshine, the view before us was a lovely one indeed.

Away to the south lay the peaks of the great Sierra Madre range, stretching far into the interior of Chihuahua. To the southeast the graceful, conical peaks of the Florida Mountains were to be seen, while, nearer, isolated ranges and solitary Picatchos, rugged and bare, raised their heads like huge rocks emerging from the quiet blue of the ocean.

To the east, more than a hundred miles distant, the peaks of the Organos reared their huge basaltic columns, which were distinctly visible in the clear morning light.

Immediately in front of us lay the Burro range, while high above their tops towered Cook's Peak, its jagged sides clothed with the enchantment that distance always lends. To the northeast the Mimbres range rose high in the air, while farther north the Pino Alto, with their dark-green pines, could be seen in bold relief against the snow-clad peaks of the Mogollon range, far to the north of the Gila, yet seemingly immediately behind them.

To the northwest the solitary peak of the San Francisco, with its *compadres*, the Dos Cabasas, were plainly visible; and far beyond them Mount Graham, with its bald old summit strove to pierce the clouds, while at our very feet the great plateau of the West, with its sand-fields sparkling in the sunshine, stretched out as far as the eye could reach.

It was a most beautiful picture that Nature had this morning unrolled for our inspection; nor did we commence our descent until we had thoroughly, and I hope appreciatingly, enjoyed its beauties.

About ten o'clock we reached the level of the vast plateau, which extends for nearly three degrees westward from the Rio Grande, and is considered one of the best natural routes for a railroad ever seen, though a more barren and desolate range of country does not exist on the American continent.

Imagine, if you can, an endless, parched-up waste, with only an occasional patch of grass to be seen; then miles of gray alkali plain, relieved by stretches of earth perfectly bare, and so light that the least breath of air drives the dust before it like a simoon, almost suffocating the unfortunate traveller who chances to be in its course.

Not a living green shrub to be seen, nor a drop of water to be found upon its surface, save in the lowest spots, where it sometimes collects for a few days, soon becoming stagnant, and emitting a most offensive odor. Yet this cesspool is the resort, while it lasts, of both man and beast. Deer, antelope, wolves, and coyotes share with the weary traveller the thickened, stagnant impurities; flocks of birds frequent it; geese, ducks, teal, and, in fact, everything that requires water, partakes of its foul unwholesomeness.

The great plateau certainly presents but few attractions to the wayfarer. Just after reaching the level of the plain, we witnessed a most remarkable mirage.

We saw distinctly reflected animals of all kinds, from the stately giraffe to the homely ox; tents, which we afterwards found standing near the Soldier's Farewell, twenty miles away, were transformed into snow-clad peaks; tufts of grass, into magnificent forest trees; every *playa* into a beautiful lake, with its rippling waves and showery sprays, while on its banks were terraced citadels, stately columns, and ruined castles, such as might be found in Greece or old Rome. It was a wonderful sight, and one never to be forgotten.

We soon arrived at Barney Station, where, through the

kindness of the keeper, we obtained water and grain for our animals.

After a short rest we again started for the Soldier's Farewell, which we reached just as the sun was setting. The station was situated in the midst of this vast barren plain, and was as desolate and gloomy a place as one would care to find in any country. The nearest water fit to drink was forty miles away, and had to be hauled in hogsheads by mule teams. The stock drank the water that collected in a couple of holes, called tanks, and this is the only watering-place on the route of the Overland Mail across the great plateau on the line of the 32nd parallel.

The whole place and its surroundings were so palpably desolate and forbidding that we no longer wondered at the peculiar name which the station bore.

For myself I could readily imagine with what joy a soldier would utter his farewell to a locality so entirely devoid of attractions. Yet here we were, and here we had to remain for the night.

The next morning we bade adieu to the Soldier's Farewell at an early hour, nor did we feel any pang of regret at the leave-taking. Even our mules seemed to exhibit signs of pleasure at once more starting for the Rio Grande, and galloped along the dry, dusty road with a speed that was remarkable. Resting on the Mimbres, the evening of the next day, we finally reached La Mesilla, thankful to have escaped

A MIRAGE ON THE GRAND PLATEAU

the dangers which had encompassed us on all sides, and overjoyed at the opportunity offered for rest after our long and tedious journey.

Jimmy was frantic in his expressions of joy, and many were the fabulous stories he told of his travels through the wilds of Arizona; nor did he forget old José, the "king," as he continued to call him, who always came in for a good share of Jimmy's imaginative descriptions.

We passed a couple of weeks very pleasantly in La Mesilla, where we frequently met the officers stationed at the United States military post, known as Fort Fillmore, situated five miles below the town, on the opposite bank of the river.

Shortly after our arrival here, I was waited upon by a Mr. White of Philadelphia, who informed me that he had recently received the appointment of sutler to the U. S. Military Post of Fort Buchanan; and learning that I had just returned from a visit there, he had called to inquire concerning the state of the roads, condition of the country, whether he should be likely to encounter Indians, etc., etc.

Mr. White stated that he was accompanied by his wife and child; that Mrs. White found it so tedious travelling with his train, he had left it behind; and taking two Mexican servants, his ambulance, and four mules, had driven on in advance, intending to reach the fort as soon as possible.

I urged him to remain over night with us, at the same time informing him that I thought the journey far from a safe one for himself and family.

After some little hesitation he was induced to remain in Mesilla until the next morning, and we gladly gave him a room in our house, quite delighted with the good fortune that had once more brought us in contact with an American lady; for American ladies in that country are like angels' visits, few and far between.

I found Mrs. White a charming little woman, about twenty-five years of age, refined, and highly educated. She informed me that this was the first time she had ever left her father's roof for an absence of more than a few weeks at a time; yet now with her babe she had left her luxurious home in the old Quaker City, and for nearly two months had been "roughing it" on the road from Lavacca, Texas, and she appeared overjoyed at the prospect of being so near her future home, which she was exceedingly anxious to learn all about. Innumerable were the questions she asked concerning it, to all of which I gave as favorable replies as possible, descanting largely upon the magnificent climate, the beauties of the Sonoita Valley, and the kindness and hospitality of the officers stationed there.

At Mr. White's request I made no mention of the danger to be apprehended from Indians, he deeming it at once unnecessary and injudicious.

We passed a most enjoyable day in company with Mr. and Mrs. White, and deeply regretted that they could remain no longer than the morrow with us.

It was nearly noon the next day when they took their departure, the doctor and myself accompanying them some miles on the road, leaving them about three o'clock in the afternoon to pursue their tedious journey, while we returned to Mesilla, delighted with our guests, the doctor declaring in the fulness of his heart that he would willingly ride over to Fort Buchanan any time for the pleasure of spending a day in the presence of such a "right clever" lady as was Mrs. White.

Early the next morning we were awakened by the sound of the great drum as it was beaten in the plaza. As this drum was only beaten for the purpose of arousing the inhabitants to arms, I sprang to my feet, and hastily dressing, made my way to the plaza, where I found assembled about a dozen Mexicans, listening to the tale of a couple of *rancheros* who had just arrived from the Mimbres.

They told us that about midnight, while coming in from their ranche, they had found the dead bodies of two men, one an American, the other a Mexican, lying by the roadside scalped; and at a little distance from them, the remains of an ambulance; also a fire still burning. Trunks broken open and rifled of their contents were scattered by the roadside, and evidences of a massacre were everywhere visible.

The *rancheros* had brought with them such articles as they could collect, some of which I recognized at once as belonging to Mr. White. The men were confident that the bodies of neither of the women were there, which fact made it evident that they, with the child, had been carried away by the savages.

Requesting the alcalde, who by this time had arrived upon the ground, to have them continue beating the drum for a time, I mounted a horse and started at once for Fort Fillmore, to inform the officers stationed there of the occurrence. Meeting Lieutenant Howland of the First Dragoons near the fort, I reported the facts to him, and he informed me that as soon as possible he would dispatch a squad of dragoons in pursuit.

Returning to Mesilla I found about fifty Mexicans assembled in the plaza with their horses and rifles, ready to start at once in pursuit of the Indians; and knowing well that some delay must necessarily occur before the troops would be ready to accompany them, both the doctor and myself, as well as half a dozen other Americans present, volunteered to go with the party, and urged so strongly the necessity of an immediate start, that Captain Pardilla, the commandant of the Mexican force, gave the necessary orders, and we set forth, accompanied by Don Jesus Armijo, and Don Manuel Chabes, two of the most celebrated Mexican guides in the country, as scouts.

A ride of two hours and a half brought us to the scene of the massacre. The bodies of Mr. White and his servant, the former half devoured by the wolves, lay by the road-side pierced by many arrows and fearfully mangled, while all around were discernible traces of the desperate efforts with which the two men had resisted the attack.

Pausing at the place only long enough to decently bury the bodies, the guides, who had been thoroughly searching the ground in the vicinity of the massacre, discovered that the party consisted of fifteen Indians; that Mrs. White, with her babe and servant, had undoubtedly been carried away with them; and that the whole party had gone in a southerly direction, towards the Florida Mountains in Chihuahua.

Swiftly and silently we sped on our sad errand of mercy. Not a word was spoken; not a sound was heard, save that of our horses' feet as we galloped over the hard, gravelly soil of the plains. Not a moment did we pause, except when the guides dismounted to examine the trail more closely than the rapid nature of our pursuit would permit them to do when mounted. Thus passed the day.

Just before nightfall we came to a beautiful green valley, through which meandered a stream of clear, sparkling water. Here we dismounted, that our tired animals, as well as ourselves, might obtain a little rest after the exhausting journey. It was about eleven o'clock, and some time after the moon had risen, that we again commenced the pursuit.

The trail soon led us through a cañon in the mountains, which we followed; and just after daylight we reached a spot where, from the confusion and number of tracks visible, it was evident the savages had halted but a few hours before.

While watering our horses at a little spring which bubbled out from under a huge rock close by, one of the Mexicans came running up with the dead body of Mrs. White's babe, which he had found lying behind a little bush near the spring, thrust through and through a dozen times with Apache spears. It was indeed a sickening sight. The nude body of this boy-baby, with its gaping, ugly wounds, that silently but eloquently appealed to every spark of manliness in our breasts for revenge upon its foul murderers, and the low, excited *carrahos* of the Mexicans, told more forcibly than words could have done, that the sight had stirred even in their dull breasts unwonted fires of rage.

We decided to push on at once, without waiting, as we had intended, for the military to overtake us; and tarrying here barely long enough to rest our animals, we started on the still fresh trail once more.

Two hours' hard riding brought us through the cañon and out into the open plain beyond, when far in the distance our guides pointed to a thin, blue, vapory smoke ascending from among a range of low *picatchos*, which seemed to form a portion of the Florida range, whose graceful peaks rose in stately majesty just behind them.

Making a long detour, in order that we might approach their camping-place without detection, we managed to get within a few miles of the spot, when, taking advantage of the shelter afforded by a spur of the mountains that projected far out into the plain, our guides suggested that we should dismount, and permit our horses to rest, while they made a reconnoissänce of the Apaches' camp.

In vain did I urge an immediate attack. Nothing that I could say would alter the determination of the guides, who would permit no one to accompany them, lest a single misstep or a careless word should betray their presence to the wary foe. After enjoining the utmost silence and care upon all, the guides departed; and nothing could be done but wait for their return.

We threw ourselves upon the ground, and gazed into the bright blue dome over our heads, or watched our tired animals as they greedily cropped the green grass, while we listened to marvellous tales told by some of the men of the skill and cunning of the guides who had gone to the enemy's camp.

Thus the long hours dragged wearily on, without any news from the guides. The afternoon was far advanced when one of the men reported that a new smoke had been started in the same place where we had seen it in the morning, which seemed to indicate that the Indians intended to remain encamped there for the night.

It was almost dark when the guides returned. They reported that there were twelve Indians in the camp about four miles distant. They had obtained a good view of it, and saw both Mrs. White and her servant, who, worn out with the toil and fatigue of their terrible journey, were apparently sleeping. They anticipated no trouble in rescuing them, but thought it safer not to make the attempt until later in the night, when we should probably find the Indians asleep. Deferring to the opinions of the guides, we possessed our souls with patience as best we could, anxiously waiting for the hour to come which should determine for weal or woe the fate of the prisoners, while we discussed the plan of attack.

Our party was to be divided so that we might completely surround the Indians, and thus prevent their escape. We were to take position on the sides of the hills which surrounded their camp, and at a given signal — the cry of the whip-poor-will twice repeated — each man was to select an Indian and fire; it being hoped that by waiting until a late hour the moon would throw the full light of its rays directly into the camp, thus enabling us to see the condition of affairs there.

No signs having been discovered of the military, we

mounted our horses about nine o'clock, and quietly rode to a point about a mile distant from the enemy's camp. Here we dismounted, leaving our horses with six men, who were detailed to take charge of them.

The party now separated, the portion in charge of Don Manuel making a wide detour, in order to reach the opposite side of the camp undiscovered, while the rest of us accompanied Don Jesus, and were to wait the expected signal from Don Manuel.

Quietly and expeditiously we made our way to the *picatchos*, behind which the enemy were encamped. Not a word was spoken; not the sound of a footstep could be heard. Occasionally, as the sharp, quick "st!" of Don Jesus fell upon our ears, we paused to hear his words of caution uttered in whispered tones, or to receive more explicit directions as to the course we were to pursue.

At last we reach the foot of the *picatcho*, which we are to cross. It rises rough and dark before us, its outline marked plainly against the light of the moon, which has not yet risen above its top.

Slowly and cautiously we make our way up its steep side, exercising great care lest the least noise should betray our proximity to the unsuspecting foe upon the other side. Stealthily we creep towards the top of the bluff. Not a breeze moans through the tall pines above our heads; nothing disturbs the death-like silence that reigns around us; and at last the camp with its occupants is before us.

How eagerly we peer down into it from behind the dark rocks, the shadows of which makes the blackness more intense. By the bright light of the moon we can count one, two, three, four, five, six, seven, eight, nine recumbent forms. Two more are crouching over the embers of the fire, their blankets wrapped tightly around their shoulders, as though for protection from the chill night air; but nowhere can we see the prisoners.

Where can they be? Don Jesus, as though anticipating our question, silently points to a thick clump of pines but a little distance from the fire; and ere he removes his hand, as though answering the question himself, a tall naked savage steps out into the bright moonlight from this very thicket of pines, and inclining his head in a listening attitude, hurriedly casts his eyes around the camp. Instinctively we raise our rifle to our shoulder. But a warning gesture from Don Jesus restrains us from taking advantage of the splendid mark thus presented, and the Indián disappears within the shadows of the pines again.

Not a movement is visible in the camp. Not a sound is heard. The hour which drags itself along while we are waiting for the signal from Don Manuel seems an eternity.

Will it never come? At last, from the hill upon the opposite side of the camp, we hear the low, mournful notes

UPPER PORTION OF THE CAÑON.

of a whip-poor-will, so natural and so truthful that it seems to us it must be the cry of the bird itself. But in an instant we hear the sharp click of Don Jesus' rifle, and we ask ourselves the question, — Can that be the signal from Don Manuel? Will it be repeated? In the excitement of the moment we almost forget to breathe. Every sense is on the alert. Yes, there it is again — a low, plaintive, yet perfectly distinct cry. Now the answer comes from the lips of Don Jesus, to be again repeated from the bluffs beyond; and then the quick, sharp ring of twenty rifles disturbs the stillness of the night.

In an instant the sides of the hill seem alive with men. As the sound of rolling rocks, the crash of tumbling men, and the yells of excited Mexicans fall upon the ears of the half-awakened savages, they utter a feeble yell of defiance, and we see three or four dusky forms rise from the ground and hastily make their way into the woods.

Pell-mell we rush for the camp; hurriedly we push our way to the thicket of pines, in which we expect to find the prisoners. Are they there? Yes! we can distinguish their forms even through the deep shade of the pine trees. They are asleep. The sound of the struggle has not yet awakened them from the heavy slumber into which they have fallen. We speak. No answer. Can it be death? We place our hands upon the bodies. They are warm; but an indescribable something about them causes us to hastily call for a torch; and when it is brought, what a sight it reveals. Great God! The remembrance even at this late day causes me to sicken at the horrors revealed by the light of that torch.

Upon the ground lay the bodies of Mrs. White and her servant, pierced with a dozen wounds, from each of which the life-blood was fast ebbing. Both were dead, although the still warm bodies bore testimony to the sad fact that the sound of our rifles had proved their death-knell.

Seven of the Indians were found dead in camp. The rest had fled, no one knew where or whither, leaving everything behind them. A portion of our party was at once dispatched to secure their animals, nineteen in number, and they were shortly loaded with all the plunder of the camp, including the articles stolen from Mrs. White.

A couple of rude litters were made, by stretching blankets over lance-poles, and the bodies tenderly borne to our place of rendezvous. Under the shadows of the cold gray rocks of the Florida Mountains, beneath the tall pines that will ever sing their mournful requiem, we left the bodies of Mrs. White and her servant in one grave. And there they repose to-day,— the elegant, accomplished, and refined mistress by the side of her servant, their grave unmarked and unknown.

Sadly we left the lone grave, and returned to our homes

upon the Rio Grande. We did not meet the military, as they deemed it useless to follow us.

Nearly a year afterward, a friend in Tucson sent me a portion of the case of a little watch that had been taken from a recently captured Apache. It bore the name of E. J. White.

Reader, my sad tale is told.

While tarrying here, I determined to put into execution a long-cherished plan that I had formed,—to visit the scenes so graphically described by old Father Niza, in his report to the Emperor Charles V., concerning the great city of Cibola (or, as it was called by the Spaniards, Zuni,) and its inhabitants.

At the time of the author's residence in Arizona, the Territories of Arizona and New Mexico were one, and as one we propose to regard them, although in the year 1863 our sapient legislators at Washington, knowing about as much of the geographical formation of that country, or the real needs of its inhabitants, as a bear knows about Sunday Schools, declared the eastern boundary of the Territory of Arizona to be an imaginary line, supposed to run somewhere near the thirty-second degree of longitude west from Washington, and giving all that portion of the Territory east of said line, to New Mexico.

As the Zuni country is situated west of the Rio Grande, and about three hundred and eighty miles northwest from

Mesilla, we determined to ascend the valley of that river, and start upon the expedition either from the town of Albuquerque, or from Santa Fé, as we should find most convenient.

Our government had so recently whipped the Navajoes into a peace, that we anticipated no trouble from them; and the other tribes residing in the country were generally Pueblo Indians, and more disposed to cultivate the soil than take to the war-path; therefore the journey promised to be a pleasant and peaceable one, unless by accident we should encounter some marauding band of Apaches.

After recruiting our animals, and laying in a goodly quantity of camp-stores from the extensive stock of our friends Grandjean and Moran in La Mesilla, and from Hayward and McGrotys at Fort Fillmore, Dr. Parker and myself, with Jimmy as cook, groom, and general factotum, turned our backs upon Mesilla, bound for Albuquerque, two hundred and forty miles distant, from which point we expected to penetrate into the "Zuni country," where we should find the celebrated city of Cibola, which with its six sister cities, De Niza visited as early as 1539, and which Coronado conquered in 1540. Their reports are the first really authentic history of the kingdom, although as early as 1526, nearly a hundred years before the landing of the Pilgrim Fathers, one Don Joseph de Bazemzalles crossed the kingdom of Cibola, and penetrated the country as far as the pueblo of Zuni, or what was then known as the city of Cibola. Of his expedition we have no reliable information.

Upon the western slope of the Sierra Madre, and not far from the still existing pueblos of Acoma and Laguna, of which we shall speak in a succeeding chapter of this work, stands a very remarkable rock, called by the Spaniards "*El Moro*," and by the Americans "Inscription Rock," which is thus described by the Abbé Domenech:—

"The front of this rock, which faces the northeast, is vertical, and of a natural polish up to two hundred and ten feet of its height. On this side the base is covered with Indian hieroglyphics and Spanish inscriptions. The opposite declivity has the form of a bastion, and possesses a spring of translucent water, which bubbles up at its foot from amid a circular basin surrounded by verdure. The summit of the rock is of white sandstone, interveined with yellow. It is perpendicularly split in several places, so that at a distance it perfectly resembles the turrets of a moresque castle, from which circumstance it evidently derives its name of 'El Moro.' Upon the smooth surface of this rock the Indians, as well as the old Spaniards, were accustomed to record the object or success of their journeys through the country."

The oldest inscription to be found upon it is in the lower left-hand corner, and is almost effaced by time and the elements, while it is most effectually concealed from careless eyes by the underbrush which has grown up around it. It is simply this: "Don Joseph de Bazemzalles, 1526."

Lieutenant Simpson, in the report of his explorations through this country in 1849, says: —

"I spent much time, and took great pains, to decipher and interpret many inscriptions upon a very remarkable rock, as well as to arrange them as nearly as possible in their chronological order."

I purpose to give in this work, however, only a few of the many score to be found thereon. The most ancient of all is that of Bazemzalles, in 1526. Then come the following:—

"Passed by this place with dispatches, 16th day of April, 1606."

"J. Aparella, 1619."

"Governor and Captain General of the province of New Mexico, for our Lord, the King, passed by this place on his return from the pueblo of Zuni, on the 29th of July, of the year 1620, and put them in peace at their petition, asking the favor to become subjects of His Majesty; and anew they gave obedience. All of which they did with free consent, knowing it prudent, as well as very Christian."

"To so distinguished and gallant a soldier, indomitable and famed, we love . . ." (The balance of this inscription is so completely obliterated, that it was impossible to decipher it.)

"Here passed General Don Diego de Baragas, to conquer Sante Fé for the Royal Crown, New Mexico, at his own cost, in the year 1692."

The only two inscriptions to be found in English, are these: —

"O. R., March 19, 1836." The other that of Lieutenant Simpson himself, bearing date September 18, 1849.

Whatever became of Bazemzalles and his band of adventurers, if he had any, none can tell. How they perished, or where their bones lie bleaching, are alike unknown.

The simple inscription upon the side of "El Moro" seems to be the only record of his journeyings extant.

Marco de Niza, a Franciscan monk before referred to, gives us the first information concerning this country and its people.

On the 7th of March, 1539, he was dispatched by Francisco Vasquez de Coronado, a nobleman of Salamanca, and governor of the province, "to descry the country." He took with him the friar Honoratus, and an Arabian negro, called Esteva. Starting from Petatlan, a town of Culican,— so called because its inhabitants lived in houses built of matted rushes, called *petates*,— he went "following as the Holy Ghost did lead," passing through "great deserts, and meeting Indians who marvelled to see him, having no knowledge of any Christians, or even of any Indians on the other side of the desert."

The inhabitants were numerous and intelligent. The women wore petticoats, or dresses, of deer-skin, but they had no idea of Christianity. They called Niza "*Soyota*," or man come down from heaven, and would try to touch his garments. They informed him that he would soon come to a great plain, full of large towns, which were inhabited by a people clad in cotton, wearing gold rings and ear-rings, and "using little blades of the same metal to scrape the sweat from their bodies."

About this time the negro Esteva, who had been giving the good father "great trouble on account of misconducting himself towards the women of the country, and only thought of enriching himself," was sent away by Father Niza on a voyage of discovery, accompanied by some "emancipated Indians."

Four days after Esteva's departure, he dispatched two messengers to Father Niza, acquainting him with the discovery of a wonderful city called Cibola.

These messengers the good father called *pintados*, because their faces, breasts, and arms were painted. They told him that a man might travel in thirty days to this great city of Cibola, which was the first of the seven cities.

They also informed him that they often went there after "turquoise and ox-hides," which they received as "wage for tilling the ground." They said that the inhabitants of Cibola dressed in "gowns of cotton down to the feet, with a button at the neck; that they girded themselves with girdles of turquoises, or hide of kine," all of which reports so greatly pleased the good father, that he determined to follow on after Esteva.

He continued his journey for five days, "always finding inhabited places, and great hospitality."

Before reaching the desert, he arrived at a very pleasant town, where he found many people, both men and women, "clothed in cotton, and some in ox-hides, which generally they take for better apparel than that of cotton." He says:—

"All the people of this village go in *caconados;*" that is to say, with turquoises hanging at their nostrils and ears, which they call *caconas*. The lord of the village, and others beside him, were "apparelled in cotton, in *caconados*, with a collar of türquoises about their necks."

They gave him "conies," quails, maize, and nuts of pine-trees, and offered him turquoises, ox-hides, and fair vessels to drink in, which he declined.

They informed him that beside the seven cities of Cibola, there were three other kingdoms, called Marata, Acus, and Totonteac, and that in Totonteac were great quantities of woollen cloth, such as he himself wore, made from the fleece of wild beasts, which were about the size of the two spaniels that he carried with him.

The next day he entered the desert; and when he came to dine he found "bowers made, and victuals in abundance."

These the Indians provided for him all the way across the desert, which was four days' journey.

Then he came to a valley "inhabited by a goodly people. It was well watered and like a garden, abounding in victuals sufficient to feed about three thousand horsemen."

Through this valley he travelled five days. Here, too, he found a man born in Cibola, having escaped from the governor-lieutenant of the same. "For," he says, "the lord of the seven cities liveth and abideth in one of these towns called Ahacus, and in the rest he appointeth lieutenants under him."

This townsman of Cibola was a white man, of good complexion, well advanced in years, and of far greater intellect than the inhabitants of this valley or the others left behind.

He says: "Cibola is a great city, inhabited by a great store of people, and having many streets and market-places. In some parts of the city are certain great houses, five stories high, wherein the chief of the city do assemble themselves on certain days of the year. The houses are of lime and stone, the gates and small pillars of the principal houses are of turquoises, and all the vessels wherein they are served are of gold. The other six cities are like unto this, and Ahacus is the chiefest of them all.

"To the southwest is a kingdom called Marata, where there be great cities builded of houses of stone, with many lifts Likewise the kingdom of Totonteac lieth to the west, a very

THE APACHÉ PASS.

mighty province, replenished with infinite store of riches; and in the said kingdom they wear woollen cloth made of the fleece of animals, and they are a very civil people.'' They showed him "a hide half as big again as the hide of an ox, which belonged to a beast with one horn. The color of the skin was like that of a goat, and the hair was a finger long.'' Father Niza was still fifteen days' journey from the great city of Cibola, following in the course of the negro Esteva.

He started once more on the 9th of May, determined to accomplish the journey without any further delay. He travelled for twelve days, when he met one of the Indians who had accompanied Esteva, and "in great fright, and covered with sweat,'' he hastily informed Father Niza that the inhabitants of Cibola had seized the negro, and after imprisoning him, had put him to death, together with several of the Indians of his party.

This statement greatly disconcerted the good father, who much feared to put his life in such jeopardy. Still, with the indomitable pluck that always characterized those early adventurers, he determined to *see* the great city, if he could not *enter* it. To this end he made one more day's journey, where, ascending a mountain, he viewed the city.

He says: "It is situated upon the plain at the foot of a round hill, and maketh show to be a fair city. It is better seated than any I have seen in these parts. The houses are builded in order and all made of stone, with divers stories and flat roofs."

Having ascertained these facts, and seen the city with his own eyes, Father Niza at once retraced his steps; and after many days' journey, during which he experienced nothing but kindness from the hands of the Indians, he finally reached the province of Culican, where he straightway made report to the governor of all the strange things he had seen. The Abbé Em Domenech, in his work on the deserts of North America, says, in speaking of Father Niza's journey:—

"The information given by Father Marcos is so vague that it is scarcely possible to state precisely the route he followed, or to indicate the geographical position of the countries through which he passed.

'There would seem to be, however, good authority for supposing that his journey was made through the valley of the Gila, instead of the Rio Verde country; across the Colorado Chiquito, thence through the Mogollon Mountains, and across the great plateau to the western slope of the Sierra Madre."

That he visited the *Casas Grandes*, already described in a preceding chapter, there is no doubt, as it is most probable that they would be included in that portion of country called the kingdom of Marata. Niza says in his report before referred to, "And these people of Marata have, and do, wage war with the lord of the seven cities, through which war the kingdom of Marata is for the most part wasted, although it yet continueth and maintaineth war against the others."

This being the only information we have concerning the early settlements on the Gila, it is much to be regretted that Niza's report is not more explicit.

Upon his return, it would seem that he decided to visit the kingdom of Totonteac, which was undoubtedly comprised of those towns lying upon the Rio Verde and Pueblo Creek; but from fear of the Indians, he did not go into it, though he saw it from afar off, lying in a low valley, "being very green, and having a most fruitful soil, out of which ran many streams."

Of course this is mostly conjecture, founded principally upon the fact that no other ruins are known to exist in the direction given from Cibola, by Father Niza.

The wonderful reports of Father Niza so fired the patriotic heart of Captain-General-Governor Francisco Vasquez de Coronado, that he determined to view with his own eyes this wonderful city of Cibola. To this end he commenced at once to organize an expedition, which he proposed to lead in person, having for its object the conquest of the kingdom of Cibola.

This army he assembled at the town of Compostella, in the province of Culican, and was composed of one hundred and fifty horsemen, two hundred archers, the flower and chivalry of the province, together with eight hundred emancipated Indians.

The army set forth the day following Easter, 1540, and marched to the outermost limit of the province of Culican, where it halted for rest. Coronado, however, could ill brook even this delay; so he determined to push on ahead, in company with Father Niza, fifty chosen horsemen, and seventy archers, entrusting the command of the remainder of his army to one Don Tristran de Arellano, with instructions to remain in camp fifteen days, and then follow the route pursued by himself.

CHAPTER XVII.

AFTER forty days of toil and privations of all kinds, Coronado arrived at a place he calls "Chichilticall," which signifies Red Town, a name which seems to have been given by Coronado himself, on account of "a very large house there of red color, inhabited by an entire tribe that came from towards Cibola, where the last desert begins."

At this point Coronado's troubles seemed to have begun in earnest. He lost some of his horses, as well as a number of his men, for want of food; and his army became greatly discouraged, and clamored loudly to return to Culican.

But Coronado was made of no such stuff, and was bound to proceed. After the delay of a week at Red Town, he with his followers continued the march. In two weeks' time they had arrived at a point within twenty miles of Cibola.

Here for the first time they met several natives of the kingdom; but they, becoming frightened, immediately took to flight, spreading the alarm throughout the country by means of great fires, which they kindled on the high mountains (a custom followed by the Indians of Arizona and New Mexico to this day).

At this point Coronado seems to have tarried for a time, in order to enable Don Tristan d'Arellano, with the remainder of his army, to overtake him. After waiting in vain for some weeks, he at last determined to advance to the walls of Cibola without reinforcements.

In his report to the Emperor Charles V., he says: "After we had passed thirty leagues of the most wicked way, we found fresh rivers and grass like that of Castile, and many nut-trees, whose leaf differs from that of Spain. And there was flax, but chiefly seen on the banks of a certain river, which, therefore, we called El Rio del Lino.* At last I did arrive at the walls of Cibola, and I sent a messenger thither, who was ill-treated and fired at." Coronado found that the people of the province were all assembled, and with "steady attitude" awaited his coming.

He valiantly attacked the city, and after a desperate fight, in which he was struck by a large stone and unhorsed, and only saved from bodily harm by the strength of his armor and the devotedness of his friends, Garcia Lopez de Cardenas and Horonardo de Alvarado, who shielded him with their bodies, while some others helped him up,

* Flax River.

the city capitulated, and Coronado marched in and took possession.

He found neither old men, women, nor children under fifteen years of age, in the town, they having been taken to the mountains before the assault began. He found, however, plenty of corn, of which they were greatly in need.

While waiting here for the arrival of Don Tristan and his command, Coronado dispatched one of his officers, by name Garcia Lopez de Cardenas, with a handful of men, to visit the Moquis villages situated at the distance of a few leagues from Cibola. De Cardenas, however, seems to have lost his way; and after travelling for twenty days through a broken, volcanic country, with insufficient food for man or beast, he suddenly came to a "great cleft in the earth's surface, which prevented them from going any farther."

De Cardenas describes the cleft to be "deeper than the side of the highest mountain; while the torrent below was scarcely a fathom wide. Two men tried to descend its steep, precipitous sides; and after experiencing the most terrible difficulties, they managed to climb down perhaps a quarter of the way, when their progress was stopped by a rock, which seemed from above to be no greater than a man, but which in reality was higher than the top of the cathedral tower at Seville."

Never had they seen such a sight before; and not knowing what might be in further store for them if they proceeded down the chasm, they straightway returned, that they might report this wonderful impediment to Captain Cardenas.

In the mean time Don Tristan and the men under his command were slowly, and in the face of most trying obstacles, making their way along towards Cibola, where they hoped to effect a junction with the general-in-chief.

Hunger assailed their ranks, and many of the men died from absolute starvation, which so affected Don Tristan that he changed his route to one farther north, hoping thereby to better the condition of his army.

This course soon brought him among a very depraved class of people. "The women painted their chins and around their eyes. The men were very wicked, and intoxicated themselves with wine made from the pitahaya or maguey, which grew in abundance throughout the country."

After passing through almost insurmountable difficulties, Don Tristan and his army finally reached Cibola, and joined Coronado, who was much dissatisfied with the results thus far obtained.

He says in his report, "It remaineth now to testify whereof the Father Provincial, Niza, made report to your majesty. And to be brief, I can assure your honor he said the truth in nothing that he reported; but all was quite contrary, save only the names of the cities and the great houses of stone. The seven cities are seven towns, all made of these kind of many-storied houses. They all exist, and within four leagues of each other, and are called the kingdom of Cibola."

He further says, "They eat the best cakes I ever saw, and have the finest order and way of grinding. One woman of this country will grind as much as four women of Mexico. That which these people worship, as far as we hitherto can learn, is the water; for they say it causeth the corn to grow, and maintaineth their lives."

Becoming tired of the inactive life at Zuni, Coronado determined to start forth in the hope of finding yet undiscovered territory. With this object in view he started eastward, into the valley of the Rio Grande.

He soon came to Acoma, or, as he calls it, "Acuco," a town on an exceedingly "strong hill," four leagues from which he met with a "new kind of oxen," * "very wild and fierce, of which the first day they killed four score, which supplied the army with flesh,— for all the way was as full of crooked-backed oxen as the mountain-sierras in Spain are of sheep."

"Coronado now took measures," says the Abbé Domenech, "to push his conquest, by taking possession of the province of Tiguex, on the Rio Grande." This province he

* Buffalo.

captured after a fight of fifty days. It consisted of twelve towns, the principal of which were Pecos, Querra, Abo, and Gran Quivera.

Pecos was a fortified town of several stories. It was built on a high mesa, and overlooked the country around for many miles. Here stood the large Mexican temple, Montezuma's church, which was three stories high, and

PECOS.

where burned the sacred flame day and night. The Indian legend is, that Montezuma built this pueblo himself, and with his own hands placed the sacred fire in the *estufa*, at the same time warning his people that when they allowed it to go out, death would come. Before he left them, he took a tall tree, and, inverting it, planted it near the *estufa*, saying, if they did not permit the sacred flame to be extinguished until the tree fell, men with pale faces would come into the country from the East, and, overrunning it, would drive their oppressors, the Spaniards, from the country; when he himself would return and build up his kingdom, the earth should become fertile, and the mountains yield rich harvests of gold and silver. All of which predictions these Indians claim have been literally fulfilled.

Late in the year 1542, Coronado, becoming tired of conquest, organized a series of festivals for the amusement of his army and the Indians; and at one of them, held at Tiguex, Coronado himself was thrown from his horse while "running the ring" with one Don Pedro Maldonado, and severely injured. This accident seems to have been the primary cause of a great desire on the part of Coronado to reurn to his province of Culican. His army became greatly demoralized in consequence of this fact becoming known, and soon disbanded, scattering throughout the newly-discovered country. Few of them were ever afterwards heard from. Coronado, with a few trusty followers, arrived in Culican in April, 1543.

I had long entertained a desire to see the ruins of this country, and many facts and incidents connected with them, related to me by Major Ruff of the U. S. Army, who commanded an expedition through the Navajoe country in '57, so strengthened the inclination, that I should have made the trip alone, had I been unable to find anybody to accompany me.

The preceding pages contain the early history of the country which we proposed to visit at this time, and we asked ourselves the questions many times over,— Shall we be able to recognize the different localities from the slight knowledge we have of them? Shall we find, inhabiting the pueblos, descendants of the people so minutely described by Father Niza and Coronado, possessing any of the characteristics and habits of their ancestors?

Reader, will you accompany us in our journey, or shall we part here? Do you care to encamp with us at each stopping-place we make on the long dusty drive to Albuqurque, or will you be content to know that we crossed the long *jornada* of ninety miles without water, in safety? That on our right hand we saw each day the peaks of the Sierra Blanca, the Organos, and the Oscruro; and on our left those of the Mimbres, while afar off, to the north and west, the snow-clad peaks of the Sierra Madre range glistened each day in the bright sunshine like huge cones of crystal, stretching from seven to nine thousand feet in the air; that after a weary journey of five days we were at last delighted with a sight of the twin spires on the church in Albuqurque; that we found here one of the neatest, and at the same time most interesting towns we had yet seen in the country; that we accepted the generous hospitality of our friend, Judge Baird, who for thirteen years had resided there; that nearly every house in the city had a piece of land or garden well filled with peach, apple, and plum trees of nearly every variety, or with vines growing the most luscious grapes? Shall I tell you of the little American colony which we found here;

KIT CARSON.

and that here we saw and talked for a long while with the veritable Kit Carson himself, a little weazen-faced, light-haired, wiry, active frontierman, who wore his hair long, and swore in a horrible jargon of Spanish and English, and who didn't "fear no Injun a livin'?"

We passed three days very pleasantly at Albuqurque, and through the kindness of Judge Baird obtained the services of a Mexican named Rafael Orrantia, as guide; a man thoroughly acquainted with the entire country through which we were to pass, and who could take us to the ruins of every pueblo, and knew the shortest and best route to every spring or stream of water to be found in that region. In short, a most valuable man, especially as he bore the reputation of being an honest one,— a qualification rarely to be found among men of his class.

Jimmy was much pleased with our new acquisition, and gravely informed me the morning after I had engaged him, that he was an "illegant cook," and would "relave him of a great daal of the risponshibility a ristin' on his shoulders," a relief that I very much fear Jimmy did not experience in as great a degree as he had anticipated.

As our guide informed us that we should have to descend the Rio Grande as far as Isletta, a small Mexican village nearly twenty miles below Albuqurque, if we desired to visit Laguna and Acoma, we decided to move down the valley that day, in order to be ready for an early start the next morning.

The valley of the Rio Grande, from Santa Fé for nearly four hundred miles south, as well as far to the north, bears every evidence of having at one time supported a dense population

In speaking of the former population of New Mexico and Arizona, the Abbé Domenech observes: "When New Mexico was discovered, the country extending from the Pacific on the one side to the Rio Grande on the other, was but a succession of towns, villages, and habitations, joined together by cultivated fields, orchards, and roads. But the great multitude of human beings have almost disappeared since the conquest. The silence of the wilderness has succeeded to the joyful songs of the extinct population, and the aridity of the desert replaces the fertility of the soil. Wormwood and artemisia now grow where fields of rose-trees and Indian corn formerly flourished. The cactus, mesquit, and the dwarf cedar vegetate on the remnant of the pine and fruit trees, reduced to powder by constant droughts. The sun darts its perpendicular and scorching rays on the arid and barren rocks, which sparkle by day like gigantic diamonds. All the smiling nature, so lovely in by-gone days, has retained nothing of its former glory but a melancholy beauty, not unlike the sickly hues of a flower washed by the waves of the sea."

He also estimates the population residing between the thirty-fourth and thirty-sixth degrees N. lat., and extending from the Canadian River through to the Gulf of California, to be at least one hundred and forty-nine thousand souls, as late as 1856. This estimate is generally believed to be largely in excess of the actual population, though less than one-tenth of the number who inhabited it at the time of Coronado's conquest.

The Pueblo Indians in the valley of the Rio Grande, who in 1790 numbered twelve thousand, in 1864 numbered less than six thousand, and they are steadily decreasing in numbers every year. Not many years will elapse before this industrious, semi-civilized race will become extinct, and the places that have known them for so many hundred years will know them no more forever.

Bidding good-bye to our friends in Albuqurque, we started about ten o'clock in the morning for the little village of Isletta, where we were to cross the Rio Grande, our new guide riding some distance ahead of us on a tough little mule that one could almost have carried under his arm, had it not been for his kicking propensities, which, to our cost, we found largely developed.

At Isletta we found a very neat, well-to-do village, the houses being of adobe, and nicely whitewashed, giving to the place a cheerful, pleasant aspect, rarely found in Mexican towns. They were large and well-constructed; the acequias nicely kept, and the vineyards yielding abundantly, all the result of Indian labor.

We were soon encamped in a shady, pleasant spot near the river-bank, and enjoying a most excellent repast, which Jimmy, in company with Don Rafael, had provided for us, not forgetting a generous supply of Isletta wine, as well as some very fine grapes sent us by Don Jesus Barela.

In talking over the matter with Dr. Parker, we concluded that our first objective points should be Laguna and Acoma, and that from these pueblos our course should be for Zuni by the most direct and easily travèlled route. After making these points we should be guided by circumstance, having supplies sufficient to last fifty days.

We retired to rest quite early, as we naturally expected some delay in fording the river at this place, which was about three hundred feet wide, though not more than three or four feet deep.

The Rio Grande is one of the most uncertain streams in the known world, owing to the peculiar nature of the soil through which it runs. Its bottom is nothing less than a mass of quicksand; and as we had been informed that the ford here was hazardous and very uncertain, it was with no enviable feeling that we looked at the muddy, turbid water, and realized the difficulties we might encounter in getting our mules and heavily-laden wagon safely across the stream and up the steep bank on the opposite side.

Early in the morning we were awakened by the loud cries of Jimmy, who was exclaiming in a loud tone of voice that "millions wouldn't timpt him to take another stip in such a damned counthry ez this; for if 'twasn't thim bloody Injuns 'twas somethin' ilse, and he was goin' home imma jately, this blissed minnit," at the same time calling loudly upon the "howly saints for protiction." It was some time before we could ascertain the cause of Jimmy's great excitement, for he certainly talked very unintelligibly. Finally, however, he became sufficiently calm to ask, "An whare's the river?" Upon our pointing in the direction in which it was supposed to be, Jimmy at once interrupted us with, "That's jist it; the d—d thing is behind us; and how the divil did it git there, is what I want to know."

Sure enough the river was flowing between us and Isletta, scarce half a mile distant, as calmly and quietly as though it had occupied its new bed for the past hundred years. It was with difficulty that we could convince ourselves that such was really the fact, so silently had Nature effected this wonderful change. The only damage done, was the destruction of a portion of Don Jesus Barela's vineyard, and a fine field of Indian corn.

The banks of the Rio Grande being of an exceedingly friable nature, and very sandy, offer but slight resistance to any freak the river may take. Sometimes it destroys whole villages, demolishing corrals, *haciendas*, ranches, in fact, anything that happens to be in its way when it starts on its "bender,"—now covering fields of rich alluvial soil with sand and rubbish, again tearing its way through a forest of tall cotton-woods and sycamores, or, selecting a piece of low, rich bottom-land, it takes from one man only to give to another.

Within a year of the time of the occurrence just mentioned, it suddenly started around Mesilla, leaving both La Mesilla and Las Cruces on the same bank, while before, it ran between them, making them rival towns, and engendering the same bitter feeling that is experienced in Eastern towns simi-

THE RIO GRANDE AND JIMMY ON A BENDER.

larly situated. Thus it performs the office of peace-maker, while it takes from the rich and gives to the poor; and it certainly verifies the old paradox, that "it is sometimes dangerous to be safe."

In the case cited, we learned that the charge had long

been expected, a circumstance that robbed it of much of the seeming mystery, and permitted us to attribute to natural causes what to Jimmy's excited mind still seemed supernatural to a wonderful degree.

We crossed the old river-bottom as easily as did the Children of Israel pass through the waters of the Red Sea. It was a long while though before Jimmy recovered from the consternation occasioned by his discovery, and not until we were far on our road towards Laguna, did we succeed in convincing him that it was not "the divil's own wark," instead of a long-expected and natural change in the course of events.

CHAPTER XVIII.

AT last we were fairly on our road to Laguna. Soon after leaving the Rio Grande we fell in with an old Mexican *ranchero*, who was going out to look after a flock of some four thousand sheep, which were feeding on the range in the valley of the San Juan, a branch of the Rio Puerco. We found him, like all Mexicans, extremely ignorant of everything but his own immediate business.

For about ten miles our road, gradually ascending, lay

through a country quite destitute of vegetation, and presenting altogether a most barren and cheerless aspect. Suddenly it began to descend, and we at length found ourselves in the valley proper of the Rio Puerco.

This valley is quite extensive and very flat, and is covered with a species of coarse grass, valuable for sheep and goats, thousands of which were seen grazing on every side. Each flock was accompanied by one or more herdsmen — wild, gaunt, half-naked creatures, whose clothing consisted of a sheep-skin tied about their loins, and whose only weapon of defence was a "sling" similar to that with which David of old slew the great Goliath; a weapon which they use with great dexterity and wonderful effect. Their feet were covered with sandals of rawhide, and their bushy, matted locks gave them a ferocious aspect, quite at variance with their general character.

These herders frequently spend months with their flocks far away from the settlements, with only their sheep and dogs for companions, the last-named animals being nearly as intelligent as their masters. I have seen one of the latter with a single word send his dog among a flock of several thousand in pursuit of some sheep that had chanced to stray from a neighboring flock, and invariably the quick-witted animal would single out the intruder in an almost incredibly short time. Many of the *rancheros* intrust their flocks entirely to the care of these sagacious creatures, who daily conduct them to the range, and as faithfully lead them back to the corral at night.

The soil and climate of New Mexico are particularly adapted to sheep-raising, and since the Navajoe Indians have confined their depredations to the more southern and

NEW MEXICAN SHEPHERD.

western portions of the Territory, the Rio Puerco has become a favorite grazing region for the *rancheros*.

To give a slight idea of the depredations committed by the Navajoes on the settlers in New Mexico, I subjoin the following table of estimates from the report made by the United States Territorial marshal, for the year 1850:—

"Between August 1st, 1846, and October 1st, 1850, the Navajoes stole and carried away from the settlers in the Rio Grande Valley alone, 12,887 mules, 7,050 horses, 31,581 head of horned cattle, 453,293 sheep."

In fact, the thieving operations of this tribe became so extensive that the government sent no less than three expeditions against them, the sole object of which was to lay waste and destroy their fields of grain and immense flocks and herds, as starvation seemed the only way of effecting their subjugation.

For eight years the Navajoes remained masters of the situation, until at last, harassed on all sides, they reluctantly yielded to the superior prowess of Uncle Sam, and accepted the overtures made by the government. For two years a general peace prevailed, rendering it safe for both the traveller and *ranchero* to sojourn within their borders.

On our arrival at the Puerco we found but little water, and that, of an extremely poor quality. The banks of the stream near our camp were not more than twelve or fifteen feet high, and were composed of sand and gravel hills with but little vegetation. This camp was at best a dreary one, and the long, tedious hours were enlivened by the stories of Don Rafael concerning the extraordinary quantity of game which we might expect to encounter during our next day's journey. These wonderful narrations made such a deep impression upon Jimmy's plastic mind that he at once insisted upon putting every available gun and pistol in working order before retiring for the night. Even an old double-barrelled shot-gun, which we always carried unloaded in the bottom of our wagon, was speedily made ready for active "service."

Nothing disturbed us during the night, save the quick, sharp bark of an occasional coyote, and the answering yelp of some shepherd's dog from the distant hills, or the peculiarly mournful note of the whip-poor-will, as he strove to make cheerful the oppressive silence of the vast solitude around us.

We broke camp on the following day, taking up our "line of march" through a portion of country more or less covered with pine forests, through which roamed large numbers of black-tailed deer, antelope, and rabbits, while the trees seemed fairly alive with squirrels of every variety.

As we were approaching one of these magnificent forests, Jimmy, who had been riding for some time on Don Rafael's mule, suddenly declared his intention of "huntin' daer as it was dun in the ould counthry;" whereupon he seized his double-barrelled gun, and putting spurs to his animal was soon lost to sight.

In a short time we were startled by a loud halloa, and there soon emerged from the dense underbrush a fine buck, of the black-tailed species, who headed directly for us, closely followed by Jimmy, who was wildly urging forward his poor bewildered mule.

Dr. Parker immediately took aim with his carbine, and, as good luck would have it, brought down the buck at the very first shot, to the great discomfiture of Jimmy, who had nearly reached the scene of action. At this juncture a little cloud of dust arose, and for a time both mule and rider were hidden from view. As it cleared away, Jimmy was discovered some distance in advance of his animal, which had unfortunately stepped into a gopher-hole, throwing him into mid-air with a velocity which well nigh deprived the poor fellow of breath. As soon as he had collected his scattered senses, he began a vigorous search for his gun, which he at length succeeded in finding far from the place of his disaster.

Upon coming up with Jimmy, we rallied him upon the way in which "they killed daer in ould Ireland." He finally acknowledged that the gun had missed fire twice before the deer had taken to the plain — a bit of information in no wise surprising, when upon examination we found, that in loading his piece, he had carefully placed a bullet at the bottom of each barrel, quite forgetting the powder which should have accompanied it,— an omission which Jimmy explained, by boldly and unblushingly declaring that "the powther had all laked out."

JIMMY'S HUNT.

Soon after this little adventure we entered the valley of the Rio San José, a pretty little stream, upon which stands the old Pueblo of Laguna; and as we journeyed along its pleasant banks, we passed through a grand and magnificent cañon, that soon widened into a fertile valley; and just as the sun was sinking behind the horizon, we reached the Pueblo, which, standing as it does upon the top of a high limestone bluff, seems not unlike some of the old German cities of the Rhine.

The houses here are most quaint in appearance. They are built of stone, plastered with mud, and, like most of the buildings in these old pueblos, have terraces or "lifts," each story being narrower than the one below it, thus leaving a promenade, to which one can only ascend by means of ladders. At night these ladders are drawn up, and then the occupants are completely isolated from the world.

This pueblo is one of the oldest in New Mexico, and at the time of our visit contained a population of about one thousand souls. The only public building of any importance within its limits is a church, or temple of Montezuma, from the top of which we had a wide-spread view of the surrounding country. Thirty miles to the north could be seen a rugged mountain-peak, which the Indians told us was the crater of an extinct volcano. Near by, Mount Taylor uplifted its bald head, until it seemed to pierce the very clouds, while the table-lands around, seemed as smooth as the waters of one of our great inland lakes. Here and there huge rocks of sandstone, bearing a striking resemblance to domes and towers, were thrown promiscuously over the vast plain. In close proximity to these were truncated cones, broken columns, and enormous vases of strange device, that looked as if they might have been fabricated by giants, ages before.

ACOMA.

Dr Parker and I spent nearly an hour gazing at this strange scene, and it was not until darkness had descended that we bethought ourselves of the supper which Jimmy and Don Rafael had provided for us on the banks of the San José.

We passed a quiet night, and the next day set out for Acoma, which lies about twenty miles west of Laguna, and is undoubtedly the "Acuco" mentioned in Coronado's report, to which reference is made in a former chapter.

Our route during the first day lay through a wild and desolate region, inhabited only by coyotes, black-tailed deer, and antelope. About two o'clock in the afternoon we came in sight of Acoma, which is a city much the same in appearance as Laguna. It stands upon the top of a rock, at least three hundred and fifty feet above the surrounding plain, and seems from its situation to be almost impregnable. This pueblo can be reached only by means of a staircase, containing three hundred and seventy-five steps, cut in the solid rock. At the upper end of this, is a ladder eighteen feet long, made from the trunk of a tree, in which notches have been cut for the feet. Corn and other cereals, together with peaches and apricots, grow near the foot of the rock, their thrifty appearance showing a degree of knowledge in the cultivation of the soil which greatly surprised me. Here also we found cisterns or tanks built of stone, and thoroughly cemented. These were used for holding rain-water, and their capacity was perfectly immense.

This town is composed chiefly of blocks, containing sixty or seventy houses each, generally three stories in height, and built after the same style as those of Laguna. The centre of the town has a plaza, in which stands a once respectable but now neglected Catholic church, upon whose walls hang several very fair paintings. The people seemed to be industrious, frugal, and happy, although they bore a very bad name among the inhabitants of the neighboring pueblos, who regard them as little better than robbers. We, however, found them kind and generous as well as hospitable, and anxious to do whatever might contribute to our comfort. Many of their women would not have been uncomely in appearance were it not for the fact that they padded their legs to an enormous size, thus rendering them anything but attractive.

We spent two days in Acoma and its immediate vicinity, more to see the result of a wooing in which Jimmy was interested, than for the purpose of resting; although the delay gave us an opportunity of ascertaining something of its governmental machinery.

The governor is chosen from among the old men by universal suffrage, the only qualification necessary for the position being wisdom. He holds his office during life, and presides over the council, which is composed entirely of old men. The decision of this official is regarded as law in all matters.

Next in rank is a war-captain, who arranges all companies and takes charge of every expedition. He also exercises supreme control over all the horses belonging to the pueblo.

Then comes the treasurer, or fiscal chief, who has charge of the council-house, church, etc., and who superintends all outlays for repairs, and exercises a supervisory power over all expenditures of whatever nature.

The government of Acoma is in many respects similar to that of all the pueblos, and is universally regarded by those most deeply interested in its success as a very beneficent one.

After we had made all preparations for leaving Acoma, we were considerably surprised at hearing Jimmy declare his intention of remaining behind, "for he had naarly succaaded in conthractin' a mathrimonial alliance with a daughther of one of the cooncel," a huge, unwieldy piece of adipose tissue, whose well-stuffed legs caused her to roll about in walking, with a motion very similar to a ship in the trough of the sea during a severe storm. The promise of this tawny, unkempt damsel's hand, together with a flock of sheep and some cattle, had so won upon Jimmy's susceptible heart, that he had determined, here to set up his earthly tabernacle for the remainder of his days. We remonstrated with the enamored wight; we told him of our needs, how necessary he was to our comfort and well-being in general; in fine, we used every available argument against his wild scheme, and at last, after a lengthy war of words, he reluctantly relinquished his fond dreams of love and affluence, and consented to depart with us in the early morning for Zuni; for daylight found us far on the road towards ancient Cibola.

CHAPTER XIX.

WE could have witnessed no more beautiful or enchanting sight than the sunrise which burst upon us ere we were half a dozen miles from Acoma. Before us rose the peaks of the Sierra Madre one above the other, each of an entirely different hue, reminding us of the ladder which Jacob of old saw set up between the earth and the heaven, or of some vast staircase constructed by the Afreets, to enable them to ascend to the very gates of Paradise. The highest of these rugged peaks were just tinged with the golden beams of the god of day, while a light purple mist hugged the bosom of the plain so closely that we seemed to be journeying through a perfectly motionless sea, whose stillness had never been disturbed by a single ripple or a swelling wave. Occasionally a mass of sandstone or a huge granite boulder could be seen rising out of the blue haze, sometimes taking the shape of a graceful turret, or again assuming the proportions of a castellated fortress, while the high mesas, molded as they had been, by the winds and storms of a thousand years, into the most picturesque and fantastic forms, were dimly seen, crowned with curious volcanic and basaltic formations.

The heavy vapor which enshrouded all things was at last dissipated by the full, broad rays of the sun, thereby revealing in all its naked, barren deformity the parched, arid desert which we were crossing, at an elevation of more than six thousand feet above the level of the ocean. Not a sound could be heard in this vast solitude, save the footsteps of our animals; not a living thing met our gaze, save an occasional antelope, as he fleetly bounded away from us, or a prowling, tawny-colored coyote, as he stopped at a safe distance to examine "the situation."

Don Rafael, who had been riding ahead, suddenly halted, and on reaching him, he informed us that this was the very place of places for breakfasting; we accordingly dismounted and refreshed "the inner man," our mules meanwhile cropping the sweet though scanty herbage which grew around us.

After resting here for a brief time, we resumed our journey; nor did we pause again until we reached a small rivulet, which our guide called Agua Frio, or cold water, and most grateful did we find its sparkling coolness. This little stream rises in a bed of lava, at an elevation of nearly seven thousand feet above the level of the sea. After flowing through this rocky bed for a mile or two, it sinks entirely from sight.

As the day was considerably advanced, our guide proposed that we should tarry here for the night, which was swiftly approaching. In a short time our animals were relieved of their burdens, supper was made ready, our blankets spread, and our pipes lighted,— everything promising a good night's repose.

The moon, which was at its full, soon arose; and as I strolled away from the camp, and seated myself upon a fragment of lava at some distance, I could but acknowledge that I was in a fair way to gain some experience of the peculiar influence which fair Luna is said to exert over all who gaze upon her regal beauty. The silence was oppressive; it overwhelmed me, as does the thought of the Infinite. I fancied myself shut out from the whole world, wrapped in an impenetrable veil of mystery.

Scarcely a breath of air sighed through the tall spires of grass around me. Even the melancholy chirp of the cricket was hushed; the cuckoo and the plaintive whip-poor-will had forgotten their songs; not even the rustle of a leaf disturbed the quiet which reigned supreme. Nature seemed

PUEBLO OF LAGUNA.

not only to have lost her voice, but to have plunged into an eternal sleep, from which there was no awaking, — a slumber at once so painful and mysterious, that I could have easily fancied the whole world dead, and I alone the only living, breathing thing left upon its pulseless surface. No words of mine can give an adequate idea of the terrible agony with which this dread silence filled me. I could not speak aloud; I felt as though a nightmare was oppressing me.

For more than an hour did I seem thus bound hand and foot; nor did I emerge from the Lethean waters which seemed to have overwhelmed me, until the quick, snarling bark of a coyote, upon some far-off mesa, fell upon my ear. With a thrilling sense of freedom and relief, such as I had never before experienced, I hastily sprang to my feet, and made my way back to the camp, shouting at the top of my voice.

Upon reaching camp I found that my shouts had aroused my comrades, who were greatly exercised as to the cause of the disturbance. Some trivial explanation satisfied their curiosity, and we all sought our blankets. Dr. Parker soon fell into a heavy sleep; but "Nature's sweet restorer" held persistently aloof from my lids, and I lay in my blankets gazing at the moon. Suddenly I was startled by a deep moan, as of some one in great anguish. Listening intently, I soon became convinced that the sound came from the lips of Jimmy, who lay at a little distance from Dr. Parker and myself. Upon speaking to him, he crawled slowly from his blankets and came towards me, his face presenting the most perfect picture of abject misery that I had ever seen. I was considerably surprised at this new and inexplicable phase of Jimmy's character, as the reader may well imagine.

"What is the matter, Jimmy? Are you sick?" I kindly asked.

"Indade an' I am, juge," was the plaintive reply.

"Where do you feel sick, Jimmy?" I inquired.

"It's here, surr," he said, placing his brawny hand on his heart; "and sick I am, bedad, at losin' the chance I have."

Even after this explanation I failed to understand the cause of Jimmy's illness; and the sight of two big drops slowly stealing down the poor fellow's weather-beaten cheeks so enlisted my sympathy and commiseration that I aroused Dr. Parker, and urged him to immediate action in Jimmy's behalf. After what seemed to me a very hasty and insufficient examination, he declared that nothing whatever was the matter with the son of Erin, and coolly turned over in his blankets and composed himself to sleep, to my great disgust at his want of feeling.

After plying Jimmy with questions for some time, I became convinced that he was suffering from an acute attack of a disease very common in the East, and but rarely met with on the plains, — a disease popularly known as "love-sickness."

"O, surr!" he exclaimed, in faltering accents; "to think what an illegant chance I've lost to sitooate misilf for life, — wid foine flucks and hards, and a be-u-tiful wife wid legs

JIMMY IN TROUBLE.

as big as a wather-boocket: it makes me wape intirely wid thinkin' ov it."

These words so awakened my sense of the ludicrous, that it was with the greatest difficulty I maintained my gravity. After all, the "beautiful wife" was but a secondary consideration, and his sighs and moans were wasted on the "flesh-pots" of Acoma, as well as on his dissipated dreams of love.

I meted out to Jimmy what crumbs of comfort I was able, for which he manifested much gratitude. It was very late when we "turned in." Jimmy was soon lost to all his troubles; and slumber, which had kept so coyly aloof, soon visited my eyes.

When I awoke in the morning the sun was high in the heavens. Don Rafael was busily collecting the mules, preparatory to setting out on our journey, while Jimmy, who had apparently recovered from his severe indisposition, was engaged in broiling bacon for our breakfast, at the same time merrily whistling a few bars of "Rory O'Moore." Dr. Parker was sitting in his blankets, with unkempt hair and unwashed face, plucking gray hairs from his long, flowing beard, which, truth compels me to avow, were neither few, nor far between, in my own. As I turned towards him, he slyly remarked that Jimmy seemed in excellent spirits after his severe attack of the previous evening, at the same time quietly insinuating that both he and myself had been partaking rather too freely of the contents of a certain demijohn, which, it was expressly understood, was only to be uncorked in case of sickness, — an insinuation which I treated with the silent scorn it deserved.

Breakfast well over; our large leathern bottles freshly

filled from the cool, sparkling waters of the little stream, and firmly lashed under the wagon; the extra mules started under the guidance of Don Rafael, and we were once more on our "winding way." The constantly ascending route gave us a wide-spread view of the plain across which we had passed. One of the most interesting features of the landscape was the town of Acoma, perched high on its cliff, like the eyrie of an eagle, though we could scarcely realize, from the distinctness with which it was visible, rendered thus by the intensely rarefied condition of the atmosphere, that it was more than a couple of miles distant. The sight of its terraced walls seemingly so near by, brought from Jimmy's breast a sigh that sounded like the wailing of the night wind through a forest of pines.

We reached the summit of the Sierra Madre range at about two o'clock in the afternoon, when the vast extent of country stretching far away towards the mighty Pacific burst upon our view. Mountains, valleys, and plains were here spread out in chaotic confusion. The eye lost itself in immensity, so boundless was the view which confronted us.

We paused here for an hour or more to give our animals rest, and then started for the Carizo Springs, which were about five miles distant. We were now descending the western slope of the Sierra Madre range, towards the Pacific.

Thus far we had been singularly fortunate during our journeyings, for we had not encountered a single hostile

Indian, nor even a wild beast, with which the country was said to abound. Shall we be similarly favored for the remainder of our travels? Alas, no! for we were destined soon to meet both of these much-dreaded and dangerous foes of civilization. But let me not anticipate. Evils at best come fast enough, and we were still many days from the longed-for goal.

Our course down the mountain-slope was, necessarily, slow and somewhat difficult; and it was nearly five o'clock ere we reached the springs, at which we proposed to encamp for the night.

At this point we saw indications of a camp, the first one we had found since leaving the Rio Grande. Don Rafael immediately pronounced it the camp of white men, and also inclined to the opinion that women were of the party, – an assertion which we received with much incredulity, though it afterwards proved to be true.

The spring here was not a very large one, but its waters were sweet and pleasant, and amply sufficed to furnish all that was needful for our own use and that of our animals, while the grass in the vicinity was very abundant, and of an excellent quality.

The adventures and lessons of the night I propose to leave for another chapter, assuring the reader that if he has followed us with interest thus far in our travels over deserts and mountains, and will bear us company still farther, as we penetrate into the wild fastnesses of this far western country, he will find that he has not spent his time wholly in vain: for many novel and wonderful sights await us; many strange adventures, which may perhaps be common enough in the country of which I write, yet to one unfamiliar with the exciting and adventurous life upon the Mexican frontier, will possess no little interest, while at the same time they will afford the inquiring mind, in its search after a correct knowledge of this most wonderful portion of our marvellous country, an exact description of the Zuni country as it was in 1860.

CHAPTER XX.

OUR camp at the Carizo Springs was destined to be neither an agreeable nor a profitable one, as the reader will readily understand, when I relate the adventures of the night.

After we had partaken of our supper, and had seen our animals safely picketed where they could obtain good grass, we seated ourselves around the smouldering camp-fire, and, smoking our pipes, enjoyed the calm beauty of the night. The moonbeams silvered with mellow light each rugged rock, each overhanging cliff, each bristling yucca, until it required no great stretch of the imagination to fancy that we were really standing on one of those fabled mountains of silver, the expectation of finding which had led the bold adventurers of the fifteenth century into such incredible toils and hardships.

I retired to rest at an early hour, and was soon in the

peaceful "world of dreams," from which I was suddenly awakened by feeling a hand laid upon my shoulder. I sprang to my feet, revolver in hand; but the bright moonlight revealed to me the fact that it was no one but Jimmy, who in whispered tones told me that "she was a-callin' him." For a moment I fancied that Jimmy had gone mad, when to my surprise a low wail, like that of a child in dire distress, fell upon my ear, apparently so near at hand that I was at once startled and confounded.

"D'ye hear it?" exclaimed Jimmy, excitedly. "The poor crayther's a follerin' me, and it's lost she is, intirely!"

Once more that plaintive cry fell upon my listening ear.

"D'ye hear it?" he again repeated. "She's a-cryin' for me, surr; and will yez not be afther hilpin' me foind her?"

Just at this moment the unmistakable bray of a mule in extreme terror and suffering answered the cry; and for the first time I now realized that the peculiar moans I have described proceeded, not from Jimmy's Acoma charmer, but from a ferocious panther.

Immediately arousing Dr. Parker and Don Rafael, we hurriedly grasped our rifles, and listened intently for the sound to be repeated. At last we heard a low, satisfied growl, as though the creature which had uttered it was congratulating himself upon an unexpected and extraordinary piece of good fortune.

We slowly and cautiously started in the direction whence

the sound had emanated. After proceeding a short distance, we saw Don Rafael, who was a few steps in advance, suddenly halt, and heard his low, muttered "*Carraho!*" The panther had attacked and killed one of our extra mules, which had been picketed beyond the others, and was greedily

PANTHER HUNT.

devouring such portions of his flesh as seemed to him most palatable. His eyes, resembling coals of fire, gleamed angrily as he occasionally raised his head, lashing his sides with his long, powerful tail. So intent was the animal upon his feast, that evidently he had not observed our approach.

Don Rafael hastily signified that he desired me to fire with him, while Dr. Parker and Jimmy should reserve their charges until the result of our "rifle-practice" should become known. We accordingly raised our rifles, and taking good aim, fired. An angry growl, and the panther was confronting us, scarcely thirty feet away. We saw him crouch, ready for a spring. Dr. Parker now raised his piece, and aiming directly between his eyes, hastily fired. One convulsive spring into the air, a single yell of mingled agony and rage, and the ferocious beast fell dead. Jimmy immediately discharged both barrels of his shot-gun, sending the entire contents into the carcass of the defunct mule.

This panther was a most magnificent specimen of the American leopard, measuring nine feet and eleven inches from his nose to the tip of his tail.

The next morning a close examination revealed the fact that neither the bullets of Don Rafael or myself had touched a vital point, but that Dr. Parker was the fortunate man who was entitled to the skin.

Don Rafael carefully removed the smooth, glossy covering from the carcass, and we took it with us to Zuni, where the doctor readily found an Indian who nicely tanned it for him; and for years he exhibited with no small degree of just pride, the beautiful skin of the American leopard, which he killed upon the western slope of the Sierra Madre Mountains.

We rallied Jimmy about permitting Don Rafael to remove the skin from his Acoma lady-love, and his reply was quite worthy of the man: —

"It's only turnin' the tables, it is; for if I'd married her, she'd a taken the hide off me intirely, surr."

It was so late before we were ready to resume our journey, that we decided not to attempt to make Zuni until the following day; but to drive only as far as El Moro Valley, where stands the celebrated "Inscription Rock," mentioned in a preceding chapter of this work.

A drive of a few hours on a descending grade served to bring us to this point. We found a most delightful camping-ground, by the side of a spring of water which bubbled up from beneath the very corner of this rock, upon which are inscribed some of the most important events in the history of this wonderful country.

Reclining upon the luxuriant carpet of verdure which Nature had spread on every side, watching the dying rays of the sun as they gilded the stately towers of El Moro, we could but speculate concerning the fate of those gallant cavaliers, who, hundreds of years before, had placed their names upon the smooth, polished surface of this remarkable rock. Who could recount the heroic deeds of "Don Joseph De Bazemzalles," who in "1526," three hundred and forty-seven years ago, inscribed his name on the lower left-hand corner of El Moro? Whence came he, and what was his fate? And what was the name of him who, as the record says, "passed by the place with dispatches on the 16th of April, 1606"? Who could tell us anything concerning the history of "Juan Gonzales," who in "1629" engraved his name on these tables of stone? Or that of "Dr. Don Martini de Cochea, Bishop of Durango, who, on the 28th day of September, 1736, arrived at this place?" What was his mission in these wilds of the West? For how many years had this old rock thus stood, looking calmly down upon the beautiful valley with its ever-changing scenes?

But there was no one to answer these questions and the thousand others which suggested themselves to our minds as we lay beneath the black shadows of El Moro. If the old rock could have spoken, what marvellous tales might it not have unfolded! But it stood grim and silent, vouchsafing no reply — a very Sphinx of the desert.

When at length the red and golden tints had faded from the sky, and the moon and stars appeared "in the infinite meadows of heaven," casting a pale, ghastly light over all things, we could almost fancy we beheld the gay and glittering cavalcade of "Don Diego de Bargas," with its richly caparisoned steeds and fluttering pennons, as it "passed by in 1692 on its way to conquer Santa Fé for the royal crown, at their own cost." Indeed, we could almost see the stalwart, well-knit form of Don Diego himself, as he quaffed a goblet of water from the spring which mur-

mured so melodiously at our side. And with him rose to view the bronzed, war-worn countenance of the old Indian fighter, "Don Felix Martinez," who "on the 26th day of August, 1716, passed by on his way to reduce and punish the Apaches."

Poor old Don Felix! Such a task was better fitted for a Hercules, than a cavalier of the seventeenth century. He it was who thus described the Apaches:—

"They are most cruel to those who chance to fall into their hands. They go entirely naked, and make their incursions on horses of great swiftness. A skin serves them for a saddle. They begin their attacks at a great distance, with loud shouts, in order to strike terror to the enemy. They do not naturally possess much courage, but depend upon artifice rather than valor. In case of defeat they submit to the most ignominious terms, but keep their treaties only as long as suits their convenience. His Majesty has ordered that if they desire peace, it shall be granted them; but this generosity they think proceeds from cowardice. Their arms are the common bows and arrows of the country. The chief object of their incursions is plunder, especially horses, which they use not only for bearing burdens, but for food, the flesh of which they esteem as one of their greatest dainties."

One thing is certain: If Don Felix failed to "reduce and conquer" these Indians, he gained a thorough knowl-

EL MORO—OR INSCRIPTION ROCK.

edge of their nature,— a dearly-bought knowledge, it may be, for who can tell the plight in which the warrior returned; or of his thinned and decimated ranks; or of the dead and wounded left behind?

It was late that night when we sought our blankets; but

FROM INSCRIPTION ROCK.

sleep soon visited our weary eyes, amply repaying us for the vexations and disturbances of the night before. The sun was high in the heavens before we awoke from our heavy slumbers, and went forth "to pastures new."

A short distance from our starting-point we came upon

the ruins of a very ancient pueblo, constructed in a manner which betokened a knowledge and skill in the art of building which we had hardly expected to find. Some of the walls were still standing to the height of six or eight feet, the masonry being in a state of perfect preservation. The timbers were of cedar, and had the appearance of having been hacked with sharp stones, rather than cut with tools, a peculiarity belonging to all of the timber found in the ruins in this country, particularly in those of the *Casas Grandes* on the Gila. Fragments of handsomely painted pottery and arrow-heads of obsidian are said to have been found among these ruins.

The country here abounded in plants of the rarest and most beautiful varieties, many of which were peculiar to this portion alone.

Passing down the valley of El Moro, we entered that of the Rio Pescado, upon whose banks stands the ancient pueblo of Zuni. This whole valley has at some time been cultivated by irrigation, though for many years the Zunis have depended wholly upon the rains that fall in the spring and summer.

In this vicinity we found the ruins of two pueblos, so ancient that this people knew nothing concerning their origin or inhabitants. Indeed, this whole extent of country bears upon its face every evidence of having been at no very remote period the abode of an immense population —

a people who were not only versed in manufactures and agricultural pursuits, but civilized to a far greater degree than are the inhabitants of the valley at the present day.

As we expected soon to reach the city of Zuni, I took occasion to caution Jimmy against attempting to form any matrimonial alliances with the fair daughters of Zuni, assuring him, upon the word and honor of a traveller, that it was the custom of the people to put before strangers "the fairest of their fair," for the purpose of inducing them to remain in the pueblo and marry, only to be put to death as soon as the unfortunate victim who should have listened to the voice of the siren, had been left by his comrades in their midst.

In support of the truth of my statement, I boldly related to Jimmy the old Indian legend, that the Zunis are indebted to the Welsh for their light hair, blue eyes, and clear complexion. The legend runs after this way:—

"A company of Welsh miners having accompanied Prince Madoc in his voyage of discovery early in the twelfth century, by some means found their way into the kingdom of Cibola with their women. The people extended to them every kindness and courtesy, and finally induced them to take up their abode with them permanently. After a brief residence among them, the Zunis massacred every man of the party, and taking their women to wife, had finally succeeded in producing the present blue-eyed race of Indians."

I also referred Jimmy to the sad fate of the negro Esteva,

who accompanied good old Father Marco on his first visit to Cibola.

To be sure these examples were rather old, yet they produced the desired effect, so far as to induce Jimmy to make a solemn vow that "he wouldn't spake to a faymale if we stayed in the haythinish place a month; nor would he permit *one* of the desateful crathers to spake to him, if he had to run frum her, bedad!" This vow, it is hardly necessary to state, he failed to keep.

In the waters of the Rio Pescado (Fish River), there is a singular fish found, somewhat resembling the wall-eyed pike of the Northwestern lakes, concerning which the Indians relate the following story:—

"Two Indians were returning from a visit to the sacred well or spring. One of them had made a vow that he would never eat any meat which had been touched by water. In passing down the banks of the stream, they saw an animal sitting upon the branch of a tree which overhung it. Being hungry they killed it, and it fell from the tree into the stream. After securing it, however, both Indians ate of the flesh — he who had taken the vow allowing his appetite to overcome his conscientious scruples. Hunger soon gave way to thirst, and the prevaricator begged his companion to bring him water to cool his swollen, parched throat. Experiencing no relief, he jumped into the stream and drank his fill, after which he suddenly called out, 'I cannot see; come and look at me!' His companion rushed to his assistance, when he saw his poor friend being rapidly changed into a fish. Thus had the Great Spirit of the water punished the perjurer, as he is said to, all who break an oath taken at the Sacred Spring."

I recounted this fable to Jimmy, telling him that we should visit this spring during the day, where he would be required to renew his vow. To my great amusement he flatly and persistently refused to have anything to do "wid the divilish wather."

A ride of a couple of hours through the valley of the Pescado, and we merged into that of the Rio de Zuni, a valley dreary and desolate enough to dampen the ardor of the most enthusiastic searcher for knowledge; and yet, perhaps, the most fertile of all the valleys lying west of the Rio Grande.

CHAPTER XXI.

HE valley of the Rio de Zuni, with its lofty cliffs of black metamorphic rock, — some of which, separated from the great mass, rise high in air like the huge chimneys of a vast manufacturing establishment,— presents a most sombre and gloomy appearance. Notwithstanding its forbidding aspect, no valley is to be found between the waters of the Rio Grande and the Pacific coast more fertile, or with climate better adapted for purposes of agriculture, than is this in which is found the pueblo of Zuni.

Here for the first time we caught sight of the town, distant about four miles, situated upon an eminence near the upper end of the valley, and which really presented, as

Jimmy expressed it, "a strange resimblince to the moighty castles ov ould Ireland."

We had not proceeded far in the direction of the town before we discovered some of the inhabitants driving towards the pueblo a number of *buros* (small jackasses), laden with wood, or with panniers filled with vegetables. This wood is obtained from the mountains; nor is it an uncommon thing to bring it twelve or fourteen miles tied upon the backs of these hardy little animals. The vegetables are raised in large quantities in the fine arable land with which the town is surrounded.

Among the natives we here met was one who could speak a little broken Spanish; and from him we gleaned some information of himself and his companions, although the difficulty we experienced in interpreting his jargon so disgusted Jimmy, that, quite forgetful of the enthusiasm which so recently had filled his soul at the fancied resemblance to his "dear ould Ireland," he exclaimed, in loud tones of contempt, "Why wouldn't a sinsible-lookin' mon like that, be spakin' so that a gintleman wud know what he wuz talkin' about, instid of a lingo that would desave the praste himsilf?" Dr. Parker's remark, that the language seemed full as intelligible to him, as that of the Irish tongue, caused Jimmy to turn away, muttering anything but complimentary opinions regarding the doctor's taste.

Notwithstanding all this, we learned from our Zuni friend that the fine fields of waving corn, so gracefully nodding their tall, tasselled heads before the gentle breeze then sweeping down the valley, were cultivated entirely without irrigation; that large quantities of garden vegetables were also raised; that melons, pumpkins, beans, chilli, onions, and garlic thrived finely, while our own eyes discovered, not only valuable and extensive vineyards, but magnificent orchards of peach and apricot trees stretching far away in the distance. Our friend furthermore informed us that he was a gardener, and would be most happy to supply us with such vegetables as we might need,—a proposition that we at once accepted, although he charged the most exorbitant prices for everything that we desired.

We soon learned to leave all bargaining to Don Rafael, whose superior knowledge of the habits and customs of the people rendered him peculiarly fitted for the office of major-domo, in which position he was immediately installed, much to Jimmy's chagrin and mortification, who regarded the appointment as a palpable infringement upon the rights connected with his position as chief cook and purveyor-in-ordinary.

Driving to within a short distance of the town, we encamped near a little stream of clear, cool water, that meandered quietly through the plain, until it finally lost itself in the waters of the Rio de Zuni, a mile or more below us. Scarcely had we pitched our tent, before we received a visit from Don Juan Maria, the cacique or governor of the pueblo, who called to learn the object and purpose of our visit.

We found him to be a fine-looking old man, dressed

THE CACIQUE.

à la Zuni, with clear, intelligent-looking dark-blue eyes, and a magnificent head of iron-gray hair. The old man seemed as happy and simple as a child; and when we informed him that we had no purpose in our journey except to see Zuni and its people, his wonder seemed to be unbounded.

He at once invited us to visit the city at any and all times, and offered to show us any objects of interest that existed in its vicinity, an invitation that we at once accepted; for by so doing, we had an opportunity to familiarize ourselves with the character and habits of this interesting and most remarkable people.

The cacique informed us that "three suns" before, a party of Americans, with four wagons, had passed down the valley to the westward, and that women were among them. He cautioned us against permitting our stock to wander over the plain at will, as many deep pits had been dug, as a protection against the Navajoes, who were in the habit of frequently raiding upon the Zuni stock.

Under his guidance we at once commenced an examination of the pits, which were scattered around the plain in the vicinity of the four trails leading into the town, and so located that they testified very clearly to the engineering skill of the Zunis.

The pits were about ten feet deep, and large enough to contain a mule or horse. The bottom was filled with sharpened sticks set upright in the earth, and the whole artfully concealed by being nicely and most ingeniously covered with brush, grass, and dirt, in such a manner that their existence would have been entirely unsuspected by a casual observer. We could easily understand that they would prove a most dangerous and effective mode of destruction to any body of cavalry, as well as greatly impede the movements of infantry.

Upon returning from our visit to the pits, the cacique rejoined his attendants, who had been most patiently awaiting his coming at a short distance from our camp; and again urging us to visit the town on the morrow, he returned to the pueblo.

The town itself is much larger than either Laguna or Acoma, though its situation is not so favorable for defensive operations. The houses are of stone, well constructed, and covered with a kind of stucco made of mud and gravel. They are terraced in the usual manner, some of them being five stories high. The ascent is accomplished by means of ladders, as there are neither doors nor windows in the lower stories.

Many of these people have light hair and blue eyes, and it is extremely difficult to convince one's self that they have Indian blood in their veins. Very few of them are familiar with the Spanish language, and we found it exceedingly difficult to communicate intelligibly with them.

In this connection, Don Rafael proved a most valuable assistant, not only as an interpreter, but also in the capacity of major-domo; for we found the Zunis close and very sharp traders, although it was rarely that Don Rafael did not prove their equal in his bargains with them. A sheep that a Zuni would unblushingly ask me *cinco pesos* (five dollars) for, Don Rafael would purchase for seventy-five cents; and all other articles at proportionately low prices.

As a tribe, the Zunis are a finely-formed and intelligent race. They wear their hair knotted behind, and bound with gay ribbons or braid. In front it is cut square across, so as to completely cover the forehead,— a custom common to all the Pueblo Indians of New Mexico, and one which easily distinguishes them from the wild Indians who lawlessly roam through the country. The only covering that they wear upon their heads is a handkerchief, tied like a band from the forehead to the back of the head; this is sometimes decorated with feathers.

The Zunis claim to have inhabited their country since the world was made, and that as it grew, they became separated from the other tribes, and have ever since maintained a distinct organization.

Many of their women are really handsome,— so good-looking, in fact, that I soon began to fear the effect their charms might produce upon the too susceptible heart of Jimmy; and had I not placed great faith in the fear which my stories of their cruel and inhuman treatment towards their prisoners had aroused in his breast, I should have felt very certain that negotiations for another "matrimonial alliance" would have been immediately commenced, — negotiations which we feared might result in a most disastrous manner to our present plans. Deeming it judicious to keep an eye on him, I requested Don Rafael to inform me of the first intimation of a return of Jimmy's weakness, for I was determined to nip it in the bud.

The Zunis have a regard, amounting almost to veneration, for the eagle, which they catch in the mountains when young, and successfully domesticate. I have seen as many as fifty at one time on the terraces, basking in the bright sunshine, and lazily flapping their great wings, or circling high in air over the town, and uttering their shrill cries. They serve the purpose of scavengers, keeping the alleys and plaza very clean, and completely ridding the town of vermin of every description.

During the day our camp was visited by many of the people, including not a few of the women, to whom we made presents of cheap and showy jewelry, which we had provided ourselves with, before leaving Mesilla.

In less than an hour from the time our visitors first came into camp, I detected in the hands of one of them, a bright, fair-haired maiden of some thirty summers, a rosary and cross that I had frequently seen on Jimmy's neck, and which I had often heard him say he valued more than all others of his earthly possessions, because it had been "blissd by the Pope." Supposing she had either found or stolen it, I called Jimmy's attention to the fact. His reply somewhat disconcerted me, I must confess, for he said:—

"Shure, sur, the poor craythur axed me for it, and I wouldn't be afther refusin' her the thriflin' thing."

"But, Jimmy, you were not to speak to a female while we remained here," I said.

"Indade, sur, I wouldn't be a gintleman, sure, if I didn't answer when she spake to me."

Knowing very well that Jimmy could not speak a word of Spanish, much less understand the Zuni tongue, I asked him what she said. He replied:—

"Indade, sur, when a lady spakes to a gintleman, you wouldn't have him bring disrespict upon his ashociates by refusin' to answer her, would yez?"

"No, Jimmy; but you were to run away if one spoke to you."

"Shure, sur, I didn't know ov thim pits, thin."

"But, Jimmy, you don't speak Zuni. Now how did you know that she asked you for that rosary?"

"Indade, sur, but 'twas the eyes that wus more spakin' than the tungue."

Nor did I succeed in getting any further satisfaction from him.

The pueblo contains a population of about four thousand souls, and in the plaza, or public square, is situated a small Catholic church built of adobes, and containing, among other property, a really meritorious picture of "Our Lady of Guadaloupe," the patron saint of Mexico.

The governor, or cacique, who is also the chief priest of the Zunis, lives in a large four-story house, in the lower rooms of which is situated the council chamber. The council consists of four persons, who have a general supervision over all public matters. The office is hereditary, the son succeeding the father. The youngest member is, *ex officio*, the war-chief; the next younger, the chief of police, the others act as councillors with the cacique.

Not quite a mile south of the pueblo a large mesa rises abruptly from the plain, at least a thousand feet in height. The top of this mesa was the site of ancient Zuni, or the former city of Cibola, the ruins of which are still plainly discernible.

In a small grotto at the foot of this elevation is the "Sacred Spring" before referred to. It is about ten feet in diameter, and walled around with stones neatly laid. The water of the spring is remarkably pure and clear, but neither man nor beast is ever permitted to drink of it; there is a tradition to the effect that the spirit of the spring avenges such a desecration by instant death; and so sacredly is this superstition regarded, that I do not believe a Zuni could be persuaded to drink of it, even if perishing with thirst. It is held sacred to those animals that live in the water, such as frogs, snakes, turtles, and lizards. Once in each year, during the month of August, the cacique, accompanied by the council, visits the spring and performs certain religious rites, the nature of which I could not clearly ascertain. With their own hands they thoroughly clean it out, and afterwards, with many mysterious ceremonies, place an elegantly ornamented *tenaja*, or water-jar, — which has been previously prepared by the hands of the high priest — inverted upon the wall

THE SACRED SPRING OF ZUNI.

surrounding the spring, as an offering to the spirit, who is supposed to make it his habitation until another one is placed there for his convenience. Many of these *tenajas* remain on the wall, while the ground around is strewn with fragments of those that have crumbled from the effects of age.

The cacique told me, that if a Zuni should make a vow at the spring, and fail to keep it, the spirit of the spring would send the lightning from heaven to destroy him. Thus all vows made at the spring are regarded as sacred, and are most religiously observed.

During the time that the cacique and his council are performing the sacred rites at the spring, all those residents of the pueblo who have lost friends by death during the preceding year, assemble just as the rising sun gilds the top of the lofty mesa, and slowly wend their way in procession to its summit, there to spend the entire day in communication with the spirits of the departed, who are supposed on that day to revisit the earth, and hold sweet converse with their friends and relatives, who carry them offerings of flour, corn, and bright blossoms,— a custom not dissimilar to that of "All Souls' Day," of Catholic observance.

No Zuni ever approaches the spring for any purpose, without the presence of the cacique, or a member of the council, who always performs an incantation before venturing near it; nor is a guard necessary, such is the veneration in which it is held.

Being aware of this custom, imagine our consternation at seeing Jimmy deliberately lie down upon its brink, and quaffing a most copious draught of its limpid coolness, exclaim, as he arose, "Bedad, but that's foine wather!"

The cacique, who had accompanied us in our visit, was apparently horrified at this wanton desecration; while the doctor and myself fairly trembled at the thought of the consequences that might ensue from this deliberate disregard of the customs and usages of the people.

As the cacique did not speak to us of Jimmy's act, we did not mention it, but waited for a more favorable opportunity to reprimand Jimmy for his temerity.

From our manner, however, Jimmy became convinced that he had done something to incur our displeasure; and making an excuse that "he thaught he'd betther be afther retarnin' to tha camp for tha purpose ov protictin' it durin' our absince," he beat a hasty retreat, leaving the doctor and myself alone with the cacique.

Upon our return, an hour or more afterwards, we found the camp deserted, and Jimmy nowhere to be seen. After a long search, with the aid of our glasses we discovered the missing man sitting on the third-story terrace of one of the houses in the pueblo, busily engaged in sunning himself, with the fair recipient of his rosary and cross, in company with a couple of tame eagles, and apparently quite unconscious that he had in any manner rendered himself liable to the penalty incurred by those who offend the spirit of the spring.

We afterwards ascertained from Don Rafael, that Jimmy had betaken himself to this eyrie that he might overlook the trail which led to the spring. Unfortunately for him, we had returned by another route; and Jimmy, quite unconscious of the fact, with anxious eyes still watched for our coming until long after the shades of evening had descended, and we had partaken of the supper which Don Rafael prepared for us.

It was quite late when Jimmy was seen approaching the camp from an opposite direction to the pueblo; and his perturbation of mind was very evident, when he discovered the doctor and myself quietly enjoying our *otium cum dig* with our pipes, while we congratulated ourselves that we had at last "caught him."

As he approached, consternation, doubt, and Irish cunning seemed chasing one another in quick succession over his features. Not a word was spoken; the doctor and myself completely ignoring his presence.

At last Jimmy mustered sufficient courage to say, "Will I be afther gittin' some supper for yez gintlemin?"

My reply, in a tone of the utmost astonishment, "Why, Jimmy, what do you mean! Don't you know that we ate our supper more than two hours since?" was rather too much for him, for he at once commenced to apologize, saying:—

"Bedad, sur, I jist walked out for a wee bit ov ixercise, an' I didn't think ye'd be here so soon, sur."

As we made no reply to this piece of voluntary information, he left us, evidently disconcerted at our silence. As he passed Don Rafael, we saw his head incline to one side in a manner that seemed to indicate a desire for a private interview.

At a nod from Dr. Parker, Don Rafael arose and followed him, soon returning, however, and informing us that Jimmy was very anxious to learn if either of us were aware of his whereabouts during our absence, or mistrusted that he had visited the pueblo.

As he obtained no information from Don Rafael, he had apparently satisfied himself that we were ignorant of his visit; for he went whistling about the camp, busying himself with some trivial occupation, to show us how entirely unconcerned he was; and at the same time by his manner endeavoring to convince us that he was utterly unconscious of having in any way given cause for displeasure.

Dr. Parker and myself had determined to say nothing to Jimmy, but for a time to allow him to rest in his fancied security, well satisfied that our silence would soon draw from him a full explanation of his actions, and of the motives that had prompted them. We therefore smoked our pipes as we lay on our blankets, enjoying the beautiful moonlight, and calmly awaited the glimmer of the spark that was to fire the train that would spring the mine.

It made its appearance much sooner than I expected, and in a manner that neither of us had anticipated.

While engaged in conversation relative to the peculiar manners and customs of the Zunis, the doctor remarked that he could scarcely believe the apparently well-authenticated reports of the inhumanity and cruelty with which the Zunis always treated their captives; and that he was almost inclined to doubt the truth of the legend he had heard me relate relative to the miserable fate of the Welsh miners, especially after having been with, and seen the people themselves.

Of course I stoutly and loudly maintained the truth of the legend, repeating other apparently well-authenticated instances of their diabolical cruelty, for the especial benefit of Jimmy, who was lying on the ground a short distance off, attentively listening to our conversation, and betraying, by the earnest expression on his face, a very strong desire to ventilate the subject from his own stand-point, in his own peculiar manner.

The doctor and myself argued for some time, *pro* and *con*, with Don Rafael and Jimmy for attentive and interested listeners, when we were unexpectedly interrupted by a howl from Jimmy that was almost enough to startle a dead man from his grave, and could have been heard at least a half mile.

We were considerably alarmed, and rushing to the spot where the unhappy youth lay, we found him with both hands grasping the leg of his pants with a grip like death, while yell after yell almost deafened us, quite preventing Dr. Parker from obtaining any answer to his oft-repeated inquiry as to what was the matter, until finally the doctor, becoming thoroughly exasperated, gave vent to a volley of oaths, that, in their vehemence and power, completely silenced the unfortunate victim of his displeasure, and gained this reply to the question:—

CHAPTER XXII.

SHURE, docther, it's quite kilt I am," said Jimmy; "for I've a rattlesnake in my trousers leg." And another yell announced that Jimmy again imagined he felt the venomous serpent's teeth inserted in his flesh.

An announcement like this, did not fail to carry with it a degree of terror even to us, who had escaped the terrible doom that seemed to have overtaken poor Jimmy, who loudly asserted that he "could fael the ugly crayther a-crawlin' round and round him," while he begged in piteous tones for us to "take the divil away from him," a task that I am frank to admit, I was far from willing to undertake.

"Does it feel cold and slimy?" asked the doctor.

"No," yelled Jimmy; "it's hotther then fire; hotther than

hill-fire!" And another howl attested the truth of his assertion.

After this exclamation, the doctor ventured an examination of Jimmy's condition, and discovered that in lying down he had carelessly thrown himself upon a nest of small black ants, which abound in that country; and they, to revenge the destruction of their home, had formed in battle array, organized an assaulting party, and attacked the enemy with such energy and determination as to completely rout him, much to our amusement and Jimmy's chagrin.

"For," said Jimmy, "if I'd only known ov that it wuz only thim little divils, divil an inch would I a moved for 'em, and I only regret that circumsthances are sich,— "

At this juncture a stray member of the attacking party inflicted a gentle reminder upon Jimmy's body, that caused him to bound at least four feet into the air, with a howl that would have done credit to Barnum's Royal Bengal tiger, while he exclaimed, with a frightened and agonized expression on his face, "There they are agin!" at the same time executing a lively and complicated double shuffle, accompanied by most frantic gestures with his arms and head; nor did this performance end until he had disappeared in the darkness, going at a rate that would have distanced any Navajoe pony, while the rest of us were so convulsed with laughter that no effort was made to check his mad career.

It was fully an hour before Jimmy returned from his evening tramp, looking exceedingly chagrined and chop-fallen at the unfortunate dénouement of his vaunted valor. As he came up to us, I remarked,—

"Well, Jimmy, have you returned? We thought you had probably planned and were executing an elopement, from the sudden manner in which you disappeared an hour or two since."

This remark drew from the doctor the observation that it was as clear a case of *intimidar* as he had ever seen.

"And what does that mane?" said Jimmy.

His reply, "A badly-frightened man," did not tend to satisfy him in the least; and the loud laugh with which the party greeted the explanation, seemed to rouse Jimmy to that extent that, for the first time in my life, I saw him quite vexed; and he remarked that "in a very short time he'd be able to eschape from all the unplisint and thrying sarcumstincis wid which he was thin surroundid."

Upon asking him what he meant by such insinuations, he promptly and exultingly announced his approaching nuptials. I said to him:—

"Well, Jimmy, what's the fair damsel's name?"

"It's no matther, sur; it's no matther to you, sur."

"But it is, Jimmy, a matter of great importance to me. What is her name?"

"Shure, sur, I couldn't tell you."

"Yes, you can, Jimmy; don't prevaricate."

"Yis, sir," said Jimmy; "that's the name, I think. And it's engaged we've bin since yisterday." And stretching out his great brown hand, on the little finger of which I recognized one of the identical brass rings that we had distributed among the women, he exclaimed,— with an air that seemed to say, "This settles it,"—"And there's my bethrothel rhing, the plidge of me affictions."

Turning to him, I angrily exclaimed, "Now, Jimmy, I'll have no more of this nonsense! There's no such thing as an engagement. Of course you can't marry a Zuni woman, for you've drunk from the Sacred Spring."

"What the divil hez that got to do wid it?"

"Only this, that you are liable to be taken by the cacique, any moment, and executed for the crime of drinking holy water; besides, Jimmy, an engagement to a woman whose name you don't even know, is simply ridiculous."

"Shure, sir, you spoke it yoursilf." And the big tears fairly chased one another down his cheeks, until, taking pity on him, I told him to go to bed, and that we would finish the conversation another time.

After he had left us, Dr. Parker and myself concluded that it would be best for us to see the cacique, and ascertain if Jimmy's visits to the pueblo could not be prevented.

With this object in view we started for the town, and

were fortunate enough to obtain an interview with the governor, when matters were soon arranged to our entire satisfaction, the cacique promising to have Jimmy arrested and sent into camp, whenever he should find him in town unaccompanied by one of us.

JIMMY'S ARREST.

With this understanding we returned to camp, and sought our blankets, when I soon fell asleep; nor did I awake until the sun was at least two hours high.

As this was the day determined upon for our visit to old Zuni, I sprang to my feet, and the first sight that met my gaze was Jimmy, standing a short distance away, firmly held in the tight grip of two stalwart Zunis, who were patiently waiting for me to awake, that they might deliver the prisoner into my charge.

Upon inquiry, I learned that Jimmy had been arrested just at the break of day, as he was entering the pueblo, for the old cacique had given his orders with such promptness, that Jimmy, who had absented himself so quietly that we should never have known it, had been fairly caught in the trap.

At a signal from me, the Zunis released him, and I bade him go and prepare breakfast, while I rewarded the men so liberally that I felt confident that Jimmy would hereafter stand but little chance of evading their sharp eyes, should he attempt to renew his visit.

As for Jimmy, he showed so plainly his shame and mortification at his unsuccessful attempt to disobey orders, that I resolved not to speak of his unfortunate escapade, unless he should give further cause for complaint, by his efforts to seek an interview with the Zuni damsel.

Breakfast over, Dr. Parker and myself, accompanied by a member of the council and Don Rafael, left camp for the purpose of paying a visit to old Zuni.

Following the same trail, and going through the same gorge travelled the day before, we passed the Sacred Spring, and commenced our ascent along a steep and almost inaccessible path that led to the heights.

At the height of about two hundred and fifty feet, we came upon a broad ledge of rock, around the edge of which the ruins of an old stone wall were plainly discernible.

This wall seemed to have been used by the Zunis, not only as a protection from an attacking party, but also as a formidable engine of destruction; for by rolling portions of it down the steep and precipitous bluff, it could not fail to carry death and destruction in its path to the plain below.

We discovered no less than three of these ledges in the course of our ascent, all bearing evidence of having, many years previous, been similarly fortified; the stones, without doubt, having been used to repel attacks.

After two hours of toil and perilous ascent, we reached the top of the mesa, nearly twelve hundred feet above the level of the plain beneath.

Once fairly on the plateau, what a glorious sight burst upon our view!

To the northeast, and stretching far, far towards the south, lay the magnificent range of the Sierra Madre which we had so recently crossed, its regularly graduated peaks, seeming to rise one above the other, reaching from the earth to the very heavens, until we finally lost sight of them in the fleecy clouds that drifted athwart the morning sky.

Far away to the southwest rose the symmetrical peaks of the Mogollon range, the dark-green verdure of their sides contrasting most beautifully with their snow-capped summits, that sparkled and glistened in the sunshine like great white crystals.

Farther to the westward, the San Francisco peak stood like a mighty giant vigilantly guarding the priceless treasures concealed within its bosom; while its aerial summit, like a great white plume, seemed gracefully suspended in the blue ether of heaven's bright dome, and offering a most grateful relief to the eye while tracing the enormous ravines, steep mesas, deep cañons, volcanic peaks, arid deserts, and overthrown rocks of the vast country lying to the westward, and stretching into such boundless immensity of space that one utterly failed to comprehend its magnitude, while it required but little stretch of the imagination to fancy that beneath the far-distant horizon could be seen the bright, sparkling waters of the blue Pacific, as they gently kissed its sandy beach a thousand miles away.

Occasionally a lovely green valley could be seen peeping out from its yellowish-gray surroundings, like a beautiful emerald in a setting of topaz, or resembling an oasis in the white, sparkling sand of the desert.

Seemingly at our very feet lay the pueblo of Zuni, quietly dozing in its quaint, strange solitude, its dark-brown walls completely encircled by the sombre foliage of its magnificent peach orchards; while the river, looking like a thread of silver, wound around through the valley, here

ZUNI.

flowing peacefully through green meadows, now concealed from our view by the rugged and black walls of a cañon; again losing itself in the waving corn-fields, or hiding beneath the golden-tinted branches of the apricot trees, to finally disappear in a deep gorge, dashing over its rocky bed, until its white foam was lost to our view in the great mass of lava that stretched far away to the southeast.

It was s me time after we reached the summit of the mesa before we could bring our minds to the examination and contemplation of the objects more immediately around us, so completely were we lost in admiration at the sight of the wonderful and magnificent picture, painted by the hand of the great Creator, that had thus suddenly and unexpectedly been revealed to our view.

A comprehensive survey of our surroundings discovered the fact that we were upon a level plateau comprising many acres, upon which was standing a magnificent grove of cedars, surrounded by crumbling walls, evidently of great antiquity, some portions of them eight and ten feet in height, while in other places but a few inches were to be discerned peeping out from the luxuriant vegetation, that seemed striving to conceal from human ken all vestige of the ancient ruins with which the top of the lofty summit was covered.

Towering high upon the side of this mighty mesa, two singularly-formed columns of sandstone rose almost to the level of the plateau on which we stood, each covered with what, at first sight, appeared to be human figures, of colossal size.

Of these remarkable formations our guide gave us the following history, which I shall here relate, hoping that it may prove as interesting to the reader as it did to us.

"Ages before the first appearance of the white man, a dreadful flood visited the earth. Water fell from the heavens, gushed forth from the earth, and rolled in from the east and from the west, until the whole earth was submerged, destroying not only man and beast, but the wild Apache and the tawny coyote as well.

"Many of the people of Zuni rushed to the top of this lofty mesa; but by far the greater part, being unable to reach it, miserably perished in the surging waters.

"In the midst of all this terrible flood, darkness came upon the earth. The sun forgot to rise, and gloom and desolation reigned supreme.

"Still the waters rose higher and higher, the Great Spirit thus showing himself to be exceedingly wroth with his children, who must offer him a fitting sacrifice, in order to appease his anger, and induce him to abate the flood that he had so suddenly and disastrously visited upon them.

"After much hesitation, and many forebodings of evil, they at last determined to offer the only son and daughter of their cacique, the most beautiful youth and maiden in the tribe, as a propitiatory sacrifice.

"Binding their victims hand and foot, they carried them to the edge of the bluff, and hurled them into the seething waters below.

"In a short time the flood was assuaged, having reached the line, at this day distinctly visible, about thirty feet below the top of the mesa.

"The small remnant of the people of Zuni, who had sought and found a refuge on the summit of the mesa, were thus saved; and they here built the town, the ruins of which were around us, and erected the two monuments before spoken of, to mark the spot where the beautiful victims were made an offering to appease the wrath of the Great Spirit, that the remembrance of this terrible catastrophe might be perpetuated to the end of all time."

These pillars, although bearing a very strange and most remarkable resemblance to human figures, are, without doubt, the work of Nature; yet they are greatly venerated by every Zuni.

We now started to visit the cedar grove, some little distance from the spot where we had been standing.

As we drew near the place that contains the sacred altars where many of the religious rites and ceremonies of the Zunis are celebrated, a singular appearance of mingled veneration and fear came over the countenance of the old councillor who accompanied us; and as he approached the spot with hesitating footsteps, he took from a small bag, that hung suspended from his neck, a quantity of white powder, and placing it upon a small silver plate which he took from his girdle, he turned his face towards the south, holding a small portion of the powder between his thumb and fore-finger; and, while muttering some mysterious words of

ZUNI ALTARS AND INCANTATION SCENE.

incantation, gently blew it into the air, after which we were permitted to enter the sacred precincts of the grove.

We were afterwards informed that the scene we had witnessed was a most solemn invocation to the spirit of Montezuma that he might shortly fulfil the promise made to his people, to once more return and lead them; that the powder used was obtained in some mysterious manner, known only to the high-priest; and that the offering thus made so pleased the Great Spirit, that he always gladdened the earth with rain, and then blessed them with bountiful crops.

We found many of these altars in the grove. They were generally oval in form, between two and three yards long, quite low, and the head, which was designated by a feathered arrow and a kind of net-work screen, always stood facing the south, towards which point of compass Montezuma was supposed to have gone when he left his children of the pueblos.

The foot of the altars was indicated by a cedar board, or stake, standing about three feet above the ground, while in the centre of the altar lay a small piece of cedar, elaborately carved.

The outside of each one of the altars was marked by a row of shells, or rare stones, or by arrows beautifully feathered and painted. Many of the altars were very ancient, having probably existed hundreds of years.

Under no circumstances is a stranger permitted to touch one of them, or even to visit them, unless accompanied by a proper escort. I very much regretted that it was impossible for us to more definitely ascertain the nature of the peculiar rites and ceremonies performed here. We only learned that they were entirely of a religious character, and that one of them was supposed to be instrumental in averting dire calamity, like that which befell the people in 1852, when nearly half the entire population perished from the ravages of the small-pox.

The people of Zuni cling most devotedly to the old customs and traditions, as well as to the religious rites of

TENAJA TAKEN FROM THE RUINS OF OLD ZUNI.

their ancestors, notwithstanding the fact that they permit a Catholic church to exist among them.

Indeed, they attributed by far the greater portion of all their temporal prosperity, and the immunity of their country from severe droughts, to these observances; consequently, there are but few apostates among the Zunis.

They firmly believe in one Great Spirit, and that Montezuma is his son, who, at some future time, will come and lead them, as he has most faithfully promised.

The ruins which surrounded us consisted for the most part of stone walls, covered, in places, with a kind of stucco made of mud. They extended over an area of about thirty acres, and showed traces of great beauty in their architectural strength and design. Of their great antiquity, there can be no doubt.

Many remnants of painted pottery have been discovered, some being quite similar to those found upon the Gila. The accompanying cuts show the general form of the vessels.

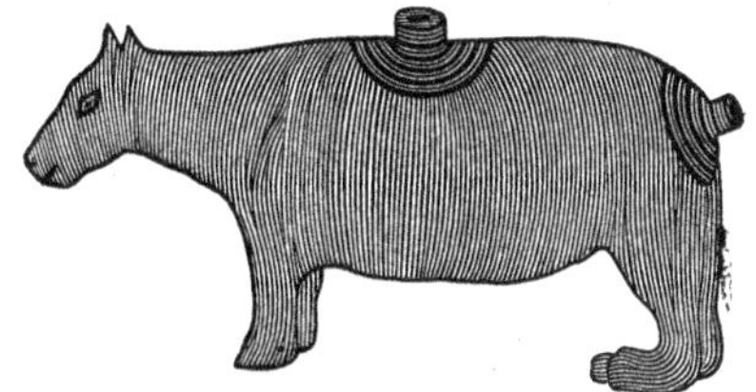

DRINKING VESSEL FROM OLD ZUNI.

The earthen spoon, a cut of which is also given, was dug out from beneath a pile of broken pottery found in these ruins. Many arrow-heads of obsidian have also been found here.

Our guide proved a most intelligent and well-informed man, speaking the Spanish language with sufficient fluency to give us much valuable information concerning the customs and traditions of his tribe.

While reclining beneath the shade of the whispering cedars, he gave an account of the Zuni belief of the creation, which I found so interesting that I purpose to give it in the succeeding chapter, hoping it may prove as entertaining to the reader as it did to me—listening to it, within sight of the sacred altars, and upon ground consecrated by the ancestors of the man who related it, with an earnestness and solemnity that did not fail to inspire us with a deep sense of the abiding faith that the narrator placed in its authenticity.

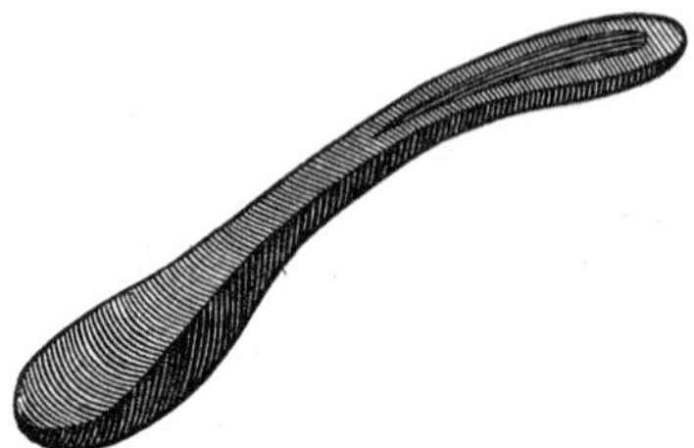

EARTHEN SPOON FROM OLD ZUNI.

Should the reader be tempted to smile at this somewhat amusing history of the creation of the sun and moon, and of the manner of embroidering the stars in the firmament, let him remember that our own religious belief is a simple question of faith, and that the creed of the Zuni is as dear to him as is the Biblical account sacred to Christian people.

CHAPTER XXIII.

IN the beginning, the Zunis, the Navajoes, the Pueblos, and the Americans, all lived peacefully together in a hollow portion of the San Francisco Mountain.

Here they subsisted upon meat alone, for the Great Spirit had beneficently given them all the beasts of the plain and the birds of the air to do with as seemed best while they should be confined in the cave.

The walls of the cave were of solid silver, and reflected the light in such a faint and mysterious manner, that a sort of dim twilight prevailed a certain portion of the time, which answered for their day. Among the Zunis living in the cave was a blind old man, whose sense of hearing was so wonderfully acute, that one day, as a huge eagle was flapping its great wings, he accidentally struck the top of the cave with one of them, which attracted the attention of the blind man, who fancied it gave forth a hollow sound.

Perplexed and wondering at the phenomenon, he mentioned it to one of the old men near by, and the two conceived the idea of discovering, if possible, the cause of this singular sound.

After much hesitation and many surmises, they called to their aid a woodpecker, and sending him up to the spot, he attempted to force a hole into the wall with his bill, but it so effectually resisted his efforts that he finally decided that it was an impossible thing to accomplish, so returned to those who had dispatched him on the errand.

Not despairing of ultimate success, however, the two men prevailed upon the eagle to try his strength. He flew to the top of the wall, and striking a tremendous blow with his strong beak, succeeded in cracking it, so that a moth worm, on being sent up, after much difficulty forced an entrance through the opening thus created.

Upon emerging from the crevice, he found himself upon the outside of the cave, and completely surrounded by water; so he immediately threw up a little mound of earth, and sat down upon it, to consider his situation, and ascertain what was before him.

As soon as his eyes became accustomed to the gloom which prevailed over all things, he saw four great white swans, stationed at each of the cardinal points, and carrying an arrow under each wing.

The swan from the North, upon observing the worm, immediately came towards it, and, thrusting one of the arrows through its body, quickly withdrew it. After examining it very attentively for a while, he exclaimed, in a loud voice, "This worm is of our race," and then sailed majestically back to his station in the North.

The poor worm was obliged to undergo this terrible ordeal three times more, until each one of the four swans had, in this cruel and barbarous manner, ascertained to their satisfaction that he belonged to their race.

As soon as the last swan had returned to his station, a terrible noise was heard, accompanied by such a commotion in the water, that the worm gave himself up for lost; when suddenly, out of the noise and confusion, four great aroyas were formed, extending to the north, south, east, and west, which drained off all the waters; leaving a hard, pebbly bottom of dry ground.

Upon seeing this, the worm returned to the old men in the cave, and made report of the wonderful things he had witnessed, showing his wounded body as a proof of his statements.

After deliberation, the old men determined to send the bear up, and he was forthwith dispatched, with orders to enlarge the crevice and force his way through to the other side. With a great deal of hard work, he finally succeeded in digging a hole sufficiently large to admit the passage of both men and animals. The old men, upon learning this fact, summoned all the residents of the cave, and consulted with them, when it was finally decided to emerge from their present home into the newly-discovered country above.

The Navajoes were the first to come forth, and when fairly upon the outside, instead of assisting the others, they organized a game of *patole*, which they are passionately fond of, and play with great dexterity to this day.

Next came the Zunis, who immediately commenced building houses. Then came the Pueblos; and, in order to distinguish themselves from the Navajoes, who had so selfishly deserted them, they cut their hair straight across their foreheads, and also induced the Zunis to imitate their example. Last of all came the Americans, who no sooner succeeded in obtaining their freedom, than they started off by themselves in the direction in which the sun rises, nor have they ever been heard from until very recently.

Up to this point, all the people who inhabited the cave spoke the same language; but no sooner had they separated, than, in some mysterious manner, their dialect was changed, each tribe speaking a language that was not understood by the others.

As the birds and beasts came forth, they at once betook themselves to the woods or to the plains, and there made their abode. The Great Spirit, in pity for their helplessness, gave them the domestic animals, and these have always remained with them as their servants.

At the time the earth was first peopled, it was very small, and there existed neither sun, moon, nor stars. As the light was quite insufficient for the needs of the inhabitants, a council of all the old men was held to ascertain if something could not be done to remedy this most serious inconvenience, and they finally decided that it was necessary, not only to have a sun, moon, and stars, but also a firmament in which to place them.

This decision having been arrived at, each nation was allotted its share of the work of construction.

The Navajoes preferred their claim for the first choice, as they were the most daring, and were the first to take the risk of venturing forth from the cave.

The old men recognized the justice of their claim, and to them was assigned the task of building the sun; but as the Navajoes knew nothing of the art of house-building, the Zunis volunteered to help, to the extent of erecting for them a building of sufficient size to serve for a workshop. This being completed, the Navajoes shut themselves up with the materials they had gathered together for tools, and went to work at their task.

To the Zunis was allotted the building of the heavens, and placing therein the moon, which they were also to construct; while the Pueblos contracted to supply the stars, and broider them in the firmament. The Americans, on account of their hasty departure, and the evident desire manifested by them to escape the toil and labor necessarily following in such a work of creation and organization, were assigned no task, the old men declaring they should have no hand in the construction or management. Thus it came to pass that the Americans lost much prestige at the outset.

The heavens being completed, they were at once elevated to their place, where, owing to the pressure of the ascending air from the earth, they have ever since remained.

The Navajoes met with a great many difficulties in the completion of their work, and were finally obliged to call to their assistance the Zunis, who, with a spirit of liberality quite wonderful, when the fact of the selfishness of the Navajoes is taken into consideration, cheerfully acceded to their request, and at once sent a deputation of their most skilled workmen to aid in completing and elevating to its place the great luminary that shines for all.

How they accomplished their work, or what means were used to cause it to so admirably dispense its light and heat, is a subject that our informant did not enlighten us upon. The sun and moon were both placed in charge of the two oldest Zunis in the tribe, who have been carrying them ever since; and as the earth grows each year, they are obliged to remove with them farther back so that they may not scorch its surface. At the time of their construction, the sun and moon were made precisely alike, but the man who carries the moon has got so far from the surface of the earth that we no longer feel the heat from that orb.

In the mean time, the Pueblos had been most vigorously at work manufacturing stars, and had a large number ready for broidering in the firmament.

This they had commenced to do in the most beautiful manner, so as to represent bears, fishes, women, etc.; and while engaged in the pleasant occupation, a coyote chanced to pass by, and seeing the great lot of stars, and the delicacy of the operation of embroidering them, said, "What's the use of taking so much trouble with these stars? Stick 'em in anywhere." And, suiting the action to the word, he bounded upon the pile, and in an instant had scattered them promiscuously all over the face of the heavens. This is the reason why we have so few constellations, and why the stars are scattered in so singular and wonderful a manner over the firmament, instead of having the beautiful images that the Pueblos originally intended.

Thus is here given, in a most satisfactory and comprehensive manner, the solution of the problem that, I venture to say, has puzzled quite as many of the leading astronomers, as it has children of all ages and conditions, who have loved to watch the heavens on a starry night.

The springs of water found upon the surface were made when the earth was small; and the Sacred Spring at Zuni, being the first one made, is the great mother spring of all, and hence the Great Spirit has taken it under his especial care and protection, demanding that people of all nations shall hold it sacred.

As the earth grows, the springs become stretched farther and farther apart each year, and this is the reason they are so scarce on the earth's surface.

After the sun, moon, stars, and the heavens had been created, and were each filling their appropriate sphere, the old men called a council for the purpose of seeing how they could benefit their children, who were so dependent upon them for all the good gifts they might enjoy.

After deliberating a long while, they finally, with their own hands, constructed three *tenajas*, or water-jars, one of which they ornamented with figures of most elegant design and brilliant coloring; this they filled with worthless trash, bits of wool, and articles of no possible value.

The other two were of precisely the same size and shape, but made of very coarse common ware, and entirely unornamented: one of these they filled with flocks and herds and implements of agriculture; the other with tools and all kinds of useful articles. After covering the three *tenajas*, so as to effectually conceal their contents, they called together the different tribes, and said unto them, "Choose! And as ye choose, so shall it always be with you through life."

The Navajoes, having preferred their claim to the first choice, upon its being allowed, immediately chose the beautiful *tenaja*, which they carried in triumph away, leaving the two plain ones to become the property of the Zunis and Pueblos.

The Zunis, choosing next, found their jar filled with agricultural and mechanical tools, as well as other useful articles; and the Pueblos, upon opening the remaining jar, found it to contain flocks and herds, and articles with which to manufacture clothes, besides others of less value.

The Navajoes, after witnessing the opening of the plain jars, were quite jubilant at the prospect of the good things in store for them, and it was with no small degree of ostentatious pride that they proceeded to remove the covering from the beautiful jar of their choice.

Imagine their chagrin and disappointment upon finding it filled with worthless trash, and containing not a single useful article. After the choice had been made, and the jars opened, the old men addressed the assembled tribes as follows: "Thus shall it ever be with you. You Navajoes shall always wander over the plains without permanent homes or habitations; you were pleased with the outside, and stopped not to consider that it was but the shell which covered the meat; you permitted your eyes to lead you, to the exclusion of all other senses, and you must now abide the result of your own selfish acts."

To the Zunis and Pueblos they said: "You Zunis and Pueblos shall have fixed residences, be blessed with flocks and herds, and find food in the ground; you shall be an industrious and frugal people, and always enjoy the favor of the Great Spirit. He shall send you food and give you clothing, and thus shall you reap your reward."

Up to this time the people had no grain or fruits, but only the flesh of animals, and such roots and herbs as they had been able to obtain from the ground.

One evening, while the Zunis were sitting around their camp-fire, they heard a great noise, and looking up to ascertain its cause, discovered a beautiful white hen-turkey flying into their midst from the place where the morning-star rises.

This turkey alighted in the valley, upon the very spot where the pueblo of Zuni now stands. The beautiful bird was permitted to remain undisturbed, the people regarding her as a messenger from the Great Spirit.

Early in the morning, while dressing her plumage, an ear of corn dropped from under her wing; which was taken possession of by the Zunis, and divided into three parts. The small end was given to the Navajoes, who, to this day, raise very inferior corn; to the Pueblos was given the middle portion, and they have much finer corn than the Navajoes; while the larger end was kept by the Zunis, who have always raised very fine corn.

The next evening the turkey came again, bringing with her, fruit and cereals; but a great part of the grain which fell from under her wings was devoured by birds, and the remainder divided between the Zunis and Pueblos, who to this day raise fine fruits, as well as wheat, rye, etc.

Shortly after this, the oldest man among the Zunis determined to make a visit to his neighbors, the Navajoes. He reached their country in safety, but while there got into some difficulty with them, and they, taking advantage of their numbers and strength, and also to revenge themselves upon the Zunis for the unfortunate choice they had made in the *tenajas*, placed the old man upon a bowstring, as they would an arrow, and shot him into the clouds, expecting to see him fall and be dashed to pieces upon the ground. Their consternation was great indeed, when they discovered that he did not return. Then they realized that they had given to the Zunis a guiding spirit who would ever watch over and protect them.

After many years the old man sent his son with messages of love and affection, as well as assurances of protection for his children. The son remained with the Zunis for a great while, and they prospered, and became a mighty nation; but one evil day, having become offended with them for some reason, he went away to the South, and was absent for a long time; when he returned he brought with him the Spaniards and fire-arms, as a punishment for their wickedness.

After some time the young man died, and the Spaniards returned again into Mexico. The body of the young man was carefully laid away, and two Zunis appointed to watch it. Three days later, when they went for it, they were much surprised to find that in some mysterious manner it had disappeared, nor could it be found.

Many days after, one of the old men of the Zunis visited the cave in the mountains from which the tribes had originally emerged, and to his astonishment discovered the dead man sitting upon a block of solid silver shaped like a throne, engaged in cutting his hair after the fashion of the Pueblos. Upon speaking to him, the young man entirely ignored his question, but in a low, melodious tone spoke as follows: —

"All those who die must come down here and live with me in this our first home; for out of the earth they sprang, and to the earth must they return, where they shall dwell with me, and I with them, for this is our mother's home."

Since that day the Zunis have always buried their dead in the ground.

From this simple narration of the Zunis' legend of the

STEIN'S PEAK BY MOONLIGHT.

creation, it will be seen that they firmly maintain and cling to the idea of an entirely distinct and separate nation from either the Pueblos or Navajoes, from which latter nation they assert the Apaches are an offshoot.

If this latter assertion be the truth or not, it is certainly a fact that the distinguishing traits and characteristics of the three nations are most admirably and truthfully portrayed in the legend, and to this day are most plainly and perceptibly noticeable in the habits and customs of the different tribes.

If a Navajoe sees an object that pleases his eye or strikes his fancy, he will make any sacrifice to obtain it; although it may have no intrinsic value, or be of the least possible use. On the other hand, a Zuni or Pueblo cannot be induced to purchase anything that is not of use or has not a specific value.

Again, the Navajoes have never had a fixed residence, but wander at will over the country with their flocks and herds, without any local habitation or chief, save that the wealthiest men of the tribe are generally regarded as leaders or chiefs; each one having his own set of adherents and retainers. In this particular, they are not unlike the old feudal chiefs of the Scottish Highlands.

The Pueblos have governments of their own; the people live in well-constructed houses; all cultivate the earth to a greater or less extent, and are in some degree skilled in the art of manufacturing; while nearly all of them are the possessors of flocks and herds.

Athough I do not regard the truthfulness of the above legend to be established beyond all question, still I had been so pleasantly entertained by the narration, and so lulled and soothed by the low, crooning tone in which it had been told, that I had quite forgotten the flight of time, and was unaware how perceptibly the shadows had lengthened while I had been listening to it, nor was I roused from the reverie into which I had almost unconsciously drifted, until Don Rafael exclaimed, with decided emphasis, "Ugh! Vamose!"

Starting to my feet, I saw at once that it was full time for us to commence our descent of the steep and precipitous path that led to the plain beneath, if we would reach it before nightfall.

The sun was fast sinking to his rest behind the high table-lands, volcanic peaks, and rugged, broken country of the vast western waste lying between us and the blue waters of the Pacific; and the soft, purplish haze that so beautifully heralds the approach of an August twilight was already enshrouding the plain below us, lending an indescribably uncertain appearance to objects that an hour before had been clearly visible, but the outlines of which were now scarcely traceable through the delicate veil that seemed to have been thrown over the valley. Taking a last, lingering look at the magnificent panorama, now so gradually fading from our sight, we commenced the tedious descent, reluctantly bidding adieu to old Zuni, and its many untold beauties.

CHAPTER XXIV.

WE accomplished the descent without accident, although I never in my life remember to have paid closer attention to any command of Scripture than I did during our journey, to the warning of the Apostle, when he says, "Let him who thinketh he standeth, take heed lest he fall."

The least misstep would have precipitated us a thousand feet down the perpendicular side of the mesa to the plain below, in a manner much less agreeable than the slow, laborious descent we were now making, and which common prudence seemed to demand for our safety.

It was quite late when we reached camp, though not so dark but that we were able to distinguish two dusky forms moving hastily away as we approached, with the evident intention of escaping our notice.

Don Rafael immediately started to overtake them, while the doctor and myself proceeded directly to camp, to find

Jimmy busily engaged in preparing our supper, and whistling "The girl I left behind me."

Don Rafael shortly made his appearance in company with the blue-eyed maiden of the rosary and cross, and her mother, a well-preserved old lady of about fifty years; each of whom was well laden with sugar, tea, coffee, flour, candles, calico, jewelry, and a bottle of our precious whiskey, together with the only remaining box of "Albert biscuit."

I was thoroughly indignant at sight of them and their possessions, and somewhat peremptorily ordered them to put everything down,— an order that they did not seem in the least disposed to obey.

At this juncture Jimmy put in an appearance, and comprehending how matters stood, came to the relief of his friends, by remarking:—

"Please, sur, make out the bill, an' I'm riddy to sittle it now."

I said, "What does this mean, Jimmy; what are these women doing with those bundles?"

"Thim's the artycles, sur, wid which I've purchased mi fradom."

"Purchased what! What do you mean?"

"Why, sur, as ye've obleged me to brake mi ingagement wid the gurl, I've given her ricompinse, sur."

"How came she in camp, any way, Jimmy?"

"Faith, sur, she warked in, I suppose, wid her mother, to git the partin' gifts."

Here Don Rafael, speaking to me in Spanish, remarked that he presumed that both the girl and her mother supposed them to be wedding presents, as it was always customary among the Zunis for the groom to make, not only the bride herself presents, but her family also, just before the ceremony; indeed, that was about all there was to the marriage.

This information caused me to ask Jimmy if the girl fully understood that they were "partin' gifts."

"Indade, sur, I told her so misilf, wid mi own finghers."

I then tried to explain to Jimmy that the articles taken were worth, at least, fifty dollars, which would be the amount of two months' wages; and that, undoubtedly, instead of their being regarded as "partin' gifts," they were considered wedding presents; therefore, under no consideration, could they be permitted to take them away, as, should they do so, the cacique would have no option in the matter, but to force him to marry the girl, in which case we should be obliged to leave him behind us when we returned, and without doubt he would share the fate of the Welsh miners, black Esteva, and many hundred others who had fallen victims to laws, as unalterable as those of the Medes and Persians.

That part of my speech referring to the Medes and Persians evidently startled Jimmy, who, turning to Dr. Parker, desired to know if "thim fellers lived in the town over there?" pointing to the pueblo.

Upon being most gravely assured that they not only lived there, but that their entire occupation consisted in acting the part of executioners to the unfortunate victims of Zuni malevolence, he approached me in a very subdued manner, and remarked, in a loud whisper: —

"I guess we'd better take the things, an' sind the gurls back widout 'em."

I told him that I would do so, although I very much doubted my ability to prevent the catastrophe which we all so much feared, especially if a knowledge of the transaction should reach the ears of the two executioners before mentioned; and that if I should fail in my attempts to avert the calamity that seemed hovering over him, he could reflect, as he was led out to execution, that his untimely end had been caused solely by a wilful and persistent disobedience of orders, — a statement which Jimmy admitted was "thrue," and, he added, "the thaught of it will be a warnin' to me all the rist ov mi life, whin it happens."

Ordering Jimmy to immediately finish the preparations for our supper, we sent the women back to town empty-handed, a course of procedure which, as their manner indicated, was anything but agreeable to them.

Quite early the next morning we received a visit from the cacique, who seemed anxious to know the impression made upon our minds by the sight of old Zuni, as well as to learn if the guide he furnished us the day before had performed his duty in an acceptable manner.

Returning him many thanks for his kindness, and assuring him of our admiration of the beauties of his country, as well as surprise at the many strange sights we had witnessed in it, the old man, in an ill-disguised tone of pride, related many facts concerning it, which were indeed most marvellous.

Among other things, he told us of a remarkable spring situated in the Moquis country, about four days' journey to the west of Zuni, which he said he had once visited. This spring is named by the Zunis, "Ouahnokaitin." I have since learned that it has been called by those Americans who have visited it, "Jacob's Well."

The old man described it as a large hole in the plain, shaped precisely like a funnel. It is six hundred feet in diameter at the top, and one hundred and sixty feet deep.

At the bottom of this hole is a spring of remarkably pure cold water, which bubbles up to the height of nearly four feet, like a boiling spring,— an underground passage carrying off the surplus water.

This spring is reached by a spiral staircase cut in the rock and earth, which, though evidently of great antiquity, is well-preserved, and still used by travellers.

By whom this marvellous staircase was constructed, or

how long it has existed in this desert, we have nothing authoritative, save Indian legend.

The Moquis claim to have known it for many hundred years, and have always regarded it as one of the marvels of their country, looking upon it with that kind of awe and veneration which the Indian mind intuitively attaches to whatever borders on the strange and mysterious.

The Zuni legend of the spring is as follows.

After the waters had abated from the face of the earth, the Great Spirit saw that the vast plain which extended far away towards the place where the sun sets, and over which his children must travel if they would reach the great water beyond, had become very dry and parched, and that the springs and rivers he had created upon its surface were dried up by the heat of the sun and the warmth of the winds that continually swept over them; that those of his children who were obliged to make this tedious journey suffered terribly from thirst, and often perished with their animals.

One night a large number of them were encamped near this spot; for days they had been suffering greatly for the want of water, not a drop of which could they find on the plain; they had finally given up the search in despair; their animals lay dying around them, and with swollen tongues and parched throats they called in whispered tones upon the Great Spirit to send them water.

The Great Spirit heard their whispered prayers, and, calling to his assistance the *afreets*, in a single night they constructed this wonderful well. In the morning the weary and almost famishing travellers descended by this marvellous staircase, and quaffed their fill of the cool, delicious water that bubbled up so refreshingly at its foot.

The Great Spirit has watched over it ever since. No sun reaches it, no heat warms it, but it is always cool, sparkling, and refreshing; and as the traveller pauses upon its brink, its murmurs fall melodiously upon his ear, inviting him to descend and partake of its delicious coolness, always reminding him of the beneficence and wisdom of the Great Spirit. Therefore they call it "Ouahnokaitin," or, Blessing of the Desert, by which name it is known to this day.

At first I was inclined to doubt the actual existence of so singular a phenomenon, especially as the cacique assured me there was nothing to indicate that a settlement had ever existed near it; but I have since met with two Americans who have visited the well, and speak of it as one of the greatest marvels of this most marvellous country; nor does their description of it differ materially from that of the cacique.

The Abbé Domenech, in his work on "The Deserts of North America," mentions its existence, although he does not claim to have ever visited it.

Without doubt, the spring itself is one of those curious formations of Nature so frequently found here; and some now extinct nation sought to utilize the water by constructing the staircase that enables the thirsty and travel-worn wayfarer to slake his burning thirst with its refreshing coolness.

About eleven o'clock in the morning, the cacique, after having spent several hours in relating many wonderful facts concerning the country and its people, announced himself obliged to return to the pueblo, as one of the old men who had died the night previous was to be buried that day at meridian.

Upon my suggesting that I should be pleased to attend the funeral ceremonies, the old man cordially invited the doctor and myself to accompany him and witness the rites, — an invitation which we were pleased to accept. In a short time we reached the plaza, just as the funeral procession was entering it.

Four men, bearing upon their shoulders the corpse, dressed in its usual garb, its hair gayly ornamented with ribbons, preceded the mourners, who slowly and reverentially followed. Upon reaching the shallow grave, the body was placed therein without a covering of any kind to protect it from the earth.

In solemn silence each of the mourners approached, and taking up a handful of earth, cast it upon the body; then a number of women appeared, their hair flowing loosely down their backs, and each bearing upon her shoulders a *tenaja* filled with water.

The first one now approached, and as she stooped over the grave, her hair falling loosely about her face and body, gave to her a singularly weird and picturesque appearance. Slowly removing the *tenaja* from her shoulders, and holding it for a moment suspended in the air, she deliberately

BURIAL SCENE.

turned its contents over the body in the grave, at the same time giving utterance to the death-cry, a low, plaintive, wailing moan, which seemed to cause my very flesh to creep, so terribly distinct was it in unearthly penetration.

The women approached separately, and, as they emptied

the contents of their *tenajas* into the grave, joined in the cry, until, as their numbers increased, their voices growing louder and louder, the sad, wailing cries seemed to fill the entire air, almost paralyzing the senses with their unearthly tones. Long after they had disappeared from our sight, and distance had somewhat softened the shrill plaintiveness, it was borne to our ears on the noontide breeze, sounding like the wail of some poor soul, bereft of all hope.

We were some way on our return towards camp when I remembered that I had promised Jimmy before leaving, that while in the pueblo I would endeavor to explain his case to the cacique so satisfactorily that he would understand it, and not allow the friends or relatives of the girl to prejudice his mind, if they should make complaint to him of Jimmy's conduct; for, situated as we were, it really seemed important that no difficulties should arise between ourselves and the Zunis.

Jimmy, seeing us approach, came out to meet us, exceedingly anxious to know if we'd "fixed it all right wid the bazaque," as he styled the governor; and his disappointment was so apparent, when I informed him that I had neglected to speak to him on the subject, that Dr. Parker remarked to me, "At last we've got Jimmy scared, and we need anticipate no more trouble with him on account of the women while he's here, that's very evident." Scarcely had we reached camp ere Jimmy again appealed to me, urging me to have "matthers fixed wid the bazaque;" and so earnest was he in preferring his request, that, after consulting with the doctor, I concluded to dispatch Jimmy to the pueblo at once, and have him bring the two women into camp, hoping by this means to satisfy any demands they might think he had incurred by his flirtations with the daughter.

After supper, upon calling Jimmy to dispatch him on the errand to the pueblo, we found, to our great surprise, that he had most mysteriously disappeared, and was nowhere to be seen.

We waited for him until nearly ten o'clock, and he did not make his appearance; so we smoked our last pipe, and "turned in," in no very enviable frame of mind, quite determined to bring matters to a crisis on the morrow as far as Jimmy was concerned, to say the least.

It was a beautiful night; and after retiring to my blankets, I lay for a long time watching the stars, and tracing the constellations visible in the heavens, quite unable to compose myself to sleep. Finally the moon rose, gilding the tops of the high terraced houses with its silvery beams; the mournful cry of the whip-poor-will sounded on the night air, causing a feeling of sadness to steal over my senses, which I in vain attempted to dispel, by trying to devise some plan that would keep Jimmy away from the pueblo, where I had no doubt he was then sojourning, enjoying the glorious moonlight from the terrace of his blue-eyed maiden's *casa*, and, shall I say it, rather envying him the situation, when I finally fell asleep.

How long I slept, I could not tell. I awoke with a start, and a strong presentiment that there was something wrong.

What had awakened me so suddenly, or the cause of the presentiment, I did not know. As I lay for a moment, endeavoring to account for this singular impression, I distinctly heard the sharp, quick ring of a rifle-shot apparently on the other side of the pueblo. There was nothing alarming in the sound itself, but the feeling I had experienced on first awakening still oppressed me, and I anxiously listened for a repetition of the cause of my alarm. Nothing, however, disturbed the stillness of the glorious night, save the whip-poor-will's cry, or the occasional croak of a frog near the little stream that ran quietly by our camp.

Suddenly I heard the sound of five or six shots in quick succession, apparently coming from the direction of the pueblo; and as I knew that scarcely one in thirty of the Zunis possessed fire-arms, I was confident that whatever the occasion, there must, in any event, be a large number gathered together.

I sprang to my feet just in time to see Don Rafael appear from the other side of the wagon, rifle in hand, and to notice the dangerous glitter of his wicked black eyes. He saw me, placed his finger upon his lips, and said, "Hist! Navajoes."

Instantly rousing Dr. Parker, who was a very sound sleeper, we at once prepared to give the Indians a warm reception, should they favor our camp with a visit, though Don Rafael seemed to think we had nothing to fear from them. Telling him to call Jimmy, I learned, much to my annoyance, that he had not yet returned to camp, although it was now nearly two o'clock in the morning.

What could have become of him? I was exceedingly vexed, and somewhat anxious at his absence from camp at this particular time.

An examination of our fire-arms revealed the fact that we had twenty-one shots, without reloading or counting upon the condition of Jimmy's fowling-piece, which, experience had shown us, we were as likely to find with the powder on top of the bullets, as the bullets on top of the powder. We were quite satisfied, however, that we could successfully cope with any number of Indians that might attack us.

At this moment the Navajoe war-whoop rang out, filling the still air with its terrific sound, and in spite of our best efforts, almost curdling the blood in our veins, sending a thrill of terror to the very soul as nothing else can. An occasional desultory shot; again the war-whoop rings out, shouting its defiance to our ear; and just then Don Rafael's quick eye catches sight of a dozen or more dusky forms visible upon the plain before us. "*Carraho*, they're comin' this way," said he; "we'd better git behind the wagon."

No sooner said than done; we hastily sought shelter behind it, and waited, revolvers in hand, the coming of the foe.

We saw them approaching as rapidly as their splendid horses could bear them, each second bringing them more plainly and distinctly into view; when suddenly the foremost one, who was bestriding a magnificent gray horse, disappeared from our view like a flash, and then another and another.

"It's them pits," said Don Rafael, as he slowly raised his rifle to his shoulder. At this moment they again uttered their terrible war-whoop, completely drowning, not only Don Rafael's voice, but the sound of his rifle, as well as that of my own, and causing me, I am quite sure, to send my first shot directly into the face of the moon, that was looking so calmly down upon us, instead of into the faces of the Navajoes, for whom it was intended.

They were so near now that we could plainly hear the zip of their arrows as they flew around us on all sides; in return for which we gave them, chamber after chamber, the contents of our revolvers, to which compliment they replied by terrific yells and a perfect shower of arrows.

I felt for an instant a sharp, burning sensation in my left arm, just above the elbow; and, glancing down, discovered an arrow sticking in my shirt-sleeve, which I pulled out and threw upon the ground, never dreaming that I had been wounded.

The Navajoes kept riding round as though following a circle, each turn bringing them nearer to us. When directly opposite the camp, they would discharge their arrows at us, and then gallop to a place of safety, out of the range of our revolvers, — returning in a moment, and bending low in their saddles, to send another volley at us.

These tactics were kept up some time, probably as much for the purpose of ascertaining our strength, as to draw our fire; but under Don Rafael's directions, our fire was a most judicious one, and so well calculated to deceive them, that they fairly concluded our numerical force to be much larger than it really was, therefore beat a retreat, leaving us masters of the situation. I took particular notice that after we had ascertained this to be the case beyond all question, neither of us manifested any desire to follow them.

Indeed, I am confident that if the doctor or Don Rafael had made a suggestion to that effect, I should not have assented to it; but later in the day I had the satisfaction of knowing that there was not the least danger of such a proposition emanating from either of them, for they assured me that had I made it, they would have considered it both unwise and improper.

Once satisfied that our midnight visitors had departed, we began an inquiry into the result of the attack. Briefly, this was the situation:

A FIGHT WITH THE NAVAJOES.

The doctor and Don Rafael had come off without a scratch. I had a slight, though troublesome wound in my arm; Jimmy was missing; our wagon-cover had received a dozen or more arrows; but we knew our stock to be all safe in a corral in the pueblo.

No one from the pueblo had come to our assistance, although we were confident that they must have heard and known of the attack. Not a Zuni had we seen; nor could we understand the reason of it, because we knew that the Zunis and the Navajoes had many unsettled feuds, which were rarely permitted to go unnoticed, if an opportunity occurred for redress.

As the doctor was dressing my arm, I remarked to him that it would be a great relief to me to know that Jimmy had been captured by the rascals, for I was thoroughly incensed at his absence at such a time; and having made up my mind to no longer endure his persistent disobedience of orders, I would as lief have the matter settled in that way as any other.

The doctor's reply, that neither Navajoes, Apaches, nor devils would ever capture him, as his never-failing good luck would bring him safely through, proved true; for just at that moment Don Rafael exclaimed, "See Jimmy comin,' quick!" at the same time pointing to the plain.

We looked, and saw coming through the bright moonlight, the coatless, hatless, terrified, flying figure of a man; now running as though borne on the wings of fear, then disappearing for a second, as he fell headlong to the ground, again seemingly on "all fours," to again straighten up with a bound that would have done credit to a "jack-ass rabbit," each moment, however, managing, in spite of his frequent falls, to get nearer the camp, when, with a tremendous burst of speed, splashing the water of the creek high in the air, as he emphatically "went through it," he tumbled headlong into camp over the wagon-tongue, his hair standing on end, and with the whitest face I ever saw on mortal man, yelling out, in tones that were fairly screeches, "Howly murther, have they got me?" and dropped to the ground quite insensible.

Our efforts restored him to consciousness after a few moments, when, opening his eyes, and recognizing the doctor, he exclaimed, "Did the divil git you too? Save her, docther!" and again relapsed into insensibility.

It was not until after daylight that we were able to obtain any information relative to Jimmy's mysterious absence from our camp, and his singular return thereto.

From his statements, it seemed that the evening before, by appointment, he had met his fair Zuni charmer, and they had gone out together for a long moonlight stroll; that they had wandered down near the Sacred Spring, when the "gurl" had informed him, by "signs wid fingers," that she wished him to take an "ooath" there.

Now, as Jimmy had drank at the spring, and no disastrous consequences had yet overtaken him, he reasoned by analogy, that he might take a "lover's oath" there with quite as much impunity as he could drink from it in any event. So, said Jimmy, "I wuz jist a swearin' misilf,

JIMMY'S MOONLIGHT STROLL.

whin I heard a noise like thunderin', and I looked up, and there wuz a dozen big strappin' Injuns jist comin' toards me. And I rin and got behind a big rock, and whin they see the gurl a-standin' there all alone they giv a yill, and one of the nasty divils picked her up, and throwed her acrost his horse, jist like a bag ov male, and she yellin' like murther all the time; and thin they stopped a minit, and all rode off togither till they wuz clane gone intirely. I wanted to holler, but I didn't spake a word; I kipt as still as a did man till they wuz all gone, and thin I started as fast as mi ligs would bring me for the camp — and I had'nt got but a little ways before I see one of 'em right before me, and, Juge, I'm stone did and gone intirely. What did I iver come into this blasted counthry wid yez for? You'll save her, won't yez, Juge! Howly murther, how thim divils did rin, tho'; and I've rin ivery stip ov the way, mor'n tin miles, be gorra, and I'll niver lave the camp again, by the blissed Vargin (crossing himself), till I'm a did man, and have the breath of life in me body. If ye'll git the gurl back, Juge, from thim devils, I'll niver spake to her agin, — boo, hoo, hoo!" And at this point Jimmy burst into the most lugubrious fit of weeping that any frightened man ever indulged in.

As soon as Jimmy's incoherent tale was ended, I informed him that it would be quite impossible for us to do anything towards rescuing the girl, at the same time taking advantage of the opportunity so unexpectedly offered, to show him that he alone was to blame for the misfortune that had overtaken her, as well as himself and the whole party; and that, in addition to the other trouble to be answered for, would be that of abduction, so soon as the girl should be missed.

"Howly murther!" exclaimed Jimmy. "Will the bazaque charge me wid all that, noo, and I a good Christian boy, too? If iver I git out ov this divilish counthry, all the saints in heaven'll niver injuce me to intir into it agin; d'ye hear that, noo, Juge? I want to go to-day; lit's start."

Telling him that this was out of the question, and bidding him be quiet, the doctor and myself went out to find Don Rafael, who had gone to the pueblo, to assure himself of the safety of our animals, as well as to ascertain, if possible, why the Zunis had offered us no assistance the night previous.

Upon meeting him, he informed us that a large body of Navajoes had attacked the town upon the opposite side, and had succeeded in driving off a large number of sheep and cattle; that the party which attacked us was one that had been sent around to the rear of the town, for the purpose of making a diversion in favor of their friends, and that, without doubt, they were entirely unaware of our presence until they so unexpectedly came upon us; that matters in the town were in so much confusion, it seemed almost impossible to gain any information at present, therefore he suggested that we should visit the position held by the Navajoes in their attack upon us, and ascertain the results of our fight.

An examination of the ground revealed the fact that the

friendly pits of which we had been so kindly warned by the cacique, had been the means of destroying no less than four good horses, while we found two Navajoes, cold and stiff in the embrace of death, some little distance in front of our camp. We took from them their blankets, which were very fine ones: one of these was given to Don Rafael, and the other to Jimmy, who in a very short time thereafter was heard to give a succinct and most thrilling account of "how the bloody divils attacked him, and he fought disperately for life, until he jist murthered one ov 'em wid his gun. And," said he, "I presarved this blankit as a miminto ov the fight, to show me grandchildren. Shure, isn't it an illigant one, too?"

In fact, we often thereafter heard Jimmy relate the story of his desperate hand-to-hand encounter with the Navajoes, and how valiantly he had fought, single-handed and alone, "all the rist ov the party bein' aslape at the toime;" and so frequently did he relate it, that after a while he really came to believe it himself, and if either of us ventured to contradict it in the slightest particular, Jimmy became indignant, and charged us "wid thryin' to stale his honor."

An hour later, we found that the Zunis had but four men killed, with two men and one woman (Jimmy's sweetheart) missing, and in addition about seven hundred head of sheep and some sixty cattle had been stolen.

Four Navajoes and ten horses were found upon the plain

making a total loss to the Navajoes of six men and fourteen horses.

I thought it strange that neither of the Zunis were scalped; but was informed by the cacique that the Navajoes never scalped their victims, — a piece of information that I deemed it injudicious to impart to Jimmy, as he feared the loss of his scalp quite as much as any mishap that could have overtaken him in the country.

Upon observing that the Zunis were fitting out a party to send in pursuit, for the purpose of recapturing the stock, I expressed a desire to Don Rafael to join it. He seemed so well pleased that I mentioned it to the cacique, who was delighted at the suggestion, and immediately offered us the use of any stock in the pueblo for the expedition.

Thanking him for his kindness, and requesting him to send animals for myself, Don Rafael, and Jimmy, to the camp, we departed to make the necessary preparations.

Upon reaching the camp, I informed Jimmy that we had determined, at his suggestion, to undertake the rescue of the "gurl," and that he was to accompany us in the expedition.

Jimmy's reply somewhat surprised us, for he exclaimed:

"And what wud I be goin' wid yez fur, thin. No naed ov iverybody goin' afther one Injun gurl."

I told him that Doctor Parker would remain behind in the camp, and that he must at once get ready, for his mule would be here in a very few moments.

When the animal came, a few minutes later, we found Jimmy sitting upon the wagon tongue, looking the very picture of desolation, and declaring that he "filt unwill;" indeed, we were obliged to use not only persuasions, but threats, to induce him to mount.

No sooner did the mule feel Jimmy's weight upon his back than he commenced to "buck" in the most fearful manner, so that before he had an opportunity to settle himself in the saddle, he found himself lying upon his back, a long distance in advance of his animal.

As he made no effort to rise from the ground, the doctor approached him, and found him lying with eyes closed, breathing heavily, and to all appearances insensible.

A slight examination revealed the fact that Jimmy was "playing possum." Winking at me, the doctor remarked in a very serious manner: "Well, Judge, Jimmy is done for this time, I guess; he won't live but a few moments." My reply, "Well, send that Zuni who is holding those horses here; I want to see how the Zunis scalp a man," brought Jimmy to his feet with a bound, while he protested "there wuz nothin' the matther wid him, fur his insinsability wuz marely timporary."

After many earnest protests, Jimmy was induced to mount the mule once again, more by threats than arguments, even though he told us "that he'd niver live to rache the battle-ground, and that he'd be the very fust man shot on raching it; besides, he didn't care a d—n for the gurl, but wuz glad she wuz gone, and he didn't want to be the manes of bringin' her back to be the plig of his life, and the manes ov gittin' his frinds into throuble wid the bazaque."

Notwithstanding these many excuses, he finally mounted again, and we set out for the pueblo. Upon reaching the plaza, we found about fifty Zunis assembled, well mounted and hideously painted.

Upon our joining the party, a low, guttural exclamation of satisfaction was uttered, and each one of the number insisted upon shaking us by the hand in the most cordial manner.

All this so delighted Jimmy that he quite forgot his presentiment of evil; and I heard him telling a group of Zunis, in a loud tone of voice, of the wonderful things they should "say him do wid his shot goon," notwithstanding he was perfectly well aware of the fact that not one of the crowd understood a word that he said.

CHAPTER XXV.

A PARDONABLE curiosity led me to ascertain, if possible, the status of our party as to fire-arms. Upon asking the question, I was referred by the cacique to Don Santiago, the war-chief, who was to lead the expedition in person.

An examination revealed the fact that ten of the braves were armed with old flint-lock rifles, of the Mississippi Yauger pattern; two with horse-pistols, of antiquated make; and the rest with bows and arrows.

Upon learning that Don Santiago possessed no arms save a bow and arrow, I sent Don Rafael to camp to procure Dr. Parker's rifle, which I loaned to the chief, much to his delight.

Don Rafael and myself each carried rifles, and also revolvers; while Jimmy clung to his fowling-piece, which, he was assuring a little group of Zunis who were curiously examining its double barrel, "ud kill a thousin ov thim divils at one shot."

It was about nine o'clock when we left the pueblo, after the grand ceremony of invocation by the high-priest and his assistants; and as we started out, the cacique gravely assured me that we should return in all safety, as the spirit which had been invoked would effectually protect us.

Leaving the town, we followed a trail that led towards the northwest, in which direction Don Rafael informed me we should probably come upon that portion of the Navajoe country into which, without doubt, the thieving rascals had driven the stock captured the night before.

We rode swiftly along, as our animals were all fresh; and the Zunis, with their bright paint, and gayly-colored ribbons fluttering in the breeze, gave to our cavalcade a truly picturesque and brilliant appearance.

Occasionally a brave, desirous of showing the superior mettle of his charger, or, perchance, his own elegant horsemanship, with a shout would start his horse into a run, and, leaving the trail, dash wildly over the plain, to be followed by half a score of others, yelling like madmen, or now and then giving utterance to a fearful war-whoop, that seemed to act as an inspiration to both men and animals.

As we galloped in single file over the beautiful green plain, which extended for miles in all directions, with groves of huge pines and cedars clustered here and there over its surface, and bounded by magnificent ranges of lofty mountains, whose bases seemed to consist of masses of foliage, fairly black in its density, above which rose their rugged sides of gray, while an occasional peak, standing higher than the others, would lose itself in the fleecy clouds that floated lazily in the surrounding ether, — even Jimmy seemed to catch the *esprit de corps* that pervaded the party. Turning his mule out of the trail, he spurred the animal into a run, and swinging his hat wildly over his head, gave utterance to a loud and prolonged Irish yell, as he started to follow the braves in their mad career.

Now, whether Jimmy's mule disliked the prospect of the violent exercise he was about to be forced into, or whether the sound of the Irish yell startled him out of his usual degree of propriety, I cannot say; but certain it is, that Jimmy had scarcely succeeded in persuading him to leave the trail ere he planted both fore-feet firmly on the ground, and lowering his head, playfully elevated his hind-feet, thus inducing Jimmy to turn as complete a somersault as it was ever my fortune to see turned, in connection with a flying leap; for he struck the ground nearly ten feet in advance of the animal, who, apparently unconscious that he had aided in the performance of any unusual feat, commenced to crop the luxuriant herbage around him.

Notwithstanding his really remarkable performance, Jimmy did not seem to be at all proud of it; nor, after rising, did he approach his animal as "the conquering hero comes," but rather with an air of bashful modesty, that was hardly in keeping with the bravado which he had assumed at the outset, when assuring the Zunis of his prowess.

Seizing the animal's bit in a very careful manner, while he picked up his fowling-piece from the ground, I was amused to see him follow the cavalcade in the most humble spirit. Reining my horse out from the trail, I waited for him to come up, and then inquired why he did not mount. His disconsolate reply, that he "prefarred to wark, on account ov the ixercise it giv him," caused me to smile, as I remarked that he'd get along faster by riding the animal, instead of leading him.

Jimmy's reply was a characteristic one, for he said: "Yiz, surr; that's jist the throble. I git along too fast, bedad; that's what's the matther." Nor could anything I might say induce him to remount.

After some little delay, a Zuni offered to change animals with him, and we once more proceeded on our way.

About three o'clock in the afternoon, we came to a beautiful little stream of clear water, where it was evident that the Navajoes had tarried long enough to water their stock, for their tracks seemed to be quite fresh; and the Zuni who acted as guide to our party, unhesitatingly expressed the opinion that they had passed the place not two hours before.

Pausing here only long enough to give our animals a draught of the cool, refreshing water, we pushed on, up the valley of the little stream, winding through a rugged and somewhat broken country, towards the southern portion of what was then recognized as the Navajoe country.

Don Rafael, Jimmy, and myself were at this time near the head of the column, when we saw the guide, who had been riding far in advance, spurring his horse towards us at a furious rate; and upon coming up, he informed us that he had found the stolen sheep, grazing in a valley about two miles ahead, but had seen no Indians.

In a moment all noise ceased, as if by magic; Don Santiago hastily giving his orders in a quiet but determined tone of voice.

A dozen of the Zunis were dismounted, and sent out in different directions to ascertain the numbers and situation of the foe. Others proceeded to string their bows, arrange their quivers, and settle themselves firmly upon their animals, when the order to move cautiously forward was given, Don Santiago informing me that he intended, if possible, to surprise the Navajoes, as he particularly wished to recapture the stock.

Upon looking around, just after we had commenced our forward movement, I was surprised to see Jimmy sitting on the ground beside his animal, busily engaged in contemplating his shoes.

Upon riding up to him, I said, "Well, Jimmy, what nonsense is this; do you want to be left behind?"

"Be gorra," said Jimmy; "would ye hev a mon ridin' all day wid sthones in his shoes?"

"No, Jimmy," said I; "but hurry up, for I've informed the chief that you are going to take upon yourself the entire responsibility of the rescue of the girl."

"But," said Jimmy, "will yez jist ride along till I'm afther gittin' these sthones from mi shoes, and I'll jine yez in a viry few minutes."

Not desiring to have him remain behind, I insisted so strongly upon his mounting his animal and accompanying me, that he finally did so, although we had not proceeded twenty yards before he dropped his gun. This recovered, I saw him picking up his hat from the ground, and after every other means of delay seemed exhausted, he deliberately stopped, and began to tighten the girths to his saddle.

Upon remonstrating with him for these frequent and unnecessary delays, he finally said:—

"I'll not attimpt the riscue ov the gurl at all; and I don't care a d—n if she's riscued or not; and I'm not faylin' will, aither, so yez naedn't wait fur mi."

Leaving him, I rode on, and overtaking the party, heard that the scouts had been in, and reported the sheep and cattle quietly grazing in a meadow not half a mile from us, and that Don Santiago had distributed his men so as to completely surround the valley, ordering them to wait for a signal from their leader before showing themselves to the foe.

In a short time Don Santiago and some eight or ten braves started for the summit of the bluff, behind which the stock had been seen, while Don Rafael and myself rode slowly behind, intending to remain spectators of the scene

Having ascertained that my arm was so sore and inflamed from the effects of the wound received the night previous that it would be next to impossible for me to use my carbine, I had loaned it to a bright-looking young Zuni who was acting as aid to Don Santiago, and whom Don Rafael kindly instructed in its use.

Upon reaching the summit of the bluff aforesaid, Don Santiago and his little band uttered the Zuni war-whoop, which was instantly answered from a dozen different points; and putting their horses into a run, they dashed down the sides of the valley, yelling like madmen, and frantically brandishing their bows and arrows in the air, while the stock, apparently paralyzed by the sight and sounds, huddled themselves together in a terrified manner near the foot of the bluff on which we were standing.

We were in time to see about a dozen Navajoes, mounted upon magnificent horses, and clothed in gayly-striped blankets, which seemed to be flying loosely behind them, hurriedly betaking themselves up the side of a bluff that seemed to bound the valley on the north, pursued by about a dozen Zunis, whom we thought could have but little chance of overtaking them, on account of the very inferior character of the animals upon which they were mounted.

Riding up to speak with us for a moment, Don Santiago informed us that the surprise was a complete one; that they had recaptured all the stock, which had been left in charge of a portion of the thieves while the remainder had undoubtedly taken the prisoners by a shorter and more direct route; that he and a few braves would join the pursuing party, and make an expedition into the Navajoe country; and that the remainder of his party would return with the recaptured stock to the pueblo.

As I was not prepared to make a campaign into the heart of the Navajoe country, I decided to return; upon which Don Rafael and myself turned our horses' heads in the direction of the pueblo, and rode on in advance of the party.

Upon reaching the stream that we had crossed some hours before, Don Rafael removed the saddles and bridles from our weary animals, and permitted them to enjoy a roll in the luxuriant meadow, before making a hearty meal upon the rich grass so abundant around them, — during which time Don Rafael and myself enjoyed our lunch with much gusto. While encamped here, Jimmy rode up looking as though he felt very much ashamed of himself, and most dolefully bewailing the day that "he'd ivir consintid to jine in an expidition to attimpt to rejuce the Navajoes," loudly complaining that the fatigue and warm weather were "anuf ter kill a mule," and saying "that he should have remained wid us all the toime, hadn't he bin complately prosthrated by the iffiicts of a sun-sthroke," from which, however, he had then most happily recovered, if we might be allowed to form an opinion from the facility he displayed in concealing the provisions spread before him.

The sun was fast sinking in the western skies when Don Rafael again resaddled our horses, and we once more resumed the journey towards our camp, pushing on at a rate of speed pronounced by Jimmy to be "most fataygin," and who begged in piteous tones to be "lift behind," notwithstanding the fact that he managed to keep right in front all the time.

The moon had risen high in the heavens when we espied our little camp, nestled so quietly beneath its bright beams, under the grim, brown walls of Zuni; and it was a sight that filled my heart with gladness, while Jimmy asserted that "it wuz dearer to his eyes than would have bin ould Father O'Brady, his own parish praste."

My arm was dressed by the doctor, and I was soon in my blankets; nor did I open my eyes again until the next noon, when the doctor awakened me to say that the Zunis had arrived with the recaptured stock.

About two o'clock we visited the pueblo to find the people rejoicing over the safe return of their braves, with all the stock that had been stolen by the Navajoes; for it seemed to be generally taken for granted that the remainder of the party would return in safety, as Don Santiago was a most successful leader.

Doctor Parker was a little anxious about his rifle; but when informed that mine was in company with his own, he seemed much easier in his mind, and accepted the invitation the cacique gave us to be present at the dance that evening, with which the braves, who had returned from the expedition, were to celebrate their success.

About nine o'clock that evening, we all wended our way to the pueblo, to see the "brave man's dance," — resembling a good, old-fashioned Yankee caucus, where each candidate is permitted to state in detail the particular claims he possesses for a nomination, more closely than any gathering I had ever attended outside of New England.

It was a beautiful night. The moon, just rising, lent its pale light, so effectually illuminating the scene that every object in the large plaza was distinctly visible, without the aid of the light from the bright fire which was burning near its centre.

Four large cedar stakes, elaborately carved, had been set in the ground at each of the cardinal points, representing the four Zunis who had lost their lives in defending the pueblo.

To each stake were attached four feathers of the eagle, four of the turkey, four of the duck, and four of the crow. Those of the eagle were supposed to be typical of the gallantry and daring of the braves who had so valiantly defended the pueblo. The turkey feathers served to remind them that the Great Spirit always regarded his children with love, and ever stood ready to exercise over them his protecting care, in proof of which he had sent them corn and wheat by the turkey when they were hungry. The duck, being a water fowl, and under the protecting care of the Spirit of the Spring, reminded them that he would guard their characters from the "forked tongues" of their enemies, even as the Great Spirit most beneficently exercised his protecting care over their lives. The feathers of the crow, being black, represented to them the hearts of their foes, over whom they had so signally and gloriously triumphed.

At the sound of the tombe,* the warriors, to the number of thirty, hideously painted and gayly ornamented, entered the plaza with slow and measured step, marching towards the north corner. Here they paused for a few moments,

* A section of hollow log, about two feet long, and from sixteen to eighteen inches in diameter. Over one end of it is stretched a dried hide, from which the hair has been carefully removed. It is sounded with a stick, similar to that used in beating a bass drum, and produces a most terrific sound, which can be heard for miles on a still night.

their faces all turned towards the north, and indulged in a series of gyrations, expressive of the contempt they felt for their foes. This completed, they made the entire circuit of the plaza four times, after which they approached the fire which was brightly burning near the centre of the square.

Here they halted, and the oldest of the warriors took a position in front of the fire, between the two stakes that pointed towards the section of the country from which the enemy came. The rest of the braves, after forming a circle round the fire, commenced a low, monotonous chant, as the prelude to a dance, during which they indulged in the most eccentric and uncouth motions, interspersed with low, guttural exclamations of satisfaction.

The orator all this time was occupying the centre of this magic circle, narrating, in a loud tone of voice, and with most extravagant gesticulations, his various feats of arms.

He told of the number of enemies whose manly forms had been hurled to the dust by the prowess of his own good right arm; of their age, wisdom, position, and rank; of the grief of those who had mourned their loss, and the sorrow and misery which their tribe had felt at their death. Then he rehearsed, by pantomime, the attack, the defence, the struggle, the death, and the final triumph; after which he burst forth into a sort of chant, or pæan of praise to himself, which he recited in a high, falsetto voice, and in the most extravagant and ferocious manner, ending by an appeal to each brave in the circle to substantiate his statement; till, as Jimmy facetiously remarked, "B' gorra, yer'd jist think the mon wuz atin' thim, wouldn't yer, docther?"

After the braves had separately assured him that every word he had uttered was truth, that he neither spoke with a "forked tongue," or babbled like a woman, but, on the contrary, had spoken like a brave, and that the slain of his enemies were more numerous than the fallen leaves of the forest, he retired from his position, with the air of a conquering hero, giving place to the next oldest brave, who recounted, in his turn, his deeds of valor, and the distinguished part he had borne in the fray; and after receiving the same assurances as had his predecessor, and with quite as much satisfaction to himself, he retired, and gave place to a third; and thus the dance went on until each brave had enjoyed the opportunity thus offered to relate to his own satisfaction a history of his many valiant deeds and gallant bearing.

In short, the "brave man's dance" proved to be the assembling together of a body of Indians who evidently belonged to a "mutual admiration society," and their proceedings soon grew so tiresome that none of us save Jimmy cared to remain longer, especially as we could not discover that any provision had been made for us to tell of the fields we had won; so we retired to camp, and to bed. I lay for more than an hour listening to the sound of the tombe, accompanied by the clear, ringing voices of the braves as they recounted their exploits, until its monotony lulled me into a sound slumber, from which I did not awake until the day was far advanced.

Breakfast over, the doctor and myself, after lighting our pipes, talked over the events of the past few days, and decided that they afforded reason for congratulation in that, at least, we had effectually gotten rid of Jimmy's Zuni sweetheart, and thus escaped the annoyances and vexations that might have ensued had she remained in the peublo. Our experience at both Acoma and Zuni had convinced us that it would have been a difficult task to prevent Jimmy, with his lamentable susceptibility, from contracting a "mathrimoniahl alliance," had not the girl so providentially been removed from our immediate vicinity; and as we were to start on our return to the Rio Grande the following morning, provided the Zunis should get back with our rifles, we did not anticipate that Jimmy, in the short time that remained of our stay, would discover any new object upon which to lavish the "wilth of his affictions," and there was no probability that Don Santiago would succeed in recapturing the "gurl," who by this time was far in the interior of the Navajoe country.

No one having intimated to us that any suspicion rested

upon Jimmy as being in the slightest degree instrumental in the girl's capture, we had allowed ourselves to believe that his agency in the matter was unknown to any one save ourselves. Imagine, then, our surprise at being disturbed in the midst of our reflections by the appearance of the cacique himself, dressed in his robes of office, accompanied by two of the most woe-begone, dilapidated-looking specimens of Zuni manhood we had yet seen. Their faces were daubed with mud and ochre pigment, their clothing perfectly filthy, and resembling in quantity the original fig-leaf pattern. With these two braves was a woman, whom I at once recognized as the mother of the girl from whom I had taken Jimmy's presents. I immediately arose, and proffering the cacique a seat, asked to what fortunate occurrence we were indebted for the honor of a visit; for I had learned enough of the manners and customs of the Zunis to know that when the cacique paid a visit dressed in his robes of office, it meant business.

Seating himself upon the proffered stool, and drawing his elegantly embroidered blanket more closely around him, he turned to me with great dignity, and stated that he desired a few moments' conversation with our Don Santiago (meaning Jimmy).

I have rarely seen a more interesting study than was Jimmy's countenance, when informed by Don Rafael that the cacique desired *his* presence.

A man about to receive sentence of transportation for life, or of death at the hands of Judge Lynch, could not have appeared more hopelessly bewildered than did Jimmy at this summons; and for a moment I really expected to see him turn, and ignominiously run for the plain.

Not so, however. Jimmy was created of sterner stuff. Having made up his mind to meet the issue, he approached the cacique with the air of a man determined to bear his fate like a hero; just such an air as I fancy the lamented John Rogers wore, who was burned at the stake in Smithfield, England, as he bade adieu to his "wife with nine small children, and one at the breast."

In one thing Jimmy possessed a decided advantage. The cacique was obliged to talk through an interpreter, and that interpreter was, perforce, Don Rafael, Jimmy's friend, who knew just enough of diplomacy to shape his replies so as to please the ear of the august personage in whose presence we were.

As no one but ourselves knew aught of the moonlight stroll, the interview must have reference to the presents that Jimmy had so inconsiderately given the "gurl," and which I had required her to return; or perhaps to the draught that Jimmy had quaffed, in the presence of the cacique himself, from the Sacred Spring. In the latter case, we could not calculate with certainty the result of the investigation which it was very evident was about to be instituted; but if the former was the cause, I relied upon my own ability to satisfactorily explain the circumstances.

Taking this view of the subject, imagine our surprise to hear the cacique turn to Don Rafael, and say:—

"These men with me are the uncles of this woman's

GUILTY, OR NOT GUILTY?

daughter, and charge Santiago, there, with enticing her from her home, upon the night that it was supposed she was captured by the Navajoes. The braves who returned from the Navajoe country this morning brought with them a prisoner, one who was with the party that made the raid upon the Pueblo. This prisoner states that the party captured no female whatever, and did not even see the girl. I have come here to see you at their request, to ask Santiago what became of the girl with whom he was walking that night!"

I was thunderstruck. The whole thing was no secret, known not only to the girl's relations, but to the cacique himself. What would be the result! How was it all to end?

While Don Rafael was interpreting the above speech to him, I carefully watched Jimmy's face, to ascertain if possible the result of the request, so politely made, upon him, but he betrayed no uneasiness, nor did he seem in the least disturbed by the situation.

I don't think I have ever been able to correctly analyze my feelings, upon hearing Jimmy, for a reply to the above direct interrogatory, so clearly propounded by the cacique, as directly and positively deny that he was with or saw the girl upon the night in question; while at the same time he asserted that he was not only in camp during the entire night, but was "figthin' the divils all the time, right 'long side ov the gintilmin there," pointing to the doctor and myself, to whom he appealed to corroborate the statement.

Here was a dilemma: unfortunately the close resemblance I bear to the great and good G. W. (a resemblance recognized only by myself) has always prevented me from lying;

while to state the truth would only consign Jimmy to the rigor of a Zuni prison. I therefore determined to leave the doctor to explain matters as best he might.

While in this state of uncertainty and doubt as to what could be said, I was still more confounded to hear the cacique, after listening to Don Rafael's explanation of Jimmy's most barefaced assertion, say to the men, after a moment's pause, "Well, you have heard what Santiago says. I told you before that this thing was impossible. He was here in camp, fighting bravely by the side of his friends, against our enemies. He says so, his friends say so, and it must be so, for the white men do not tell lies."

A statement that I am sure the reader will sustain me in attributing entirely to the old man's ignorance of the "white man's" character, as well as of the customs prevailing among them. I did not attempt to dispel this charming illusion that the old man's fancy had conjured up, for I thought, at that time, at least, that, —

"Where ignorance is bliss, 'tis folly to be wise."

After addressing a few words of reproof to the men for the presumption they had evinced in making so preposterous a charge against the "brave Santiago," the cacique, in the most peremptory manner, bade them begone, and never more refer to the subject upon pain of incurring his serious displeasure. Upon which the whole party arose, and slowly left the camp, looking anything but pleased at the result of the interview, and without doubt quite as much surprised as were the doctor and myself.

The party gone, the cacique turned to me, and said he was "indeed glad for Santiago's sake that the matter had been so satisfactorily explained, for the brutes had even had the impudence to say, after they had learned that the girl had not been captured by the Navajoes, that Santiago had secreted her for the purpose of carrying her with him to his home on the Bravo, as he called the Rio Grande.

To Jimmy, who had been standing by, and most anxiously waiting to learn the subject-matter of the conversation, I briefly stated the latter part of the cacique's communication, which drew from him the most positive and earnest denial of the entire charge, to which I listened as patiently as possible. I then told him that he need never expect me to place any confidence in any statement he should make in the future, for after hearing his denial of the cacique's charge, I was satisfied that he would rather *lie* than do anything else; an opinion that the doctor fully corroborated, after reflecting upon the difficulty which frequently accompanied his exertions at rousing Jimmy in the morning.

After listening to my remarks, Jimmy coolly asked,—

"An' is it thro' I am wid all this?"

I said, "Yes, for the present." Upon which he turned away, apparently quite delighted at the thought that he had succeeded in lying himself out of the difficulty; muttering, as he went, "that 'twas a dirthy thing for thim lyin' Navajoes to thry an' injure his caracture by decavin' the good old bazaque," and intimating that in case he should "ivir mate one ov 'em, he'd tache him bitther manners than to be spakin' disrespictful, or makin' insinooations respictin' him to the bazaque."

I was amused to hear Don Rafael slyly remind Jimmy that he met one alone the other evening, and unfortunately neglected to give him any lesson at that time.

To which suggestion, he replied,—

"That he didn't know at that time that the dirthy divil'd bin lyin' about him, or he'd a given' him a taste ov a swate bit ov shillalah that viry avenin."

Here we were interrupted by the appearance of Don Santiago and his aid, who, after saluting the cacique and ourselves, respectfully returned our rifles, with many thanks for the kindness that had prompted the loan. They had found the Navajoes so much better mounted than themselves, that with the advantage they had in the start it would have been quite impossible to have overtaken them before they had reached the very heart of the Navajoe country; and he did not deem it advisable with his small force, to pursue them to their stronghold. Consequently he had returned without any information concerning the prisoners, who would undoubtedly be offered for ransom before many moons.

Nor did we ever afterwards hear from the girl; although I have no doubt that she was finally ransomed by her relatives, and returned to the pueblo, to learn of the wickedness and duplicity of her Santiago, as well as to refute the theory of the good old cacique, "that white men tell no lies."

Under the circumstances, I felt that I could not do less than produce the demijohn,—a movement that caused all parties the greatest satisfaction; and many were the exclamations of delight caused by the skilful manner in which the doctor's concoctions were mixed; while the good old cacique smiled frequently, and enlarged most generously upon his friendship for "*los Americanos*," seemingly but too happy that his "lines had been cast in such pleasant places," as he glowingly depicted to Don Santiago the bravery that his namesake (Jimmy) had shown in repulsing the attack made upon our camp, until he finally ended by asserting that he "did not doubt but the two Santiagos had together been the means of routing and putting to flight the entire Navajoe force," a statement that, while it caused considerable amusement, convinced us that Jimmy had exalted "his honor" to good purpose, as far as the Zunis were concerned.

From a consideration of Jimmy's brave deeds, the conversation drifted towards the bravery of the Zunis; and the cacique recounted many of the legends concerning his ancestors, of the intrepidity and courage shown by them in resisting the attacks of the Spaniards as well as of the Apaches and Navajoes; until, warming with the subject, he insisted upon accompanying and showing me the very spot where the attack had been made by Coronado's army, and which had so nearly proved fatal to that great chief.

The old man seemed so anxious that we should once more visit the site of old Zuni, and in his company, that the doctor and myself, nothing loth to again witness its beauties, accepted the invitation, only requiring that the visit should be paid during the afternoon, as on the morrow we had determined to start for the Rio Grande.

Expressing his regrets at our hasty departure, with many assurances of his respect and good-will, the old man left us, promising to call for us later in the afternoon.

Dinner over, we informed Jimmy of our intention, strictly enjoining upon him the necessity of remaining in camp during our absence, as well as expressly forbidding him to receive or entertain any visitors, to each of which injunctions Jimmy promised the most implicit obedience.

It was late in the afternoon when we started, in company with the cacique, to view the place which three hundred and twenty years before a little handful of Spaniards had so gallantly assaulted and carried by storm,— the ancient city of Cibola, where, as the cacique informed us, the Zunis had won a name for themselves that would never be forgotten.

Passing the "Sacred Spring," and down through the narrow rocky gorge at the foot of the mesa, we commenced to climb the steep and rugged path that led to the height above us.

We made our first halt upon a terrace, or ledge, about two hundred and fifty feet above the plain. Around the outer edge of this terrace formerly had been constructed a wall of rock, traces of which were plainly discernible, and must have afforded complete protection against any assaulting party, so perfectly did it command the only means of approach. Indeed, it seemed to us that a dozen men might have successfully held it against a thousand.

Standing upon the narrow ledge, scarcely ten feet in width, the old man depicted in glowing terms the contest, and told us how they had hurled great rocks from the wall upon the heads of the invaders of their homes; how the great chief himself had been felled to the earth by one of them, and of blood flowing like water.

Indeed, the old man seemed never to tire of the subject; and as we slowly made our way up the difficult path, listening to the earnest and impressive traditions regarding the valor of his ancestors, I could but sympathize with him when he said, "The Zunis were a happy and prosperous people until the Spaniards came among them; they warred for the protection of their homes and for the honor of their women, it is true, but the strife was never of their own seeking;* they only fought when obliged to; then they fought honestly, man to man; there was no nation that could stand against the Zunis.

Montezuma had protected them since the creation of the earth. Had he not instructed them how to manufacture their own clothing; to raise their food out of the ground; to raise flocks and herds; to build houses to live in? Were they not more prosperous than the wild tribes who wandered over the country, but to destroy and lay waste?

They had always prospered until the Spaniards came. Then all was changed. From the day that those people came, they had been cursed.

Montezuma no longer regarded them with his former love; the Spaniards had made his heart cold towards them; but the Great Spirit would again kindle the flame in his heart. It must be a punishment that he had sent upon them, because they, his children, had permitted the sacred flame to burn dimly that he had kindled with his own hands upon the altar of their *estufas;* but they relied upon the promise he had made them, that he would one day return and lead them as of old — for was not Montezuma the very embodiment of truth?

In this garrulous, simple manner the old man entertained

* A statement not confirmed by Coronado's report of the condition in which he found the adjoining kingdoms in 1540. See Coronado's report to the Emperor Charles V.

us as we toiled up the steep, precipitous sides of the mesa, enchaining our attention so completely that we gave heed to but little else, and had actually ascended the highest of the three terraces before I was aware that we were standing upon a narrow shelf scarcely twelve inches in width, although eight hundred feet above the plain.

When I at length realized the fact, I was indeed startled at the novel and perilous situation in which we found ourselves; nor were my fears in the least allayed by noticing the nervous and excited manner with which Don Rafael, who seemed ever on the alert for our safety, called our attention to the fast-growing darkness, as he urged us to at once commence the descent.

Upon our left was a huge wall of rock and earth, towering nearly three hundred feet above our heads, and apparently so smooth as not to afford footing for a living creature, while upon our right for nearly eight hundred feet below was empty space.

The dizzy height at which we stood, the narrow path before us, the vast abyss below, the growing darkness, the danger of the descent, all seemed to have been forgotten in the desire to hear the old man, who still kept on in his low monotone, utterly oblivious of everything save the Zunis and their history; when, carelessly stepping upon a small stone which rolled under my foot, before I could possibly recover myself I was precipitated over the bluff, and in a moment found myself sliding down its almost perpendicular side, feet foremost.

In the twinkling of an eye I was far beyond the reach of my companions, who, upon hearing the noise made by my fall, turned towards me, and stood aghast, but powerless to aid me. My first thought was, that I should be dashed to pieces upon the rocks at the foot of the bluff; the next, that I might possibly manage to save myself upon one of the terraces beneath.

All this time I was acquiring greater momentum, until it seemed as though I was fairly flying into the very arms of the horrible death which stood staring me so steadily in the face. Not a bush or shrub could I see growing upon the precipitous sides; there was nothing, absolutely nothing, for me to cling to, and the stones and earth which I disturbed in my descent were falling in a shower around me.

Convinced that death was inevitable, I became perfectly reconciled to the thought. My mind comprehended in a moment the acts of a life-time. Transactions of the most trivial character, circumstances the remembrance of which had been buried deep in memory's vault for years, stood before me in bold relief; my mind recalled with the rapidity of lightning, and yet retained a distinct impression of every thought.

I seemed to be gliding swiftly and surely out of the world, but felt no fear, experienced no regret at the thought; on the

I FALL THREE HUNDRED FEET.

contrary, rejoiced that I was so soon to see with my own eyes the great mystery concealed behind the veil; that I was to cross the deep waters and be at rest.

I thought I heard the sound of many voices, in wonderful harmony, coming from the far-off distance, though from what direction I could not tell.

My momentum had become so great that I seemed to experience much difficulty in breathing; and I remember that I was trying to explain to my own satisfaction why this should be so, when the heel of my right boot struck the corner of a small stone that chanced to be firmly imbedded in the earth and therefore offered so much resistance to my descent, that upon striking it I was thrown forward upon my face. This stone without doubt saved my life.

I have a clear recollection that as I was thrown forward, I instinctively threw my arms out, whether to act as a protection to my face, or to enable me to grasp something, I do not know; but one of my hands struck against the sharp edge of something, and I grasped it and clung to it with a tenacity that a dying man only can understand.

I have always since that day understood perfectly the feeling that induces a drowning man to catch at a straw that he sees floating near him.

How it was that I succeeded in grasping it, or holding it,

or managing to make it afford me a kind of support, I have no idea.

I remember of thinking that I had stopped; of being aware that I was bleeding badly; of wondering if I was dead, and why such an eternity of time had elapsed since my foot had slipped; and then darkness closed around me.

I was aroused by a sharp pain in my left arm, and opening my eyes saw two or three persons standing around me, whom I did not recognize, though I realized the fact that I was not dead, and immediately relapsed once more into a state of insensibility, to be again aroused by a terrible twinge of pain in my arm.

Opening my eyes, I saw the doctor with a pair of scissors, which I recognized as my own, in his hand, with which he seemed to be engaged in cutting my coat-sleeve, while a confused mass of something seemed above and around him on all sides. At first I could not seem to understand what it meant, then I knew them to be human faces, and then —

When I next awoke I was lying in my blankets, with, I was sure, a broken arm, and was pretty well convinced by the feeling of my body that I had not a bone in it that was not in some manner injured. The doctor was sitting a short distance from me, complacently smoking his pipe, in the bright light of the camp-fire.

I said to him, "Well, old fellow, you seem to be taking it easy."

He replied: "Yes; and if you know when you're well off, you'll do the same thing. Go to sleep again, and in the morning you shall know about it."

Reader, I obeyed orders, because I couldn't help it. I went to sleep, and in the morning heard the story that I shall relate in the next chapter.

CHAPTER XXVI.

IS it likely to die he is, docther?" were the first words that saluted my ears upon awaking, the next morning.

I lay perfectly still, and with closed eyes listened for the doctor's reply.

"Die? Not he; he'll be all right in a week."

"Faith, an' it's *wake* anuf now he is," replied Jimmy. "How long will we be here, docther?"

"Ten days at least," answered the doctor.

I fancied I could discern a tone of genuine satisfaction in Jimmy's voice in the "Thank yez, sur" with which he responded to the doctor's reply to his inquiry. Opening my eyes, I said, "I'm sorry you told Jimmy that, doctor; we have been annoyed enough by him, and if he thinks we are to remain here ten days longer, I fear we shall have more trouble with him."

"Not a bit of it," cheerily replied the doctor. "Jimmy's heart is still sore, and he's not likely to fall in love again, for the present, at least. Do you know that I believe he really had a strong fancy for that girl? Never mind that, however; it was a 'touch and go' with you, old fellow, last night. How's your arm this morning, and how do you feel?"

"Sore! Tell me about it, doctor."

"Tell you about it? I wish I could. The first thing we knew of your mishap, we saw you going down the face of the bluff on your back, at a rate of speed that would have put to shame old Pegasus himself, without even the compliment of notifying us of your intended trip. It was some seconds before I comprehended the situation, and even then we could neither of us do anything, and certainly never expected to see you alive again.

"We listened, and heard you call from away down below that you were 'all right;' and then Don Rafael started off like the wind, and almost before the old cacique or I had had time to collect our senses, and think how we could render you any assistance, he was back with half a dozen Zunis and some lariats. I declare I don't think he was gone five minutes. When you think of the distance he was obliged to travel to the pueblo and back, it seems incredible that he could have gotten over the ground in such a short space of time.

"They went to the terrace above you, and Don Rafael and one of the Zunis were lowered to the spot where you lay, attached the ropes around your body, and you were then hoisted, more dead than alive, to the ledge where the Zunis stood, after which you were carried upon their shoulders to the plain below. We laid you upon the grass, and I made an examination to ascertain the extent of your injuries, and greatly to my satisfaction and delight found that your only serious injury was a broken arm. I managed to successfully set it, after which you were brought here. It was really a most wonderful escape; the thing couldn't be done once in ten thousand times; for, with the exception of your broken arm, which isn't a bad fracture by any means, and some pretty rough old bruises, you are quite unharmed. A few days will set you all right again. I only wish I had some arnica for you."

"But, doctor, have you none? You had a bottle."

"A bottle! Yes, but not enough to do you much good, though. I would as soon think of anointing a whale with a pint of water. I have ordered you some soup, and am going up to the pueblo to ascertain if the Zunis have any remedies which they successfully use for bruises."

Jimmy soon after made his appearance with a bowl of hot mutton broth. While partaking of it, he entertained me with an amusing account of my fall, viewed from his standpoint, evidently conceiving the idea that it was occasioned by some experiment I had been making to find a shorter cut to the plain below; "for," said he, " 'twas an awful fall yer got, Judge, an' whin Don Rafael cum runnin' into the town beyant thare, and sed yer'd fall'n from the top ov the bluff, and wuz kilt intirely from the iffiets ov it, I thought I shud die misilf from the fright I got, an' I hadn't the stringth in mi ligs to stan' up at all, at all, an' ef it hadn't bin for mi mither-in-lor, I'd nivir hev raised the stringth to hev got back to camp; she's a foine nuss, mi mither-in-lor; she's bitther nor any sisther o' charity I ivir saw — a foine woman, sur."

"Jimmy, how came you in the pueblo on that afternoon? Didn't I expressly forbid you to go there?"

"Did I say I wuz there; an' how could I be afther forgittin' what yer honor said to me, an' the purticlar charges yez giv to me?"

"That's just what I'd like to know, Jimmy, what sent you to the pueblo."

"It wuz a-lookin' afther the animals, sur. I wuz fearful they might naed somethin', sur."

"But, Jimmy, what was your mother-in-law doing at the corral where the animals were?"

"Faith, sur, an' she wasn't there. I wuz at her house; I hadn't bin to say the animals yit; I wuz jist a-goin', sur.

when I see Don Rafael a-comin', and thin I wuz scart, and forgot all about 'em, sur. But I'm thankful to see yez will, sur, an' able to take yer soup."

In a very short time after Jimmy left me, I dropped into a quiet slumber, from which I was aroused by the arrival of

JIMMY'S MOTHER-IN-LAW.

the doctor in company with a woman that he had procured to give me treatment, *à la* Zuni.

The woman, by no means a bad-looking one, was about forty-five years of age, quite well preserved, and altogether a better specimen than the average of Zuni women.

She at once commenced bathing my body with a lotion prepared from herbs, which seemed to give me almost instant relief. She was remarkably neat and cleanly in her personal appearance, and the gay-colored ribbons with which her head was adorned, together with a bright scarlet jacket, gave to her quite a coquettish air.

Later in the day, when the cacique came to see me, I was sufficiently free from pain to be able to sit up and converse with him; and for an hour or more I was agreeably entertained by the many interesting facts concerning the Zunis, their legends and traditions, as well as those relating to the Moquis country, which he never tired of telling. I was especially glad to hear him discourse at some length of the Moquis, for the inaccessibility of that country had compelled us to forego an intended visit there.

Among the many legends that he related was one regarding the future state, which for poetical imagery I have rarely heard equalled. A similar legend prevails among the more northern tribes on the Pacific coast, which has been so frequently referred to by different writers as one of the most beautiful of the many traditions extant among them, that I propose to give it substantially as I find it related by the Abbé Domenech, well satisfied that it will lose none of its beauty or force when clothed in his language.

A young Zuni huntsman, distinguished for his manly

beauty and his noble pride, saw his betrothed die on the day he was to have wedded her.

He had given proof of his impetuous courage in battle, and the warriors of his tribe had long admired his intrepidity; but now his heart was without the power to endure the cruel loss he had sustained.

Since the fatal day which had destroyed his dearest hopes, he knew neither joy nor repose. He often went to visit the cherished tomb, and remained whole days absorbed in his bitter grief. His family and friends urged him to seek a diversion from his sorrow in hunting and war, but his former occupations had lost all attractions, and his tomahawk and arrows were forgotten.

Having heard that a path existed which led into the "Country of Souls," he resolved to seek it out and follow it, until he should find her whom he so sincerely mourned.

One morning he departed alone, and turned towards the south, guided only by tradition. For a long time he perceived no difference in the aspect of nature: the mountains, the valleys, the forests, and the rivers resembled those which he had so often traversed near the tombs of his fathers.

The day preceding his departure from home, a heavy fall of snow had covered the ground; but by degrees, as he advanced upon his journey, the snow became rarer, and at length disappeared altogether. The trees soon became green, the forests gay and smiling, the air pure and warm, and the cloudless sky resembled a vast blue prairie suspended over his head, while delicious flowers made the atmosphere heavy with their sweet perfumes, and birds of most brilliant plumage sang their melodious songs.

By these signs, the mourner knew that he was on the right road, for they were all in accordance with the tradition.

At last he came to a shady and sequestered path, which attracted his fancy to such a degree that he determined to follow it; and after passing through a beautiful wood, he found himself before an humble cabin, situated upon the top of a high hill.

At the door of this dwelling stood an old man with long white hair, whose whole appearance betokened great age, and whose eyes, though sunken, shone like fire. He was clothed in a mantle of swans' down, which, thrown negligently over his shoulders, fell to the ground in graceful folds, and in his hand he held a long stick.

The young Zuni began to relate his history, but before he had uttered five words, he was interrupted by the old man, who thus addressed him: —

"I was waiting for you, that I might introduce you into my cabin. She whom you seek passed here a few days since, and as she was fatigued by her journey, she rested in my poor dwelling. Come in; sit down, and I will point out to you the road that you must follow, if you would find your bride."

After the young warrior had fully recovered from the fatigue of his long journey, the old man led him out of the cabin by another door, when, pointing with his stick, he said to him: "Do you see yonder, far away beyond that gulf, a beautiful green prairie? That is the 'Island of the Blessed.' You are here upon its confines, and the only entrance to it is through my cabin; before departing from here, you must leave your bow and arrows, your dog, and your body with me; upon your return you will find them here."

The traveller immediately felt himself become extraordinarily light; his feet scarcely touched the ground, and his arms seemed transformed into wings.

This sudden and wonderful transformation seemed to extend to all surrounding objects; the trees, foliage, flowers, lakes, and streams shone with extraordinary brilliancy.

The wild animals gambolled around him with a fearlessness which incontestably proved that the hunter never entered into their countries.

Birds of all colors sang melodies unknown to him, or sportively bathed in the limpid waters of the lakes and rivers.

But what astonished him more than all the wondrous things that he saw, was to find that he walked freely through dense thickets of verdure, without being impeded by the objects that stood in his path.

By these things he understood that all the sights which

he saw were only images, shadows of the material world, and that he was in the abode of spirits.

After having walked nearly a whole day in this beautiful land of enchantment, he arrived upon the bank of an immense lake, in the midst of which he saw the "Island of the Blessed."

A canoe, made of a single white stone, and as brilliant as crystal, was moored to the shore. He threw himself into it, and seizing the oars, which were also of fine crystallized stone, began rowing towards the Island. Scarcely had he left the shore, when, to his joy, he saw his beautiful young bride, whom he had come so far to find, enter a barque like his own, imitate all his movements, and row by the side of the one in which he was floating.

As they advanced, the waves arose threatening and foaming, as if they desired to swallow up the two voyagers in their angry embraces; then they would recede to again form anew, as menacing as before.

The two lovers passed through continual alternations of hope and fear, their terror being greatly increased by seeing through the transparent water, that the bottom of the lake was strewn with the bones of the multitudes that had been shipwrecked while attempting the same voyage that they were then taking.

The Master of Life had, however, decreed that they should arrive safely, because the thoughts and actions of both had ever been good; but they beheld many others, less happy than themselves, after struggling in vain against the waves, sink helplessly into the abyss.

Men and women of every rank, age, and condition in life, embarked; some reached the port without difficulty, others perished on the way.

At last, they were permitted to set foot upon the shore of the happy island; they breathed with delight the perfumed air which strengthened them like celestial food; they walked together in meadows always green, and filled with flowers which did not fade when trodden on, but emitted an exquisite perfume that soothed and delighted the senses.

All nature, in this enchanting island, had been planned by the Great Spirit, expressly to charm the souls of those who were to be its inhabitants; cold, heat, tempest, snow, hunger, tears, war, and death were unknown; animals were hunted in the "happy hunting-grounds" for amusement only, but were never killed.

Our young warrior would have remained eternally in this happy land with his betrothed, had not the Master of Life commanded him to return to his own country, to finish his mortal course.

He could not see him who spoke, but he heard a voice like the sweet murmur of the breeze, which said to him: "Return to the land from whence you came. The time has not arrived for you to come and dwell in this blessed abode;

the duties for which I created you have not yet been fulfilled; return, and give to your people the example of a true life; you will become a great chief in your tribe; you will be instructed in your duties by the messenger who guards the entrance to this happy island.

"He will restore to you your body and all that you left in his cabin. Listen to him, and you shall one day return to join the spirit that you came to see, and whom you must leave behind you, for you were only admitted to visit with her, and to see the glories of this happy land, because you were faithful to the memory of her whom you so truly loved, and who is accepted, and will remain here always young, and happier by far than when I called her from the land of snow."

There are many of these legends among the Zunis, which might be related in this connection, some of them very beautiful, and all of them abounding in the finest poetical fancy; but the preceding legend of the "Island of the Blessed" is sufficient to give the reader an idea of them, and perhaps a glimpse of the Zunis' hereafter, which to my own mind suggests much that is pleasant for contemplation, although many of my readers, I fear, will hardly call it orthodox.

As I had felt the necessity of returning to my blankets during the recital of this charming little legend, as soon as he had finished it the cacique arose and congratulated me most sincerely upon my very wonderful escape from instant death. He took his departure, wishing me a speedy recovery, and promising to spend a portion of the morrow with me.

While lying in my blankets, I could distinctly hear the low, monotonous tones of Jimmy's voice, uninterrupted by any sound in reply, until, fancying that he must be talking to himself, I managed to so change my position that I was enabled to see him sitting upon the ground at no great distance behind the wagon, conversing by signs with the woman that the doctor had procured from the pueblo to act as my nurse, while at the same time, he kept up the incessant talking that had first attracted my attention, although he knew very well that the woman could not understand a single word that he uttered.

Curiosity prompted me to endeavor to ascertain what the subject of conversation was, and, by attentively listening, I managed to occasionally catch a word, while fancy supplied the missing ones.

In this manner I soon became convinced that he was rehearsing to his auditor a list of the many charms possessed by the "girl he left behind him" in his flight and hurried descent upon our camp on the night of the Navajoes' attack.

As I gazed at the pair, I thought that I remembered the woman's features, although I could not recall where I had seen her, as the neat and jaunty garb in which she was clothed effectually metamorphosed her beyond recognition.

I heard Jimmy say to her, "She wuz an illigant craythur, ez beautiful ez yoursilf intirely, an' me heart is broke, shure;" at the same time he endeavored by the most ridiculous pantomime to make the woman comprehend what he was saying, and endeavoring to enforce the remark upon her mind by asking every moment, "D'ye understhand that, noo?" with an earnestness that was truly amusing.

To each repetition of the above question, the woman would reply by an affirmative nod of the head, which seemed to give him the most complete satisfaction.

After watching them for some time, I once more quietly resumed my former position, and calling loudly for Jimmy, he presented himself before me.

Inquiring for Don Rafael, Jimmy informed me that he had accompanied the doctor to the pueblo for some purpose, whereat I asked Jimmy if the nurse that the doctor had brought from the town had returned yet.

"Shure, sur," said Jimmy, "she wuz jist a-goin', whin I seen her last."

"How long ago was that, Jimmy?"

"Indade, sur, I wouldn't sthate, not havin' the time wid me!"

"Well, Jimmy, has she gone or not, do you know?"

"Faix, I wouldn't like to sthate, but I'll go and say."

And the next minute he was by her side, making the most frantic gesticulations in his efforts to get rid of the poor woman, while he insisted upon continually talking to her, in a strain something like the following,—

"Ye must go right home, like a good ooman, an' I'll cum up right away, for if the Juge knows yer in camp, he'd hev me kilt immajetly at onst. Go now, there's a good ooman; don't bodder him enny longer."

After fairly pushing the woman out of the camp, and returning with a most innocent look upon his face, he remarked, "I don't say her inywhere about, sur."

I said, "Jimmy, who is the woman? I've seen her before, somewhere."

"Indade, sur, it's only me mither-in-lor."

"Who?"

"It's the mither of the gurl, sur."

"What girl, Jimmy?"

"The gurl, sur, thet thim Navajoe divils rin away wid the other night;" and tears as big as gooseberries appeared in Jimmy's eyes; as he added, "poor craythur, who can till what her sufferin's may be."

I said to Jimmy, thinking to comfort him in his affliction, "Well, I'm very glad she's here, for now you may be enabled to make the poor woman some kind of reparation for the great wrong you have unconsciously worked her, as well as her daughter."

"Wrang, sur! How did I wrang her?"

"By cruelly leaving the poor girl to be captured by the Navajoes, when you might have defended her just as well as not, and —"

"Last me scalp?" said Jimmy, in a tone of voice that clearly indicated that such a contingency had been fully considered by him, before acting in the matter.

"Certainly, Jimmy, any person should feel it an honor to lose his scalp, or his life even, in defence of his lady-love."

"An' what wud me honor amount to widout me scalp? Bedad, I'd rayther fale the wan, then have the ither," said Jimmy, inadvertently passing his hand over the top of his head, as if to assure himself that his scalp was still there. "But, sur, the poor woman is wantin' some things to make hursilf comfurtable, jist thryflin' things, sur; wee little things, that yer honor wouldn't miss at all, at all. Can she have 'em?"

"Well, Jimmy, as she's gone now, we'll talk of it another time."

"Shure, sur, she haven't gone, I giss."

"But you told me she had, Jimmy."

"Will, sur, I didn't rightly know at the time I was spakin', sur."

"Jimmy, I think you're trying to deceive me."

"Is it mesilf, sur, that wud be thryin' to decave yez,

d'ye think? I'd know I couldn't do it, sur, but can I give the woman a few things, sur?"

"Yes, Jimmy; but remember we're a long way from home yet, and our supply is none of the largest."

"Shure, sur, I know all that," said Jimmy, as he hurried away to bestow his presents, leaving me well satisfied in my own mind, and greatly relieved to think that we should have no further trouble from Jimmy's too susceptible heart.

Ere half an hour had elapsed, Jimmy returned, and seating himself by my side, remarked,—

"That's a moighty foine woman, Juge."

"Yes, Jimmy, she seems like a nice kind of a person."

"She's a beauthifool craythur, sur, and an illigant cook."

"Well, we don't want her to cook for us."

"But she's comin', this blissid avenin', sur, to cook garvies for yez; thim illigant little cakes, that looks like wasps' nishts."

Thinking it best to humor Jimmy in his desires, I made no objection to the arrangement; and away he went, to ascertain if possible what had become of the doctor, who in a very few moments appeared with Don Rafael, who reported seeing Jimmy on his way to the pueblo; nor did we see him again until he appeared, late in the afternoon, in company with his mother-in-law, who was evidently prepared to cook the "garvies," as she bore in her hand a small earthen dish or bottle, filled with the thin paste made of meal ground from corn.

As the *guayave* is an article of food very much liked by all the Pueblo Indians of New Mexico, and also one that Americans become very fond of after a short sojourn in the country, let me inform the reader how it is made and what it is like.

The woman, after selecting a smooth, flat stone, laid it carefully upon our camp-fire, so that it would gradually heat through.

After it was hot, she knelt beside it, and pouring upon it a little of the paste from the bottle, with the palm of her hand she smoothly spread it over the surface of the stone, until it was very thinly and evenly distributed; then she peeled it off from the stone, and made it into a roll resembling a large cigar, when it was ready to be eaten.

It is a very palatable article of food, not unlike the *tortilla* (described in a previous chapter) in its taste, as well as the general manner of preparation.

We made our supper, in part, of *guayaves* that night, much to the satisfaction of Jimmy, who pronounced both cook and garvies "illigant."

CHAPTER XXVII.

UPON rising the next morning, I was informed by Don Rafael that Jimmy had accompanied the nurse from camp the night before, and that he did not return until long after midnight. Deeming it best to let Jimmy know that I was informed regarding his movements, though I did not want him to think that I was inquiring too closely into the secret of his outgoings and incomings, I called him to me, and asked him his reason for absenting himself from camp the night before.

He replied that "he warked 'beside his mither-in-lor to the town beyant, in order that he might protict her from eny sthray bands of Navajoes that might be prowlin' through the counthry."

Of course, to so reasonable an excuse as this, I could offer no objections, as Jimmy had so clearly demonstrated in a previous instance both his ability and disposition to defend (?) any woman who might be in his charge from danger threatened by reason of Navajoe prowlers.

Breakfast was hardly dispatched, before Doctor Parker, who had seated himself, pipe in hand, by my side, discovered the cacique approaching, with the evident purpose of paying me his promised visit.

The doctor filled a pipe for the old man, who was no sooner seated, than he informed us, with an eagerness almost child-like in its simple earnestness, that on the morrow the Zunis were to celebrate the "Maize," or "Green-corn dance," and that it would make him "much happy" if we would do him the honor to be present and witness it.

As this dance is one of the few Montezuma festivals still celebrated by these Indians, and is regarded by them with the greatest veneration, the doctor and myself determined to attend, and see this most curious and beautiful ceremony.

I immediately signified my thanks for the invitation, and promised, if able to walk to the pueblo, to be present.

As the old man seemed in quite a loquacious mood, a few questions drew from him much interesting information concerning Montezuma and the people of the Moquis country, as well as a description of some of the extensive and singular ruins found in the Navajoe country, some ninety or a hundred miles north of Zuni, lying upon the Rio de Chelly, and in the Cañon de Chaco, which are the most northern of any in New Mexico.

Upon asking him if he could give us any reliable account of these ruins, he replied, without a moment's hesitation, "O yes; they were built by Montezuma himself, who, as he travelled over the country, was in the habit of building a town in a single night wherever he stopped; that he also planted maize at night, which in the morning was found to have grown and ripened, ready for his followers' use; that he never failed to construct an *estufa* in each town that he built, on the altar of which he kindled a flame, ever after regarded as sacred. This flame his followers were never to allow to become extinguished until his prophecies were all fulfilled; that for centuries his commands had been regarded, and the sacred flame was never allowed to go out until after that portion of his prophecies regarding the coming of the 'pale faces from the place where the sun rises,' had been literally fulfilled." *

Upon asking if he could give me any facts concerning Montezuma's origin, he informed me that Montezuma was the only son of the most beautiful woman that the Great Spirit had ever created and permitted to bless the earth with her presence.

So beautiful was she, that none but the bravest warriors

* There are, at the present time, Americans living in New Mexico who have actually seen the "sacred flame" burning in the temple at Pecos, as well as in the pueblo of Jemmez, and this some years after the United States had acquired possession of the Territory.

could look upon her, as the celestial beauty of her form and features caused all who gazed upon her to at once become her humble and abject slaves.

That the chiefs of all the tribes of the earth came and sought her hand in marriage; that they no sooner saw the other suitors, than they waged war one against the other, and engaged in furious combat for the privilege of first paying their addresses to her. She turned a deaf ear to all their entreaties, however, and refused to entertain the proposals of any of them, because she was the bride of the Great Spirit. Each of her suitors brought tribute of the finest and best productions of their lands, which were stored in great houses, built for that purpose.

In this manner she accumulated large quantities of gold, silver, precious stones, cloth, and skins; also vast stores of maize, wheat, and other grains. So immense were these supplies, that when famine came upon the land, and the people were starving, she was enabled to furnish them with food, and prevent them from dying. Thus it was that she won the love of all the people, and made herself worthy to become the mother of the great and good Montezuma.

One day, while wandering through a beautiful grove near her residence, she lay down upon the green grass, and fell asleep, failing to awake as the shades of evening approached. A gentle zephyr having displaced the snowy garment that covered her bosom, a single drop of dew fell upon one of her beautiful breasts, and she forthwith became pregnant, and gave birth to a son, who immediately grew to the stature of a man. This son was Montezuma, he who had built the many towns, the ruins of which were scattered throughout the country.

The old man informed me that he had visited many of these ruins himself, and found them "very much large;" but as Lieutenant Simpson, U. S. A., in his "Navajoe Expedition," has given so complete a description of them, I prefer to use it, rather than the somewhat faulty and confused one given by the cacique.

Simpson describes a portion of these ruins as situated in the Cañon de Chaco, and in the valley of the Rio de Chelly, two of the most southern tributaries of the Rio San Juan.

In all, there are more than thirty of these ruined pueblos, only six of which he gives a description of: Pintado, Weje-gi, Una-Vida, Hungo-Pavie, Chettro-Kettle, and Peñasca-Blanca.

He found the ruins of the pueblo Pintado "forming one structure, and built of tabular pieces of hard, fine-grained, compact, gray sandstone,"— a material quite unknown in the present architecture of New Mexico,— "to which age and the atmosphere have imparted a reddish tint, the layers, or slabs, being not thicker than three inches, and sometimes as thin as a fourth of an inch. The masonry discovers a combination of science and art, which can only be referred

RUINS IN THE CAÑON DE CHACO.

to a higher state of civilization and refinement than is to be found in the works of either the Mexicans or Pueblos of to-day.

"So beautiful, diminutive, and true are the details of the structure, as to give them at a little distance the appearance of a magnificent piece of mosaic work.

"In the outer face of the buildings no signs of mortar are to be seen, the intervals between the beds, or layers, being chinked with beautifully colored pebbles of the minutest thinness; the filling and backing of the walls is done in rubble masonry, the mortar, however, showing no indication of the presence of lime; their thickness at the base is a little more than three feet, while higher up it is less, diminishing every story by retreating jogs on the inside from the bottom to the top.

"The elevation of the walls at the present time is thirty-two feet, showing it to have been originally four stories high; the ground-plan, in exterior development, is four hundred and thirteen feet. On the ground floor are fifty-four apartments, the smallest one measuring five feet square, the largest one thirteen feet by seven. These rooms communicate with each other by means of small doors, two and a half feet wide by three feet high.

"In the second story, the doors are much larger; in this, as in the third story, were once windows. The system of flooring was unhewn beams about six inches in diameter, from which the bark had been carefully removed; they were laid transversely from wall to wall, small, peeled sticks, about one inch in diameter, being laid across them; these were covered with grass, or *tulle*, which, with a layer of mud mortar, furnished the floor to the room above. These beams show no signs of the saw or axe, but bear the marks of having been hacked off by some very imperfect instrument.

"In different portions of the ruins were three circular apartments, sunk in the ground, the walls being of masonry; these apartments measured from sixteen to twenty-seven feet in diameter, and were about six feet in the clear; were called *estufas*, and were used for the performances of the ceremonies and rites of their religion; the only entrance to them being through a small door in the top, which also admitted the light."

The pueblo Wejegi is built in the same manner as that of Pintado, and is constructed of the same kind of material. The apartments on the ground floor numbered ninety-nine; the length of the principal edifice is three hundred and ninety feet.

The ruins of Hungo-Pavie show the same nicety in the details of their masonry as do those of Pintado, the *estufa* alone being different, it having a number of interior counterforts. This pueblo was undoubtedly four stories in height.

The ruins of the pueblo of Chettro-Kettle, although

showing the same style of architecture, and built of the same kind of material, are more extensive than those already described; there are four stories now standing, and one hundred and twenty-four rooms occupied the ground floor. Many of these rooms are in an excellent state of preservation, the walls still having upon them their coating, or plaster.

The most extensive of these northern ruins are those of the pueblo of Peñasca-Blanca, which differs from the others in the arrangement of the stones composing its walls; those of the other pueblos were of uniform character, in the several beds or layers composing them, but in these there is a regular alternation of large and small stones, the effect of which is both unique and beautiful.

The largest of these stones are about one foot in length and six inches in thickness, forming but a single bed; alternating with these are four or five beds of small stones, about an inch in thickness.

The general plan of the buildings seems to have been about the same; the number of rooms traceable upon the ground floor of this pueblo is one hundred and thirty-four, while the existing walls show it to have been five stories in height.

In no single instance was either a chimney or fireplace found among the ruins, nor were there any indications of the presence or use of iron in their construction. Quantities of pottery-ware were found, the colors showing taste in their selection and style of arrangement, and being still quite bright.

It can hardly be necessary to describe the ruins found in the valley of the Rio de Chelly, as they are similar to those already described as found in the Cañon de Chaco, covering the valley for the space of twenty-five miles.

Before leaving this subject, I desire to speak of some ruins which, though lying south of the present boundary of the United States, without doubt formed a part of the wonderful system of pueblos existing in this marvellous

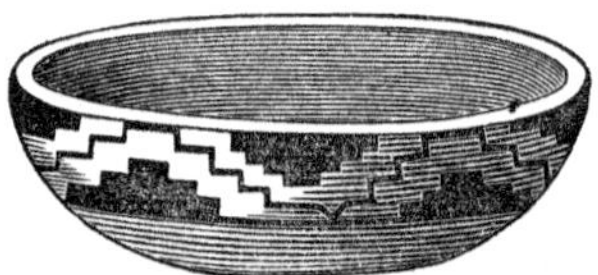

EARTHEN BOWL FROM RUINS OF THE PUEBLO PEÑASCA-BLANCA.

country, which extended throughout New Mexico and Arizona, and were once the homes of a numerous and industrious race of people.

I refer to the ruins of the Casas Grandes found in northwestern Chihuahua, and situated upon the Rio Casas Grandes, a stream that empties into Lake Guzman.

These are the ruins of the most southern of these fortified towns, or pueblos, and which the historian, Claverigo, declares similar in every respect to those of New Mexico, being constructed of three stories, and without entrance to the first floor.

Unlike any other ruins in New Mexico, save those of the Gran Quivera, water was conveyed to the pueblo from a spring some distance away, by means of an aqueduct. A large watch-tower, called by some "Castle Janos," stands about a league to the southwest of the town, commanding a wide extent of country, while along the banks of the stream are many mounds, in which weapons of stone, with many earthen vessels, handsomely painted, have been found.

Bartlett, in his "Personal Narrative," says: "The ruins of Casas Grandes in Chihuahua face the cardinal points, and consist of fallen and erect walls, the latter varying in height from five to thirty feet, projecting above the portions of ruins which have crumbled to decay. Were the heights estimated from the foundations, it would be much greater, particularly those of the centre point of the building, where the fallen walls and rubbish form a mound more than twenty feet above the ground. If, therefore, the highest walls now standing have their foundations on the lowest level, their probable height was more than fifty feet. I concluded that the outer portion of the buildings was the lowest, about one story high, while the central ones, judging from the height of the walls now standing, and the accumulation of rubbish, were probably from three to six stories.

"Every portion of the building is made of adobe, which differs entirely from that now made by the Mexicans, in that the blocks are very much larger, being about four feet in length, by twenty-two inches in thickness. Gravel was mixed with the mud, but no straw was used.

"The building consists of three masses, united by walls of one story, forming court-yards. The entire edifice extends from north to south eight hundred feet, and from east to west two hundred and fifty. The general character is very similar to the Casas Grandes near the Pimo villages, and the ruins on the Salinas. Not a fragment of wood remains; many doorways are to be seen, but the lintels have gone, and the top has in most cases crumbled away, and fallen in.

"Some of the apartments arranged along the main walls are twenty feet by ten, and connected by doorways, with a small enclosure, or pen, in one corner, between three and four feet high. Besides these there are many other exceedingly narrow apartments, too contracted for dwelling-places or sleeping-rooms, with connecting doorways, and into which the light was admitted by circular apertures in the upper part of the wall. There are also large halls, and some enclosures within the walls, and so extensive that they could never have been covered by a roof. The lesser ranges of buildings, which surrounded the principal one, may have been occupied by the people at large, whose property may have been deposited within the great building for safe keeping. Although there appears to have been less order in the *tout ensemble* of this great collection of buildings than in those farther north, the number of small apartments, the second stages and stories, the inner courts, and nearly all the minor details, resemble those of the ruins found in New Mexico and Arizona."

Who shall answer the question, when and by whom were these wonderful structures built?

In a succeeding chapter I propose to give the reader a synopsis of the many theories that have been advanced concerning these ruins by our savans, that he may, in connection with the facts here given, understand the great uncertainty that exists concerning the early settlement of this marvellous country; as well as to convince him of the truth of the statements made in previous chapters of this work, that the barren and desolate wastes now existing between the Rio Grande and the waters of the Pacific were once inhabited by a race of people far superior in the arts and in mechanical skill to any of the races that for the past century have been found within its confines.

In all these ruins *estufas* are found to exist; they were invariably built underground; were circular in form, with neither doors nor windows, entrance always being had through a small aperture in the roof. These *estufas* are of different sizes, and from six to nine feet in the clear. They always contained a kind of altar, or stone table, flat upon the top, upon which it is supposed was kept burning the sacred flame.

The walls of many of them were ornamented with rude paintings or representations of different animals or birds; such figures as the deer, the dog, the wolf, the fox, the eagle, and the turkey; in addition to which, rude representations of the sun, the moon, the clouds, and the lightning were found painted in colors.

These *estufas*, the old cacique informed me, were the temples of Montezuma, and that the cacique and their council, at the planting and before the harvesting each spring and fall, visit them and perform certain religious rites, consisting of songs and chants, which are supposed to make the offerings there given more acceptable to Montezuma, who in return therefor bestows upon his children many blessings, sending them rain and abundant crops.

I ventured to hint to the cacique that I possessed a very strong desire to visit the *estufa* at Zuni before I left; but the intimation was unheeded, nor was the subject again referred to by either of us.

The cacique had scarcely left ere Jimmy made his appearance, and seated himself beside me with such an air of importance that I was at once aware that he was about to make some communicàtion of import. Inflating his lungs to their fullest extent, and inclining his head to one side, while his face wore a very cunning expression, he remarked,—

"It is impossible for me to belave thi mony injurious reports carculated concernin' thi Injuns in thi town beyant, whin I say thi face ov thi good ould bazaque."

For a moment I was under the impression that Jimmy had been too freely partaking of the contents of our demijohn, but soon discovered, from the serious air that pervaded his whole hearing, that he meant business by his remark, and therefore replied,—

"Well, Jimmy, as we don't propose to trust ourselves among them for any length of time, the truth or falsity of the report can be a matter of no earthly consequence to us, especially as neither of us will have any opportunity to test it."

"It'll be a great satisfaction, for to do it, sur," replied Jimmy.

"Do what, Jimmy?"

"Tist it, sur."

"Well, you can't test it, so let that settle it," replied I, rather testily.

"But I think I will, shure."

"How do you propose to do it, Jimmy?"

"By thryin' it, shure, sur."

"How are you going to try it, Jimmy?"

"Well, sur, yer say I owe mi mither-in-lor some riputation for thi loss ov her gurl, an' I'm thinkin' I'll jist marry her, an' sittle down misilf right here, sur, wid thi other Injuns."

Had I at that moment heard a clap of thunder resounding through the sky, I could not have been more completely astounded, than at this piece of information. Then the utter absurdity of it struck me so forcibly, that I lay back and indulged in a prolonged and most hearty fit of laughter, much to the discomfort of my poor body, which was still very sore from the effects of my fall. As soon as I could sufficiently recover myself, I said,—

"Why, Jimmy, the woman is old enough to be your mother."

"No, sur," said Jimmy, "she's only twinty-five, an' I'm twinty-six misilf."

"How can that be, Jimmy, when she has a daughter at least twenty years old?"

"Faith," said Jimmy, looking for a moment rather puzzled, "moighty quare things hap'n in this counthry; d'ye moind thi sthory that thi ould bazaque was tellin' yez a bit ago, about Mister Montezuma's mother?"

"Yes, Jimmy, but that was only a legend that occurred a great many hundred years ago."

"Will, ef these things tuk place thin, why wouldn't they do it now?"

"That is a question which I can't answer, Jimmy; but I

can, and do tell you, to keep away from the woman, and I shall require your parole that you won't go near the town without permission."

"I'll not give it to yez," said Jimmy, firmly bracing himself, and speaking with a most determined air. "Father Donnegan giv it me, an' I'll kape it all mi life long, for he tould me to; an' it's mighty quare that a mon can't visit wid his own mither-in-lor, widout bein' obliged to deliver up his barole."

"You couldn't marry your mother-in-law, Jimmy, without breaking the law, and that would subject you to punishment for the crime of bigamy — perhaps."

"What's that, shure, sur?"

"When a man marries his mother-in-law, that's bigamy, Jimmy, which the law don't permit."

"Shure, I think it's moighty small bizness for the lor to interfere in cases ov thi affictions."

"There's no country in the world, Jimmy, where such a marriage would be legal."

"Yis, sur," said Jimmy, with great promptitude; "it wud be laghal in ould Ireland."

"O, no; you are mistaken. It is impossible for it to be legal in any civilized country."

"Yis, sur," said Jimmy. "Michael Murphy, in the county Monohon, parish ov Limerick, married his own mither-in-lor, an' Father Donnegan did it wid his own hands."

"Well, if he did do it, it's no excuse for you, and you may as well understand that, first as last."

"I'm no *peon*, shure," replied Jimmy.

"No; but you are under my care, and I'll see that the cacique puts a stop to any such nonsense."

"Is't the ould bazaque yer spakin' ov now? That for the ould haythin," said Jimmy, jumping up from the ground, and violently snapping his fingers, while he capered around like a mad man; "that for the ould haythin! Hasn't he got five wives alriddy, an' didn't he want mi mother-in-lor for another one, an' didn't she till me so wid her own mouth last night?"

"Now, Jimmy, how is that possible, when you can't understand a word she says?"

"Faith, she tould me it wid her fingers, so she did."

"Well, Jimmy, I do not propose to discuss the matter any further with you, nor do I know or care how many wives the cacique has; he is the governor, makes the laws, and has a right to have as many as he chooses; but I'll wager something that he never yet married his mother-in-law, nor can you, either."

"But I must, tho', for I'm plidged to her since last night," said Jimmy, looking very fierce.

"That doesn't make any difference; not the least in the world. You were pledged to her daughter, and on the very first appearance of danger, you left her like a cowardly puppy, and took good care of yourself alone, notwithstanding you had inveigled her away."

"What's invaygled, noo," said Jimmy.

"Well, sir," I replied, "I'll not talk with you any more at the present time; we will wait until the return of the doctor, and have his opinion on the subject. In the mean time, get me some dinner. I'm hungry, and want it at once."

"Will I go and git mi mither-in-law to come and cook yez some o' them illigant garvies yez liked so much?"

"No, sir. I don't want your mother-in-law in camp, or to ever hear of her again, and you be very careful that I don't, either. Now go and cook me some dinner at once."

Jimmy started, to return in a few moments with the announcement that Don Rafael had neglected to provide any meat, but had told him to go to the pueblo after it, a circumstance that he had entirely forgotten.

Upon his mentioning the fact, I remembered that Don Rafael had asked permission for Jimmy to go for the provisions before he had left camp, and feeling remarkably hungry I could see no way of satisfying my appetite but to permit Jimmy to again visit the pueblo. I therefore reluctantly told him to go, but bade him return as soon as possible.

Jimmy assented to this command most cheerfully, and started towards the pueblo with the air of a man who goes to perform a most agreeable errand; in fact, so quick was his step, and so light his air, that I called him back after he had proceeded some distance on his errand, to bid him be sure and not forget to return immediately, as I was entirely alone in the camp, and very hungry.

Assuring me that he would certainly comply with my most reasonable demands, he once more departed, and the setting sun was tinging the earth with its crimson benediction ere he returned to inform me that "the mate wuz gane whin he got thare." A fact that my loneliness during the afternoon had more forcibly impressed upon me than did Jimmy's bare assertion.

To say that I had made up my mind to give Jimmy a "piece of it" upon his return, doesn't do justice to the ideas that had been crowding my active brain all the afternoon long; nor can I repeat to you the withering sarcasms that had sprung unbidden to my lips, or the tremendous oaths which I had determined to hurl at his devoted head, upon his appearance.

They would have crushed a dozen stalwart forms into the dust, for I had intended that they should annihilate Jimmy so completely that he nor his mother-in-law should never again be heard from.

Alas for my determination! One glance at his bright, pleasant face completely disarmed my resentment, and I heard his story about not "findin' the mate, and goin' round to his mither-in-lor's own house, an' gittin' a chicken fur my supper that he and his mither-in-lor had picked wid their own hands; and here it is,'' said Jimmy, ''as fat as butther, noo; jest look at the beauthiful crayther, and I'll cook it fur yez illigantly, fur yez must be hungry.'' And away went Jimmy to cook the chicken.

Reader, I did just what you'd have done — ate the chicken, and heard Jimmy tell me that his ''mither-in-lor wuz a moighty foine woman.''

CHAPTER XXVIII.

IT was after I had eaten my chicken, and more than an hour after the sun had sunk behind the line of bluffs that marked the western horizon, that Dr. Parker and Don Rafael made their appearance in camp, the latter with a fine, fat antelope which he had shot that afternoon, tied to his saddle behind him.

Their arrival was the signal for Jimmy's disappearance. He was gone like a will-o'-the-wisp before they had fairly dismounted, and when wanted to take our animals to the corral he was nowhere to be found. We were much provoked at this utter disregard of our known wishes and commands, and were determined to prevent in future, if possible, Jimmy's unlicensed rambles.

While the doctor was swearing at the necessity that

demanded his presence in the culinary department of the camp in consequence of Jimmy's absence,— Don Rafael having gone with the animals to the pueblo,— to our surprise, and the doctor's great delight, the miscreant, looking as sweetly innocent as if entirely unconscious of having transgressed any command, appeared upon the scene of action accompanied by his mother-in-law, and immediately proposed to relieve the doctor of the by no means self-imposed task he had undertaken of preparing our supper. Never before did a hungry man surrender a frying-pan and its contents with as much resigned equanimity as did the doctor on this occasion. While Jimmy was engaged in finishing the cooking of our supper, his mother-in-law, seated at a little distance, quietly surveyed the operation with no small degree of curiosity.

As I lay in my blankets cogitating upon Jimmy's persistent disobedience, and endeavoring to invent some means of curing him of his troublesome infatuation, an idea suddenly occurred to me, which I proceeded to put in practice upon the return of Don Rafael from the pueblo. Calling him to me, I said, in Spanish, "Go and make yourself as agreeable as possible to the woman there. I want to see what effect your making love to her will have upon Jimmy."

Don Rafael, who apparently liked the suggestion, immediately approached her, and commenced a conversation in the Zuni tongue, evidently very much to the woman's satisfaction. Jimmy occasionally stopped in his operations, furtively watching the pair, and plainly showing a perturbed state of mind; while it was equally apparent, from the smiles that illumined the faces of the couple under his espionage, as well as the loving intonation of their voices, and their expressive gestures, that Don Rafael, if not verging upon the tender, was, at least, making himself very agreeable to the woman.

Now Don Rafael, like all Mexicans, possessed a most irascible temper, of which fact Jimmy was well aware, having had it demonstrated to his entire satisfaction on several occasions; consequently he stood in wholesome fear of rousing the slumbering demon in the Don's breast; but the present situation of affairs was getting to be unbearable. While Jimmy stood watching them, Don Rafael, perhaps for the purpose of illustrating more clearly some point upon which the conversation had turned, took the woman's hand in his own, in that peculiar manner which speaks more plainly than words.

This was the "straw that broke the camel's back," and induced Jimmy to announce "supper" in the most stentorian tones, which summons, being unheeded by Don Rafael, caused Jimmy to angrily exclaim, in a tone of voice that in its volume would have done credit to the Cardiff Giant, "Will yez be afther lavin' the woman alone thare, an' cum to yer supper, an' not be kapin' it round all the night long?" The fact that Don Rafael made no reply to the inquiry did not tend to reassure Jimmy in the least, much to the gratification of the doctor and myself, as we hoped, by thus rousing the "green-eyed monster" in his breast, to provoke a quarrel between himself and the "plidged object of his affictions."

After waiting a few moments, and no one offering to partake of the supper which he had prepared, Jimmy approached, and in most affable tones inquired for my health with so much Irish blarney that I could not fail to discover the "cat under the meal," though he tried hard to conceal it. A moment later, under pretence of arranging the blankets, the cat was let out of the bag, for, in a tone of voice intended only for my ear, he said,—

"What's he spakin' ter her, Juge?"

Innocently enough I inquired, "Who?"

"That ould black divil, Don Rafael," said Jimmy.

I replied, after listening for a few moments, "O, he's only talking nonsense."

"But what's he sayin'?" asked Jimmy.

"O, he's only telling her he thinks she's a handsome woman, and he'd like her for a sweetheart."

"An' what duz she say ter that, sur?"

"She says she thinks the Mexicans are splendid people, and that she'd rather have a Mexican for a lover than any one else in the world."

"Thi dirthy ould pig," said Jimmy, "thryin' to thraduce mi characther and win her affictions for himsilf; he can't do't, though; she's thrue to me."

"True to you, Jimmy? It may be so, but it don't look much like it. She's making an assignation with him now."

"What's that?" said Jimmy, staring at them with eyes as big as saucers; "what's a sassination?"

"O, nothing but an agreement to meet her in a couple of hours for the purpose of taking a stroll."

"Is that it?" said Jimmy. "I'll tache the dirthy black divil a lisson, at thi sassination, wid mi shot goon, that ha'll rimimber all his life long, bedad."

"You'd better not let Don Rafael hear that remark, Jimmy. He'd shoot you quick as wink, if he should get mad; and he has as much right to make love to the old woman as you have."

"No, sur," said Jimmy; "she's mi mither-in-lor, an' she's plidged ter me."

"Well, settle it between you, only take care of Don Rafael."

"Juge, will yez spake ter him aboot it?"

"No, Jimmy, I have nothing further to say on the subject."

Upon which Jimmy turned away and went out into the darkness, leaving Don Rafael and the "mother-in-law" still engaged in sweet converse.

As soon as the doctor and myself were left alone, I informed him of Jimmy's engagement, and of his determination to marry his mother-in-law, in spite of all opposition. At first he was disposed to be incredulous, and to regard the whole thing as a joke; but upon becoming convinced that with Jimmy at least it was a reality, he saw that it would be likely to cause us great annoyance and trouble should he persist in carrying out his intention.

"But," said the doctor, "we must endure it, for I am satisfied we can never cure it unless we kill him."

I most certainly deprecated resorting to any violent measures in attempting to prevent the exercise of his propensity to fall in love with every woman whom he met, though I could but acknowledge to myself that Jimmy might as well be dead, for all the service he was to us in his present nervous and dazed condition. After considering for a long time as to the best course to pursue, a thought struck me, and turning to the doctor, I asked if he had in his medicine-chest any tartar emetic.

"Plenty," replied the doctor, at the same time bursting into a hearty laugh; while he ejaculated, "By thunder! that's a capital idea. I can cure him."

"It's best not to be too hasty, doctor; but if worse comes to worst, we can certainly try its effect."

"True. There's nothing in the world that'll cure lovesickness so quickly as a counter-irritant, administered in homœopathic doses. There isn't a particle of danger in it, and I'll guarantee a cure for the malady."

"Are you perfectly sure, doctor, that no harm can result from it?"

"Of course I am. Only let me know when you want your remedy tested, and I'll administer it."

Having then and there come to a firm determination to prevent the further growth of Jimmy's affection by nipping it in the bud, the doctor and myself smoked our pipes, rather amused to see Don Rafael so literally fulfilling or carrying out the suggestion that had been made to him; while in our mind's eye we enjoyed the confusion and dismay that we expected would ensue upon the application of our proposed treatment to Jimmy.

The "mother-in-law" having at last, greatly to our gratification, signified to Don Rafael her desire to return to the pueblo, he arose and accompanied her.

Scarcely, however, had they left the camp, before Jimmy appeared, following so closely upon the heels of Don Rafael's departure that, to say the least, it suggested a suspicion to our minds that he might possibly have been concealed in so close proximity that he was enabled to witness the manner in which his "mother-in-law" received the attentions of the Don.

Striding furiously by both the doctor and myself, without deigning to notice either of us by a look even, Jimmy approached the wagon, and drawing from it his "shot gun," proceeded to examine it with the air of a man determined on desperate things. After apparently satisfying himself of its condition, he cast a hasty glance around the camp, and addressing the doctor and myself, who were amused spectators of the scene, said,—

"Where's the ould black divil gone?"

The doctor smilingly replied,—

"If you mean Don Rafael, you'll find him up at your mother-in-law's, Jimmy. He went home with her."

"Will, sir," said Jimmy, "whin he retarns, I shall inthrojuce him to the contints ov this fowlin'-pace, in a manner that'll not be very idifyin' to him."

"I wouldn't do that, Jimmy, because the Don is a good shot, and he will certainly kill you if you should fail in your attempt."

"Fail in mi attimpt!" said Jimmy. "Fail! How will I fail? The ould thafe ov the world's been thryin' to thrajuce mi characther to mi mither-in-lor, an' I'll hev his heart's blood, so I will, bedad; I'll shoot him like a dog."

At this moment I said,—

"Jimmy, I hear Don Rafael coming. Hadn't you better put up the gun before he sees it in your hand?"

With a bound Jimmy sprang towards the wagon, attempting to violently force the gun into the place from which he had drawn it at the bottom of the wagon. In the effort, one of the hammers caught, and we were terribly startled by a tremendous report as one of the barrels was discharged, seemingly through Jimmy's body, who immediately fell to the ground uttering the most terrific yells, as he kicked and floundered around like a decapitated hen, crying,—

"For the love ov God, save me, docther. I'm kilt, shure. Shot through mi body. Howly muther! I'm bladin' to dith. It's me bowels that's prothrudin'," said Jimmy, as in his agony he seized an India-rubber pillow that lay close by him.

We all rushed to him (Don Rafael, who had just returned, included) expecting to see him fearfully mangled. We were first surprised at finding no blood; but when an examination revealed the fact that the entire charge had passed between Jimmy's body and his arm, without touching him anywhere, and that the only damage that had resulted from the explosion was a bad scar, and a large rent in his flannel blouse, our wonder and astonishment knew no bounds. We all agreed that Jimmy's lucky star was, as usual, in the ascendant, and had certainly saved him this time, although he would not believe himself unharmed for a long time; nor would he then, until he had carefully examined all his clothing for blood-stains, as well as made a close and extended examination of each particular bone in his body, and satisfied himself that they were sound and unbroken.

Then he majestically arose from the ground, and casting

a withering look upon Don Rafael, who was congratulating him upon his fortunate escape, said, "Ef mi bones is not bruk, me heart is; I might ez will bin kilt thin."

"Why, Jimmy, what do you mean?"

"It's mi mither-in-lor I mane," said Jimmy, bursting into tears.

"I don't want your mother-in-law, Jimmy; I was only trying to entertain her while you were busy. She looked so lonely sitting by herself, and was waiting to see you."

"But yez squazed her hand," said Jimmy.

"O, no, Jimmy; I was only looking at a wart on it."

"Is that so? B'dad! Don Rafael, you're a rale gintilman, and can appryceate a gintilman's faylins," said Jimmy, as he grasped Don Rafael's hand in both his own, and shook it with a fervor and earnestness almost paralyzing in its effect, quite forgetting in the excitement caused by the reaction in his feelings, that it was Don Rafael's blood that he was thirsting for but a few moments before.

Matters having been arranged to the entire satisfaction of Jimmy, we all retired, but were hardly ensconced in our blankets ere we saw Jimmy rise, and silently steal away in the direction of the pueblo. We did not disturb him, but allowed him to go his way, solacing ourselves with the thought that though he might build his "Castles in Spain," they would exist only in the bright clouds with which his imagination canopied the future.

The next morning quite early, in fact, before breakfast, I was waited upon by Jimmy, who briefly informed me "that under the exhisting sarcumstances, he filt it to be his duthy to lave mi sarvice."

As I had expected this, I told him that I would talk with the doctor in the course of the day, and see him again.

"I'm roight sorry to part wid yez," said Jimmy, "but mi mither-in-lor thinks I owe her some ripotation for the loss of the gurl, an' b'dad, I'm goin' to pay it wid mesilf."

"Very well, Jimmy. I shall be sorry to hear that immediately upon leaving you, you were sold to the Navajoes, as a ransom for the girl."

"How d'ye mane? What would they sill mi fur?"

"You know that the cacique told me that the relatives of the girl demanded of him that he should require you to pay what the ransom of the girl would cost."

"Yis," said Jimmy; "but I proved mi innocence."

"Well, if you did that, you certainly owe the woman no reparation."

"Will, but she thinks I duz," said Jimmy.

"In that case, it's plain to me that there is some object behind all this; and that in some way you are to be made to suffer for not protecting the girl you were with; and if, in spite of all that has been said, you still desire to remain here, no one will make the least objection."

"Thank yez fur that,'' said Jimmy, as, with a bow and a

scrape he moved away, as happy as a lark at the idea that he had at last convinced me of the propriety of his remaining behind among the Zunis, a proceeding that would have subjected him to no danger in the least, but ourselves to most serious inconvenience.

Scarcely was our breakfast over before the cacique, accompanied by two members of his council, appeared for the purpose of escorting us to the festival, which was to commence at noon.

Sundry toddies, however, together with a smoke from the doctor's big pipe, so won upon the old man's good-nature that, at my request, he seated himself upon one of our camp-stools, and was soon deeply engaged in giving an account of the wonders of the Moquis country and its people.

When at the Apache *rancheria*, I had seriously thought of paying this interesting and curious people a visit, but had been prevented from carrying out my design. I was, therefore, very glad of this opportunity to learn something of them from one who had visited their villages, and whose knowledge of them was obtained by personal contact.

Taking a sip from his glass, and a few whiffs from the pipe, the old man commenced, in the low, monotonous tones that he always assumed in his narrations, a relation of the facts embodied in the information herein conveyed to the reader.

The Moquis country lies to the north and west of the San

Francisco Mountain, and not very far from the Colorado Chiquito. It is an arid, barren country, deeply eroded by floods, and largely formed of steep mesas, volcanic peaks, and rocky cañons, with a few fertile valleys interspersed among them.

Their villagès, of which there are seven, are built upon the very edge of some of the steepest of these rocky mesas, in so singular a manner that, at a little distance, it is impossible for a stranger to distinguish them from the rocks, of which they appear to form a part. The first three of these are built upon a bluff of solid rock, about three hundred feet high and one hundred and fifty feet in width, and are reached by steep paths and by steps cut into the rock in such a manner that they can only be approached by persons on foot.

The houses are built of stone, are generally two stories high, and are laid in a mortar made of mud which is brought from the valleys below upon the backs of men, there being no soil whatever upon the rock. In form they are similar to those of Zuni, entrance to them being by ladders, as there are neither doors nor windows in the lower stories.

The first and largest town is called Harro, and contains a population of about two thousand persons. All the towns or villages have large water-tanks, or reservoirs, constructed upon the rock, lined with masonry; they are generally five or six feet in depth, and are used for collecting and hold-

THE MOQUIS PUEBLOS.

ing rain-water. Below each of these large tanks are smaller ones similarly constructed, and connected with those above by means of a pipe, through which water is conducted for the use of their stock. This stock consists entirely of sheep and goats, which are driven each day to pasture, the nearest grass being six miles away.

The population of the Moquis villages numbers, it is supposed, something over six thousand. Their government is an hereditary one, not necessarily descending from father to son, however, but any blood relation may be selected as determined by the choice of the people.

Of their religious belief, the cacique knew but little. They believed in a great father who dwelt where the sun rises, and of a great mother who lived where the sun sets. She peopled the earth by bringing from her own home nine things, from which sprang the different races of men. First, the deer race; second, the sand race; third, the water race; fourth, the bear race; fifth, the hare race; sixth, the prairie-wolf race; seventh, the rattlesnake race; eighth, the tobacco-plant race; and ninth, the reed-grass race. That after death, they assumed the form from which they originally sprang; thus aiding to form anew the decaying elements of the earth.

They never plough or irrigate their lands, depending entirely upon the natural fall of rain; their only agricultural implement is a kind of hoe; with this they plant corn, beans, onions, melons, pumpkins, cotton, and a species of tobacco-plant in the valleys around them. They also knit, weave, and spin very nicely, as do the Zunis and the others of the Pueblo tribes.

One very singular fact in connection with the Moquis is deserving of especial mention, viz. the people of Harro, although living within two hundred yards of another large village, — the whole seven of these villages are within a radius of six miles,— speak an entirely different language from those of the remaining six villages, and seem to have preserved their manners and customs intact, as well as their language, for centuries; and another singular fact is, that while the people of Harro understand and can converse in the language spoken by the people of the other villages, they neither understand or can converse in the language spoken by the people of Harro. With these and many more interesting facts did the old cacique while away the morning hours; but as I was accidentally brought into contact on the following day with a couple of Moquis who came directly from Harro, I shall give the reader some further account of the manners and customs of this singular and primitive race in a succeeding chapter.

As the time had arrived for us to start for the pueblo, I asked the cacique if he would give us the origin or history of the "Green-corn dance," to which request he willingly assented, and gave the following account.

As soon as the first ears of maize begin to ripen, they are plucked by women, and brought to the high-priest, who alone possesses the right to strip from them the husks, for the purpose of ascertaining the degree of maturity to which they have arrived.

After the ears shall have obtained a certain age, if the promise for an abundant crop be a fair one, the high-priest sends criers through the streets, to announce to the people that as Montezuma has been kind to them and given them bountiful crops, they must assemble upon a certain day at noon,— specifying a particular day, —"and render unto him thanksgiving and praise for having so kindly provided for their comfort." This was the day he had appointed for that purpose, and the doctor and myself accompanied him to the pueblo to witness the ceremony, leaving our camp in charge of Don Rafael,— Jimmy, as usual, being absent.

Upon reaching the pueblo, we were assigned a seat of honor by the side of the cacique, on the lower terrace of the council house.

The procession soon slowly approached; the men came in single file, their bodies bent almost double, as though borne down by the immense weight of the load of maize which they were pretending to carry upon their shoulders. Around their loins was tied a small blanket, the upper portion of their bodies being entirely naked, and painted a dark-red color; their arms and legs, which were also naked, were striped with red, white, and green paint; around each arm above the elbow, they wore a band of cloth, trimmed with the tops of the pine-tree, intermingled with red pimento berries, while a similar necklace encircled their necks; their heads were elaborately decorated with eagles' feathers.

In one hand they carried a small gourd, in which were a few grains of dried corn, while in the other was a string, from which depended a number of *guayaves* tied together like a bunch of cigars; around each leg, just below the knee, was fastened a band from which depended shells, eagles' claws, antelopes' hoofs, etc., while from their shoulders dangled the skins of such wild animals that the wearer had himself slain.

One of the men had with him a "tombe," or drum, on which he occasionally beat in the most frantic manner, although the only attempt at instrumental music, was made by drawing a notched stick swiftly across the convex half of a dried gourd, the sound of which was supposed to resemble that made in grinding corn upon a *metatte*.

This party were accompanied by three members of the council, whose business it was to make a short harangue in front of each house, the occupants awaiting their coming upon the terraces, and bestowing upon them maize, which was added to the common fund provided for the occasion.

After all the houses had been visited, the party sang and danced themselves back to the *plaza*, where four large

THE GREEN CORN DANCE.

camp-kettles were hung over fires, in each of which maize was boiling. These kettles were suspended by ropes from four poles, about five feet high, which came together at the top; the poles were ornamented by twelve ears of corn, supposed to represent the twelve months of the year. Each one of the kettles were tended by four men, dressed similarly to those already described, their bodies, however, being solidly painted in white, red, green, and blue.

These men were supposed to represent the four seasons, and were selected for their sweet voices and ability to endure fatigue, being expected to sing their hymns of gratitude to Montezuma,—for whom this boiling maize, the first of their crop, was intended,—all the while beating time with a corn-stalk on the edge of the kettle around which they were dancing.

This singing and dancing continued until the maize was perfectly boiled, after which it was taken from the kettle, placed upon the fire and reduced to ashes, which were carefully collected by members of the council, and carried to the fields and sprinkled upon the earth, that they might purify and enrich the soil for the crops of the coming year.

This ceremony completed, another fire was lighted, and the kettles refilled with maize; this was boiled and distributed among the populace, and then ensued a scene of gluttony and excess that would equal that displayed at a country parson's donation visit.

No one is permitted to join in this dance who has not fasted for a given length of time, and, in addition, they are required to thoroughly cleanse the inside of the body, which is done by the free use of fermented liquors, that act as a cathartic. This practice renders them better fitted to sing their hymns of praise to Montezuma, as well as to enjoy the feast of good things that come after.

The origin of this dance is without doubt of a religious character, and seems, with the "Buffalo Dance," to have been handed down from generation to generation for centuries.

We very much regretted that we could not witness the celebration of this latter dance, as its mysteries, and the peculiar manner in which it is performed, are said to be very amusing.

We retired from the scene about sunset, and upon reaching our camp we learned from Don Rafael that Jimmy had not made his appearance there during our absence, nor had we seen him at the pueblo. We felt that his remissness was becoming so flagrant, that we must at once adopt some means to correct it, and determined to administer the first "corrective dose" that night.

Of all the dishes that our camping life afforded, none so tickled Jimmy's palate as an "Irish stew," and this night Don Rafael had prepared a savory stew of antelope for our supper. A dish of it was carefully tartarized and put one side for Jimmy when he should return to the camp, while the doctor and myself speculated on the probable results.

Some hours later Jimmy returned in a remarkably happy frame of mind, having, as he informed us, "injied thi sight ov thim naked divils widout clothes on, caperin' round wid their corn, bitther nor he wud a rale ould Irish jig, fur his mither-in-lor tould him they'd hev foine corn thi ensuin' year," telling us at the same time that he was "hungry as a bear, an' could ate a Navajoe alive," whereupon the doctor arose, and produced the stew that had been so carefully saved for him, much to Jimmy's delight.

A few moments sufficed to finish his meal, which he pronounced "viry foine," and shortly afterwards we all "turned in," and awaited further developments, which the reader will find recounted in the succeeding chapter.

CHAPTER XXIX.

"HOWLY MUTHER! it's dyin' I am," were the words that saluted my ears about midnight.

There was no response, although I could distinctly hear Jimmy's groans, accompanied by the most violent retching and vomiting.

Between these paroxysms he called loudly upon each one

of us, begging us to "wake up an' hilp him, fur the luv o' God, before he got so did he couldn't call us."

At last, in answer to his frequent calls, the doctor leisurely arose, and going to Jimmy, inquired what was the matter.

"Matther anuf, God knows," said Jimmy. "I'm dyin', docther; an' thare's no praste to absolve mi. Will yez be afther givin' mi somethin' to aze mi, docther?"

Here another violent retching spell occurred, after which Jimmy exclaimed, "D'ye say that now, docther? I'm a did mon; in liss thin tin minnits I'll be a corps; and may the blissid Vargin recave mi sowl, for there's no praste to absolve me at all, at all."

The doctor here requested Jimmy to talk less, while he proceeded to examine him; and then, calling me to see him, he informed me, with a very grave face, that Jimmy was suffering from a severe attack of "tartarus emitticus cholera," which he much feared would prove fatal.

This announcement caused Jimmy to utter a terrible groan, and then to call loudly upon the saints for "protiction from thi awful dezases that wuz a lyin' hauld ov his vitals."

Kneeling by his side, I commenced an examination, and found him looking pale, and evidently very much frightened at what he seemed to consider the near approach of the King of Terrors. After a few moments I remarked, "Jimmy, I think you must have eaten too much."

"Atin, atin too much; me atin too much!" said Jimmy. "Do I look like a mon that's atin too much?" and here another violent paroxysm of retching seized him. "May the saints furgiv yez, docther, fur standin' thare an' seein' a human craythur pirish, widout liftin' up yez hand to save him, an' on his weddin'-day, too."

"What's that, Jimmy? Were you to have been married to-day? Who to?" asked the doctor; "for I must save you, even at the risk of my own life."

"Go at it quick, thin, docther, for I've not more thin tin minnits to live. Jist look at that, now," and another fit of retching came upon him. Here I asked Jimmy if he felt qualmish.

"No, I don't fale clamish at all; but I fale as tho' mi boots had cum up thro' mi stumick."

Both the doctor and myself assured Jimmy that if he could go to sleep, he would feel better by morning; and at last he became quiet, and sank into a slumber, from which he did not arouse until late the next morning, when, pale and ghastly, he informed us that he wouldn't be able to "stir from his bid in a wake," at which statement we were much rejoiced, and also convinced that tartar emetic hath its perfect work.

The doctor having forbidden Jimmy to rise from his bed without his permission, we went to our breakfast, which we relished most heartily, notwithstanding Jimmy's doleful remark, that it was "a bruthal thing fur min to ate, whin a human craythur lay a dyin' widin tin fate ov thim."

About noon we were surprised to see the cacique approaching, in company with a strange-looking man, whom

WE TREAT JIMMY FOR A NEW DISEASE.

we at once recognized as an American, and two Indians, who proved to be Moquis.

The American was a large, powerful, haggard-looking man about sixty years of age, with a long white beard that flowed over his breast, and reached nearly to his waist. He wore neither coat nor vest, while, with a handkerchief bound tightly around his head, and his shirt covered with blood, he presented as wild and crazed an appearance as it is possible to imagine.

The instant he caught sight of us he sprang forward, and grasping our hands, exclaimed, while the tears rolled freely down his cheeks, "Thank God, friends at last!" almost at the same instant falling insensible at our feet.

A hasty examination revealed the fact that the man had fainted from excessive fatigue and hunger, also that he was suffering from an ugly arrow-wound in his right shoulder, which, although from its appearance was several days old, had not been dressed, and must have become very painful.

While the doctor was administering to the old man's needs and comforts, the cacique informed me that the Moquis had found the man wandering near the Zuni trail about twenty miles from their villages, and as they could not understand what he wanted, supposed that he desired to go to Zuni, consequently, had guided him through.

They had arrived at Zuni during the morning, and as no one there could understand who he was, or what he wanted, they very properly had brought him to our camp

In the course of half an hour he had so far recovered as to be able to take some stimulants, as well as to sparingly partake of a little nourishment, which the doctor administered from time to time. Later in the day, we succeeded in getting from him his sad, sad story.

He was a Missourian, by name Parley Stewart, and had left his home two months before, for the purpose of going to Los Angeles, California, by the thirty-fifth parallel route. Near Los Angeles he had a son living, whose wife and child were accompanying him, in addition to which his own wife and six children, the youngest being a girl thirteen years of age, made up the party, in all, ten persons: four grown men, and six women and children.

Their household effects they carried in four covered wagons, each one being drawn by two mules; and without doubt it was the party that the cacique had mentioned to us, as passing Zuni some days before our arrival there, and whose camp we had discovered at the Carizo Springs.

They had met with no accident since leaving home; had passed to the south of what they had supposed to be the Moquis country, and a couple of days' journey beyond it, without seeing any signs of hostile Indians, when, upon coming to a beautiful valley abounding in fine grass, through which ran a stream of clear, beautiful water, they determined to halt for a few days, for the purpose of giving their weary animals a little much-needed rest.

From Mr. Stewart's description of the place, the cacique, as well as the Moquis, thought that it was without doubt upon one of the tributaries of the Colorado, perhaps upon the Colorado Chiquito itself; for he described the valley as very large, and the pasturage fine; magnificent great oaks were scattered throughout, and the banks of the stream, the waters of which were clear and very cold, were entirely free from underbrush, yet skirted by trees of great size, which afforded a most refreshing shade, while the base of the rough and rugged mountains that formed the setting of this jewel of the desert, seemed to be covered with a fine growth of pine, cedar, and fir trees.

After toiling for months over the hot, dry, and dusty road across the plains, exposed to the burning heat of a solstitial sun, is it any wonder that this quiet, beautiful valley, with its grateful shade, luxuriant herbage, and cool waters, seemed to the tired and travel-worn wayfarers a little Eden, into which no serpent had yet intruded?

Is it any wonder that they should determine to pause here for a while, and enjoy the beauties with which Nature's hand had so lavishly bestowed her good gifts?

It was in this delightful spot that they, with one accord, determined to pass at least a week, in order that they might give their weary and well-deserving animals an opportunity to recruit from the toils of the past, and to prepare themselves for the fatigues of the future.

The first night one of the sons mounted guard, but nothing disturbed the solitude of their Eden. This was continued for the second night, and in the morning they all decided that it was a useless task, to keep guard while they should be encamped there. They would therefore abandon the habit, and sleep soundly at night, the better to enable them to bear the hardships of the long and desolate route they must travel before they should reach the golden sands, where the loved one was anxiously waiting to embrace them.

During the day two of the sons went out hunting, and returned ere nightfall loaded down with the spoils of the hunt, and reporting that they had seen no trace of hostile foes.

The women of the party, having spent the day in washing and mending the clothing, were all very tired, and immediately after partaking of their supper, retired to rest.

Once during the night Mr. Stewart arose and replenished the camp-fire, which had been kept burning brightly, as a precaution against wild beasts; but seeing nor hearing nothing unusual, again retired to rest.

How long he had been sleeping he had no means of knowing; but they were all aroused from their sound slumber by the terrible war-whoop of the Apaches, sounding in their ears like the death-knell that it proved to be, and so frightening and intimidating them all, that in their terror, and the confusion that ensued, they knew not what to do, the screams of the terror-stricken women and children but adding to the consternation.

Springing to their feet, they grasped their rifles, utterly

unconscious of the direction from which the appalling danger threatened them, although they had received a shower of arrows, that, in their fatal and well-directed aim, had laid low in death five of this little party: Mrs. Stewart the elder, the daughter-in-law with her infant, and two of the sons.

Before they could recover from the horror into which this murderous attack had thrown them, the terrifying war-whoop again burst upon their ears, accompanied by another and another volley of arrows, that in their deadly aim once more brought death upon their wings, for another daughter fell before the murderous fire.

Mr. Stewart and his second son, who thus far had escaped unscathed, in the mean while had been using their rifles and revolvers, though firing entirely at random, for up to this time they had not seen an Indian.

Observing that the bright light of the camp-fire prevented him from distinguishing any object beyond its immediate vicinity, while at the same time it enabled the Indians to distinctly see every movement in camp, Mr. Stewart ordered his son to extinguish it if possible. This he attempted to do, by separating the burning brands. While engaged in this task, a shot from a rifle was heard, and the son, crying out, "Father, they've killed me!" fell dead upon the dying embers of the fire, from which his body was dragged by one of his sisters.

Mr. Stewart stated that the moment he heard the rifle-shot, and saw his son fall, he gave up all hope, and hurriedly telling his daughters to conceal themselves in the water behind the bank of the river, but a few yards distant, where he would immediately join them, he discharged the remaining barrels of his son's revolver at the Indians, and hastily abandoned the camp; not, however, before receiving an arrow-wound in his shoulder.

As soon as possible, he sought the friendly river-bank, where he expected to meet his daughters.

Upon reaching the river, he failed to find either of them; therefore he hastily concealed himself as best he was able in the water, and while lying there, he both heard and saw Indians searching for him in all directions. He managed, however, to elude their observation; and after waiting an hour or two, ventured forth to resume the search for his children, which he was obliged to prosecute with the utmost caution, not daring to call upon them, lest the Indians whom he had seen at work plundering and destroying his camp should overhear him; he counted twenty of these human fiends engaged in this work of demolition, but could see nor hear nothing of his daughters.

Still quietly and cautiously pursuing his search, he waited until the Indians had completed their work of destruction, and had disappeared, going in a southerly direction. Then he carefully approached the spot where at sunset, with his family around him, they were happy in the thought that they were approaching the end of the long and tedious journey that was to restore at once a husband, brother, father, and son to the family circle, and at the same time furnish a home for him and his in their declining years.

What a sight met his horrified gaze! Upon a large fire lay the nude bodies of his wife and six children, all scalped, and fast being reduced to ashes by the flames that their bodies were feeding, and that at the same time were consuming the woodwork of the wagons, with which the bodies had been covered, seemingly for the purpose of adding to the intensity and power of the flames.

The sight completely unmanned him, and throwing himself down upon the blood-stained sward, he watched the fire feeding upon the bodies of the loved ones, with neither the ability nor disposition to attempt to stay the angry, hungry tongues that were fast lapping up, not only his household gods, but the bone of his bone and the flesh of his flesh, upon whom the love of a life-time had been so lavishly bestowed; his only consolation being in the thought that even that was better than to leave their bodies to be torn asunder and devoured by wild beasts.

Daylight found him still gazing upon the horrible pyre, and it was with an almost fiendish delight he saw that a few charred bones and a little handful of ashes were all that remained of those dear ones, who, but twelve short hours before were full of life and hope, and looking forward with bright anticipations to a happy home by the broad waters of the blue Pacific.

Childless, wifeless, homeless, and heart-broken, the old man sorrowfully started out to renew the now almost hopeless search for his two remaining daughters, but no trace of them could he anywhere discover.

Reluctantly he abandoned the search, and once more returned to the desolate scene that he had left within the hour, and which, as he said, completely fascinated him by its terrible reality. Here seating himself upon an old stool that he found, he again surveyed the scene.

The sun shone as brightly, the cloudless sky was as blue, and the grass as green as it was the day before. The leaves of the same magnificent old oak rustled in the breeze, and the little birds in its branches as gayly carolled forth their sweetest songs of praise; the same snow-clad mountain-peaks coldly arose out of their sea of verdure, that had so calmly looked down upon the happy scene of a few short hours before, but alas! now how changed. Was it not a horrid, horrid dream?

Convincing himself at last that it was indeed true, he rose, and gathering up a handful of the still warm ashes, he placed them in his tobacco-box, and prepared to leave the spot that had witnessed the termination of all his earthly happiness.

As he slowly turned away, vainly endeavoring to discover some memento of the dear ones that might have escaped the notice of the fiends who had so ruthlessly destroyed his all, his eyes fell upon a little coop containing some chickens which he had brought with him from his old Missouri home, that in some unaccountable manner had been left behind by the savages. He went to it, and releasing its occupants, turned them loose into the green valley that they might not die of starvation and thirst; then gathering up a few of the fatal arrows that had brought this terrible desolation to him, he took a last lingering look upon the scene before him, and reluctantly turned away.

Taking a trail which he supposed would carry him to the Moquis villages, he left the valley forever.

How he passed the night, or where, or if he slept at all, he could not tell; but the next morning very early he met the two friendly Moquis, who gave him the food and water which he so much needed, and kindly conducted him to the pueblo of Zuni, a three days' journey, although neither party could converse save by signs. Upon arriving there he became almost wild with joy at the sight of Americans, and fainted as I have related.

The old man's grief while relating his story was heart-rending, and during its recital the tears ran down his weather-beaten cheeks like rain, nor did he make any effort to restrain them; and so contagious was his sorrow that it was impossible to prevent the tears from falling from our own eyes.

After the doctor had again dressed the old man's wound, and given him more nourishment, he administered to him an opiate, and in a short time we had the satisfaction of seeing him in a quiet slumber, the first that he had enjoyed for four days.

Signifying to the cacique a desire to have some conversation with the Moquis who had so kindly guided Mr. Stewart to the pueblo, he at once volunteered his services as an interpreter, at the same time informing us that he was not very familiar with the Moquis dialect.

Their dress was similar to that of all the Pueblo Indians, and in general appearance they strongly resembled them, although I fancied them more intelligent looking, their faces having a frank and manly expression; in fact, save in dress and complexion, they resembled American rather than Indian nationality. They had in their possession four arrows that Mr. Stewart had given them, and which they unhesitatingly pronounced to be those of the Tonto Apaches, a statement that afterwards proved to be true, thus fixing this horrible massacre unquestionably upon that band.

I was much surprised, upon offering them some whiskey, to have them decline it, also to learn that the vice of drunkenness was unknown among them, and that they used no kind of fermented liquors, notwithstanding Neal Dow and the

Prohibitory Law were strangers to them. I also learned that the crime of murder was unknown in their nation, that they never made war, but were brave and valiant when attacked.

At home the Moquis go about their houses naked, breech-clout and moccasins excepted. Their women are very pretty, as well as industrious, and have a manner of dressing their hair, which, to the initiated, proclaims their condition in life.

If unmarried, they do it up in two inverse rolls, which gives to the head a very singular appearance, not unlike that of having horns; after marriage, it is worn in two large braids on each side of the face.

A proposal of marriage always emanates from the fair damsel herself, who, after selecting the happy youth, informs her father of her choice, and he forthwith proposes to the father of the lucky swain, who is never known to refuse to sanction the choice.

The preliminaries being thus happily arranged, the young man is required to present his bride with two pair of moccasins, two pair of fine blankets, two mattresses, and two sashes, which latter articles are considered very ornamental by them all. The young woman, in her turn, is obliged to furnish a goodly store of eatables cooked by herself, as a proof that she is capable of making home attractive, so far as creature comforts are concerned, and then the marriage is celebrated with dancing and feasting.

This union continues until one or the other of the parties become dissatisfied, when the marriage between them is dissolved by a joint declaration to that effect, made before the cacique. Should there be children, the respective grand-parents are expected to provide for them.

The women are never permitted to join in any of their dances; the place that would naturally seem to belong to them being filled by young men dressed to represent them. The faces of the dancers are always covered by a mask made of small willow twigs peeled and curiously interwoven together. Those worn by the men are colored a dark brown, while those worn by the supposed women are painted a bright yellow.

Each house has its patron saint represented by an ugly little Aztec image, made of wood or clay, gaudily painted and gorgeously decorated with feathers. These images are suspended by a string from the rafters of their houses, and are supposed to exert a great influence for weal or woe over its inmates.

Every village has an *estufa* underground, or, more properly, a council-chamber, which is used as a public room; here the people are wont to congregate, to sit and smoke and talk over the affairs of the nation. The only light or air is obtained from a scuttle in the roof, which also serves as a door.

From all that I saw or could learn of the Moquis, I came to the conclusion that they were a most simple, moral, happy, industrious, and very hospitable people, and without doubt are legitimate descendants of the Aztec race.

We gladly made them presents of such articles in our possession as we thought would please them, besides giving them a good supply of tobacco, of which they are extremely fond; and they left us very happy, and feeling well repaid for the kindness that they had shown to Mr. Stewart.

The doctor having declared that there was no longer good reason for delaying our departure from Zuni, and being myself convinced that I could endure the fatigue of travelling without any very great degree of inconvenience, I thought it a good opportunity to tell the cacique of our determination to leave Zuni, which I did, informing him that we expected to start on the following day, in time to reach El Moro, where we intended to make our camp the first night out.

The cacique expressed many regrets at the idea of our leaving so soon, which I have no doubt were somewhat mollified by our presenting him with a bale of smoking tobacco, as well as the large pipe which he had so much enjoyed during his visits to our camp.

Thanking us many times over, and promising to see us in the morning before we should start, he left, assuring us that we could have presented him with nothing that he so much desired, or would have prized more highly.

As dinner was being served, Jimmy put in an appearance,

looking a little pale and somewhat woe-begone, and almost as much frightened at the news of our departure, as he had been the night previous at the prospect of his own for the "mysterious realm."

He endeavored to persuade us to tarry another day, by assuring us that his health "wouldn't parmit 'im to start so soon afther a most dangerous and complicayted dizase like his own had attacked him," but the doctor was obdurate, and assured him that once on the road he would again be entirely well.

Finding that nothing he could say changed our determination to start on the following morning, he began to manifest a strong desire to again visit the pueblo; a desire that both the doctor and myself were determined to prevent his accomplishing, if possible; to which end the doctor slyly conveyed into Jimmy's cup of tea dose number two, which he unsuspectingly drank.

As he arose from his supper, he announced in the most careless manner possible, that he "thaught he'd take a bit ov a thramp, which he gissed wud make him fayle all the bitther," to which proposition both the doctor and myself most cheerfully assented.

As he was about starting upon his "thramp," I asked him to assist Don Rafael in packing some things that we should not again require before our departure.

This he at once proceeded to do with an alacrity that

promised well for the speedy accomplishment of the task, but alas!

> "The best laid schemes of mice and men
> Gang aft agley,"

for, long before the task was finished, Jimmy lay upon the flat of his back assuring the doctor that "this time fur thrue, he was a-dyin' fur shure."

No reasoning had any effect in convincing him to the contrary, no assurances seemed to quiet him, his time had certainly come, and said he, "If yez would only bring to mi bidside mi ould father and mither to recave mi blessin', I'd die contint, be jabers."

Assuring him that if it were possible we would gladly do it, but that as his father and mother were in Ireland, we did not see how it could be done, he declared between the paroxysms of retching that "say-sickness was hilth compared to the bastely sufferin' that he was goin' thro' wid," and said he, "Docther, I'd die contint, if ye'd till me the cause ov it."

To which request the doctor gravely and unhesitatingly responded, that his sickness was "undoubtedly owing to the malarious results superinduced by too frequent and undue exposure to the deleterious effects of the Hesperian ether while in an unacclimated physical condition."

"Howly mother," said Jimmy — retch — "is all — retch — that — retch — the matther wid me? — retch — Thin

I'll — retch — die fur shure — retch — fur I can't live wid all that — retch — in me constitootion — retch — I'll not survive — retch — an hour."

Some time after the most violent of Jimmy's paroxysms had subsided, we left him, quite well satisfied that for the night, at least, we had reason to apprehend no further trouble from him.

Upon turning our attention to old Mr. Stewart, whom we found still sleeping quietly, the doctor remarked that sleep would do him more good than any medicine; for after the terrible shock his nervous system had sustained, it was very probable that at his advanced age he would never fully rally, but long before he could by any possibility reach his old Missouri home, strangers' hands would have to perform the last sad offices that could be performed for the old man on earth.

A prediction that proved but too true, for in less than two weeks the old man's spirit went aloft, to join those of the dear ones that had gone before from the beautiful valley of the Colorado Chiquito.

CHAPTER XXX.

THE first faint streak of light in the eastern skies was heralding the approach of dawn, when my eyes chanced to fall upon a figure bowed down and dejected, as if by the accumulated weight of misfortune and grief, over the smouldering embers of our dying camp-fire. So still, motionless, and white did it seem in the gray light of the morning, that I could scarcely realize it to be a breathing object endowed with life, but almost fancied that it had been fashioned from pure white marble by the afreets in a single night, and placed in our camp that it might serve as a crowning surprise on this, the morning of our departure from a country which, for so many thousand years, Nature had reserved as the theatre in which to erect the most singular and stupendous of her many eccentric architectural designs.

Rousing myself by an effort from the dreamy, unconscious state in which I was lying, I was soon aware that it was the form of Mr. Stewart, sitting bare-headed and in his shirt-sleeves, and looking, in the pale morning light, far more wan and sad than ever before, as he vainly strove to obtain some heat from the warm ashes over which he was bending.

Knowing that exposure to the damp, chill air of the early morning would be anything but beneficial to him in his weak physical and mental condition, I quietly rose, and while replenishing the fire, ventured to suggest that he should try and obtain a little more rest, as we were intending to start in a few hours for the Rio Grande, and the fatigue incident to the journey might prove too much for him without a proper amount of sleep.

'Journey? journey?'' said the old man, looking up in a bewildered manner; ''they have gone on a long journey, and they sleep, but I can't.'' Taking from his pocket the little box he had brought with him from the valley of the Chiquito, he said, as he opened it, ''Can you see there a wife and eight children? Yet they are all there; to me they look like desolation.''

I endeavored to cheer him by assuring him that he was among friends who would see that he was comfortably provided for, and who would not leave him until they had procured transportation for him across the plains as far as Westport in Missouri, which was scarcely a day's journey from his old home. He interrupted me by declaring that he had no home, no friends, — nothing but ashes.

Referring to the son whom he had started to join in California, I asked if he would like to go to him. "Yes," said the old man, brightening up, "can you send me to Parley?" I promised him that if, upon reaching the Rio Grande, he should still desire to do so, I would take him with us to La Mesilla, and send him through to Los Angeles by the overland mail, as soon as the doctor should pronounce him able to endure the fatigue of the journey. This promise seemed to afford him so much comfort, that he permitted me to throw a blanket over his shoulders to protect him from the damp air.

After a little further conversation, I left him, and proceeded to wake the doctor, with whom I paid Jimmy a morning visit. We found him fast asleep, and looking like anything but the fresh, ruddy-cheeked Irish boy of the week before. Perhaps the doctor and myself both experienced some compunctious throbs at the sight of his pale face and sunken eyes, but they were speedily dissipated by the reflection that we had used our best endeavors to put that "tartar" where it would do the most good, and this thought went far towards quieting any twinges of remorse that assailed us.

In an hour we had completed all our arrangements for an early start. Before breakfast was over, our old friend the cacique made his appearance in camp with a couple of attendants, who brought with them a fine fat lamb nicely dressed, together with a generous supply of fresh vegetables for our trip, which the old man begged us to accept, with his best wishes for a safe and pleasant journey.

As we had been told of some singular ruins that existed on the very top of El Moro, we desired to take an early start in order to visit them. The cacique informed us that they were so ancient the Zunis knew no tradition concerning them.

It was about eight o'clock when we shook hands with the cacique, and bade him adieu, reluctantly turning our backs upon Zuni, and its kind, generous, and hospitable governor.

In consideration of Jimmy's recent illness, he was permitted to get into the wagon, and to ride with Mr. Stewart, while the doctor and myself mounted our mules, and followed Don Rafael, who was already some distance on the road. Indeed, we were very glad, by making this concession to Jimmy, to have him leave Zuni, and its many charming attractions, without causing us any further trouble, or even entering a protest against our so ruthlessly tearing him away from the "objict ov his affictions."

We had been some hours on the road before Jimmy

ventured a word; then he asked Dr. Parker if he thought it would "be a lang time intirely befoore he recivered frum thi thryin' ordael he'd bin passin' thru wid so racently?"

The doctor assured him that a day or two would put him all right.

"Aal right in a day or two," responded Jimmy; "don't I kno' that thi intire cauz ov mi sickness wuz thi thort ov bein' partid frum thi objict ov mi affictions, an' thi attimpt to bring mi mind to the siperation? It's a heart-rindin' thing, docther, fur a mon wid all the sinsible, dilikit, and complaycated falins like miself, to part wid two ov the swatest, tinderist craythurs in thi world, in thi thryin' manner that's bruk mi heart intirely," to which statement the doctor's only reply, as he rode away from the wagon, was, "You're a fool, Jimmy, and I don't want to hear any more on the subject."

Foiled in his attempt to draw the doctor into a discussion of the matter which lay so near his heart, Jimmy turned to Mr. Stewart, and for the next hour regaled him with a lengthy account of the "thrials an' sufferin's ov two fond hearts," to which dissertation the old man apparently paid but little attention, and Jimmy was afterwards heard to remark, that he "detisted a mon who couldn't apprayciate the thrials and throbles ov another person who suffered aiqually wid himsilf."

It was some time after we had forded the Rio de Zuni, and while we were threading the little cañon of black metamorphic rock through which it ran, that we heard the sharp ring of Don Rafael's rifle, and in a short time we saw him coming towards us, bearing before him upon his saddle one of the finest specimens of the wild turkey I ever saw; its plumage was perfectly magnificent, and its body as fat as the pine buds could make it. The exclamations of delight at sight of this beautiful bird caused Jimmy to slip from his seat in the wagon, and before we were aware of his presence he was by our side, and saluted us with the remark, by way of reply to the unqualified admiration with which both the doctor and myself were regarding it, "It may be a foine bird fur this counthry; but bedad, in ould Ireland, in thi County Cork, they have wild tarkeys ez big ez two ov 'im."

While Jimmy was engaged in this rhapsody upon the wild turkeys of "ould Ireland," I dismounted, and telling him to take charge of my mule, took a seat in the wagon by the side of Mr. Stewart. Jimmy was evidently much disconcerted at this arrangement, and gave me a look so full of sorrow and disappointment that I was balf tempted to abdicate in his favor, but consideration for the poor old man at my side decided me to remain where I was, and thus give him a respite from the volubility of Jimmy's tongue.

It was nearly half-past three o'clock in the afternoon before we arrived in the shadow of El Moro; and here we made our camp in close proximity to the beautiful spring which I have described in a previous chapter, and beneath the shade of the giant pines and cedars that for so many years had sung their mournful requiem for the departed glories that formerly crowned the summit of this mighty rock.

Don Rafael immediately started to ascertain if any path or means of ascent to the top of the rock could be found, while the doctor and myself prepared for the undertaking, leaving Jimmy and Mr. Stewart to get supper and protect the camp during our absence. Our guide soon returned, and reported that on the eastern side of the rock he had found a very narrow, but he thought accessible path or escarpment which led to the top, though he much doubted if with my broken arm I should be able to accomplish it. The doctor expressed himself favorable to my making the attempt, however, and we started, notwithstanding the fact that I had solemnly promised myself at Zuni to abandon all attempts at ascending until I could learn to descend with some degree of propriety.

The path was very steep, and exceedingly slippery, but after half an hour's hard toil we arrived upon the summit of El Moro. Here our eyes were regaled by a sight which repaid us for the labor and fatigue of the ascent.

To the north and southeast, stretching into illimitable space, lay the magnificent Sierra Madre range, its base effectually concealed by a long line of foliage, and surmounted by snow-clad peaks, that seemed to resemble fleecy clouds reposing upon lofty, rocky islands which rose from out a sea whose dark-green waves, gracefully undulated by the summer breeze, appeared to lovingly embrace and kiss their rugged sides as they stretched far away in the distance. To the south, extending as far as the eye could reach, peaks, mounds, and mesas rose one above the other, over which the beautiful purple haze had thrown a veil so filmy and light, that while it toned down and tried to conceal the rugged barrenness of the country, clothing it with an indescribable charm and nameless beauty, it magnified and brought into bold relief every cañon, every gorge, every rocky ridge, in delightful contrast to which appeared here and there charming bits of prairie, their bright green surface dotted with the sombre foliage of magnificent cedars and spreading oaks.

To the west stretched an unbroken line of high cliffs, elevated mesas, volcanic peaks, and desert solitudes, over which the foot of civilized man never yet trod, while occasionally could be seen the grayish-white surface of an alkali plain, upon some *playa* of which, the descending sun cast its glittering light, reflecting back its rays with a faithfulness and intensity that made it resemble a huge mirror quietly reposing in its rough setting, or some silvery lake whose waters were undisturbed by a single ripple; the whole scene forming a picture never to be forgotten.

After admiring for a time the beautiful view around us, we commenced our search for the ruins upon this aerial elevation. The top of the rock itself we found an almost flat surface, upon which lofty pines and cedars were growing, some of them centuries old. The ruins were discovered after a little search, near the southern portion of the mesa; and judging from their extent and general character, they once formed the home of a large and industrious population.

There are two distinct sets of these ruins existing here, standing about a quarter of a mile from each other, and separated by a large fissure or cañon in the rock itself. These towns had evidently once been precisely alike, showing now the same form, as well as construction and material used. Their sides conform as nearly as possible to the four cardinal points, and are in the form of a rectangle three hundred and twenty feet in length, with two sets of rooms on three sides of the rectangle, and were evidently three stories high.

The walls are faced with a hard, close-grained, gray stone, varying in thickness from three to eight inches, and about twelve inches in length; the back or filling being a kind of rubble masonry, strongly cemented with mud mortar.

The general style of the masonry is similar to that found in the ruins of the pueblo Pintado, although they lack much of the finish and general beauty of detail ascribed to those ruins. I should imagine that there could be hardly an existing doubt but that they were erected by the same people and about the same time as those found in the Cañon de Chaco.

The growing lateness of the hour warned us that we had but little time to spare for further explorations if we would reach the plains below us that night, and neither of us had any particular fancy to spend the night on the top of El Moro.

Before leaving, however, we found some very pretty spec-

A DRINKING VESSEL FROM ZUNI.

imens of pottery-ware, beautifully painted, and entirely different in style and color from anything we had yet seen. One thing that struck both the doctor and myself as being particularly worthy of note in connection with these ruins, was the immense quantity of broken pottery we found here. The earthen-ware from a dozen pueblos seemed to have been collected at this point and broken, there being huge piles of it scattered over the mesa, in proximity to these ruins.

Of the many questions that this sight suggested, not one could we answer in a manner satisfactory to ourselves. What could have induced this people to have sought so lofty and almost inaccessible a site for their town? How did they procure water, and could they have depended entirely upon the rain for their supply? From whence came the large quantity of broken pottery with which the ground is strewn in all directions, and for what purpose was it thus broken? Who should answer these and many other questions that suggested themselves?

Humboldt, in his celebrated "Essays on New Spain," locates the residence of the Aztecs during the twelfth century as being "between the thirty-fifth and thirty-seventh parallels north latitude, and the one hundred and ninth and one hundred and twelfth degrees west longitude." If this location is correct, all doubt as to the builders of these ruins is at an end In any event they discover, not only in design and material used, but also in their superior workmanship, a style of architecture far beyond the capacity of the present inhabitants of New Mexico, either Indian or Mexican.

Gregg, who was the first to call attention to these ruins, in his work on "The Commerce of the Prairies," refers to the ruins of the Casas Grandes near the Gila, and to those of the Cañon de Chaco and Rio de Chelly, as being the work of one people; boldly announcing that the assertions of the historian Claverigo are correct when he says that "all the ruins existing in New Mexico and Arizona are of undoubted Aztec origin."

On the other hand, Prescott, in his "Conquest of Mexico," says, "It is true that these remains discover a race of men superior to the natives of New Mexico of the present day, but where are the evidences of the very high stage of civilization to which the Aztecs are said, by historians, to have obtained in Anahacu? Where are the evidences of a mechanical knowledge equal to that which must have been exercised in the construction of the temple of Xochicalco, or the palaces of Tescotzinco, and the colossal calendar stone in the capital?"

In a word, Prescott seems to think that all of these ruins are of Toltec rather than Aztec origin, or are the work of their contemporaries, the Tezcucans.

Professor Bell, an English writer, who travelled through a portion of this country, in his work on "North America," devotes considerable space, and discusses to some length the question as to who were the builders of these ruins. He considers the town-building Indians as the skirmish line of the Aztec race when it was united and in the full plenitude of its power. He says: "The rich bottom-lands of the Gila were occupied and placed under irrigation; the valley of the Rio Verde, Salinas, and other streams, were taken possession of, and the Apaches driven into the mountains; these savages were undoubtedly driven into the mountains by the Aztecs as barbarous hordes, whom they found it impossible to subdue, who continually harassed them and obliged them to invent means to protect their settlements against surprise; thus they introduced the art of building houses of stone and adobe; they chose the most commanding positions upon the summits of the mesas, overlooking large tracts of fertile bottom-lands, and added story to story in such a manner that a few resolute defenders could keep almost any number of assailants at bay.''

He thinks that these town-builders gradually pushed their way north, until they were stopped by the immense cañons of the Colorado and Flax (Colorado Chiquito) Rivers, thence striking east they established the kingdom of Cibola, and pushing still farther into the wilderness of what now is the Navajoe country, they built the large towns in the Cañon de Chaco, and in the valley of the Rio de Chelly, and then by following up the head-waters of the San Juan, finally came to the beautiful valley of the Rio Grande.

Here they found such unusual facilities for their settlements, that they crowded in, in great numbers, gradually working their way down from the north, until the valley became so densely populated that they found it no longer necessary to live in fortified towns for mutual protection.

If this be the correct theory, the fact that no such struc-

A PUEBLO RESTORED BY LIEUT. SIMPSON.

tures as we have described are to be found in the valley of the Rio Grande, is thus easily accounted for.

The Abbé Domenech is of the opinion that many of these ruins show an undoubted Toltec origin, and that they were built before the invasion of their land, some time about the twelfth century. He says:—

"All these towns are so ancient that no Indian traditions of the present races make any mention of them. The banks of the Rio Verde and Salinas abound in ruins of stone dwellings, and fortifications which certainly belong to a more civilized people than the Indians of New Mexico. They are found in the most fertile valleys, where traces of former cultivation and of immense canals for artificial irrigation are visible. The solidly-built walls of these structures are twenty or thirty yards in length, by forty or fifty feet in height; few of the houses are less than three stories, while all contain small openings for doors and windows, as well as loopholes for defence from attacks."

His theory in relation to the disappearance of the immense population that formerly inhabited the country is, that it was owing in a great degree to a wonderful change in the configuration of the soil; moist and fertile valleys becoming barren solitudes, thus forcing the inhabitants to emigrate to other regions.

After indulging in many theories and much speculation regarding these wonderful ruins stretching over the vast extent of country, from the Cañon de Chaco on the north, to the Casas Grandes in Chihuahua, on the south, the Abbé says:—

"These vast monuments of New Mexico and Arizona are known to but few travellers; consequently, but few writers have speculated about their origin. Certain it is that all the pueblos of this wilderness are of an incontestable, homogeneous character; they are the work of a great people, of an intelligent nation, whose civilization was far superior to that of the actual tribes. But the question is, what became of this vast population who have left the land covered with such numerous and wonderful constructions?

"It is known that all agglomerations of men and families, on settling in a new land, build their dwellings in wooded parts, or near streams, in order to ensure these indispensable elements. Many of this population were suddenly deprived of wood and water.

"Perpetual droughts followed the clearing of the woods, compelling the inhabitants of high plateaus to emigrate into the plains; when rain failed, the wells and cisterns dried up, and the horrors of thirst drove the people from their abodes. Both rivers and their sources dried up. I have known a multitude of rivers in both Texas and Arizona which have ceased to flow; some for centuries, others only within a few years, and the banks formerly gay with verdure, plants, flowers, and trees, have now disappeared under heaps of sand,

and present a scene of desolation. The springs and rivers of the plains always flow over a pebbly bed, never over a muddy one; the waters are capricious, and often intermittent, appearing and disappearing from the soil, to appear and lose themselves again; many alter their course, or cease to flow altogether, while others suddenly rise in the midst of a desert land.

"On the other hand, the soil of these regions is often covered with agate, jasper, chalcedony, petrified trees, and masses of arenaceous lava, which, descending from the hills, absorb the water of creeks and their sources, fill up the beds of streams, and render lands barren and dry which at one time were watered and fertile.

"When these phenomena take place, the people that dwell in the country are naturally compelled to flee from these newly-made deserts, which become the abodes of sickness, famine, and death, and go to seek a more favored land. These compulsory emigrations must have been frequent, to judge from the traces the population have left behind, notwithstanding the ranks of the emigrants must have been fearfully thinned by exposure, hardships, and misery.

"If to all these natural causes of dissolution are added intestine war, the difficulty of forming new establishments, the decline of Montezuma's dominion, and its complete annihilation under the Spanish sway, it does not appear necessary to invent a different nation to account for the works of art and civilization of which the remains cover these solitudes of America, merely because their successors have less genius, energy, or enterprise.

"The Zunis and other tribes still dwell in pueblos similar to those we have described; and it is probable that to their ancestors the construction of these gigantic edifices ought to be attributed."

By the extracts here given, it will be seen that the origin of these extensive and really wonderful ruins found scattered broadcast, as it were, throughout this most marvellous country, is still a question of much doubt. No data exists among the archives of New Mexico calculated to throw any light upon the subject; all the records of the Territory preceding the year 1680 were destroyed by the Indians in their successful insurrection against the conquerors in that year; and it was not until 1695, that the Spaniards again occupied the country, although in 1692 Curro Diego de Bargas Zapata managed with a large force to penetrate as far as the pueblo of Zuni, but finding the Indians too numerous for him to retain possession of it, was obliged to again return to El Paso.

During my residence in the Territory, I spent much time in endeavoring to ascertain something more definite concerning the builders of these ruins and their fate than was afforded by the very meagre knowledge to be derived from people who were residents of the Territory; but so few persons had ever visited them, or cared to brave the dangers naturally following an attempt to penetrate into the home of the barbarous tribes who roam over this immense range of territory, together with the fact that there is absolutely no scrap of written history to be found in existence, previous to the year 1680, made my attempts quite futile.

The whole subject is shrouded in an impenetrable veil of mystery, although upon an examination of the ruins themselves, I became fully convinced that they were of undoubted Aztec origin. There is but little question that those found upon the Gila, and upon the Casas Grandes, in Chihuahua, are more ancient than the others described in this work, and were probably erected by the Toltecs or their contemporaries. This opinion was founded more upon conjecture and speculation than upon any tangible proofs which the examination afforded; nor have I ever, since my return, learned anything to cause me to change the opinion then formed. There they stand, magnificent, though decaying monuments of the energy, skill, and civilization of a mighty people who flourished but a few hundred years since, yet have now no history save the crumbling evidences of their works, to tell us of their rise and fall.

Does not the sad fate of these nations furnish us who to-day journey over the deserts which their civilization and industry caused to "blossom as the rose," ample material for reflection?

CHAPTER XXXI.

THE next morning, just as the glorious beams of the rising sun were gilding the lofty turrets of El Moro, we resumed our journey towards La Mesilla.

Emerging from its beautiful valley, we commenced the slow and laborious ascent of the western slope of the Sierra Madre range. For miles our road lay through a thick growth of stunted pines and cedars, until we finally reached the summit of the mountain range. Here we could but pause for a few minutes, to view the magnificent prospect presented from the lofty elevation of the Navajoe Pass; and then, urging our animals rapidly forward, we commenced the descent of the eastern slope, in hopes to reach the cool, sparkling waters of the Agua Frio * in season to make its banks our camping-place for the night. We were some five miles distant from our old camping-ground, when Don Rafael proposed that he should make a circuit through the forest in search of game, and join us after we should have arrived in camp. We willingly assented to his proposition, and he soon disappeared among the thick growth of pines at our left, while we drove on, reaching the camping-ground about an hour before sunset.

We had scarcely arrived when, scanning the horizon with my field-glass, I discovered a horseman toiling wearily up the steep acclivity in the direction of our camp. I watched him with some curiosity, for a stranger travelling alone was an anomaly rarely seen in that country. After satisfying myself that he was journeying in a direction that would bring him to our camp, I ordered Jimmy to prepare supper for another, informing the doctor that we should soon have company for the night. This information caused Jimmy to loudly protest against "paoples goin' a-visitin' in sich a God-forsaken counthry as that widout givin' warnin' ov their comin' at all, at all!"

The stranger seemed to be carelessly riding along, until he caught sight of the smoke from our camp-fire; then, pausing a few moments to settle any doubt which its appearance might have suggested, he suddenly put spurs to his horse

* Sometimes called "Agua Azul," or "Blue Water."

and galloped rapidly towards us. As he approached, we had an opportunity to note his *personnel.*

He was a large, powerfully-built man, about forty years old; his long black hair hung low upon his broad and massive shoulders; a full, brown beard, keen, black eyes, and an open, generous countenance, were the distinguishing characteristics of his features. He was dressed in a full suit of buckskin, gayly fringed and ornamented, which proclaimed him to be a hunter or scout; around his waist was a United States cavalry belt, from which protruded the handles of a pair of navy revolvers, as well as that of a huge hunting-knife of the "Jim Bowie" pattern; balanced exactly across the pommel of his Mexican saddle was a superb Kentucky rifle, so perfectly poised that it seemed as though a breath of wind might displace it. He was mounted upon a magnificent black stallion, whose long silky mane and tail at once attracted Jimmy's attention, and he informed Mr. Stewart that the horse looked like the horses of "ould Ireland more'n anything he'd seen since he'd been in thi counthry."

Riding up to the spot where we were standing, the stranger courteously bade us "Good-evening," and carelessly throwing one leg over the pommel of his saddle, said, in answer to the invitation to share our camp, "Wall, yes, strangers, I'll jest do that, because five is better nor one under some circumstances, and this is one off 'em. I struck the fresh trail of Apaches down below this mornin', and

I've been ridin' Major here pretty lively to git up through the pass yonder before 'em, for they're pinted this way. I reckon you'll be pretty sure to see 'em along here if you don't tell that Irishman o' yourn, to put out his fire there."

Unsaddling his horse, and carefully tying him with our

GROUP OF APACHES.

animals to the wagon, he briefly informed us that he was one of Old Bonneville's* scouts, and was on his way to the pueblo, to see if the Zunis could be induced to join the

* Referring to Colonel Bonneville, U. S. A., at that time in command of the Military Department of New Mexico.

United States forces in a campaign against the Navajoes, who of late had made themselves very troublesome to the settlers on the Rio Grande by their depredations. Early that morning he had come upon a fresh trail of what he supposed to be Coytero Apaches, which he had followed far enough to ascertain that its direction led to this pass, through which they must cross the Sierra Madre range; but he reckoned that "five Americans, even if one of 'em was an Irishman, was enough to whip the whole party."

The news which the scout brought, unpleasant though it was, produced a remarkable effect upon Mr. Stewart: from a listless, feeble old man, with one foot almost in the grave, he suddenly became young once more; and his quick step, the firm intonation of his voice, and his flashing eye seemed to speak as plainly as words could say, that in the event of a fight, he would prove a most valuable ally.

Borrowing the doctor's rifle, he petted and caressed it as he would a child, lavishing the most endearing epithets upon it, and hugging it fondly to his bosom. So singular were his actions that they attracted the attention of the scout, who viewed with so much curiosity his manner that I briefly explained to him the circumstances attending Mr. Stewart's presence in our camp.

"The old man's jest achin' for a fight; and he'll have it, too, as sure's my name's Sam Bean," said the scout. "They're plucky cusses; if there's a few scalps to be made out of it, them Apaches — but we kin giv' the red devils as good a lickin' here, as well — holloa! — there comes a Mexican, by thunder!" said he, abruptly breaking off from his remarks, as his quick eye detected Don Rafael approaching in the distance.

Upon explaining to him that it was our guide, Don Rafael, he exclaimed, "What, Rafael Orrantia from Albuquerque; he's a good man — worth a dozen common Mexicans anywhere you can put him; he'll fight Injuns like the devil, with only half a show." Just at this point Don Rafael rode up, and the greeting between the two was a most cordial one. I briefly informed him of the news Sam had brought, and without a moment's hesitation, he remarked, "We'd best be prepared for them."

We hastily partook of our supper, paying no attention to Jimmy's remarks relative to having no "hot wather to wash the dishes in," or at his grumbling concerning "min's aitin', an' Injuns all round 'em," until the scout, turning to him, exclaimed, "Shet yer yawp, you infernal red-mouthed Irishman, or I'll let daylight through that thick skull o' yourn in jest two minutes."

This outbreak so surprised and confounded Jimmy that he scarcely spoke for an hour, meekly performing his duties about the camp, and contenting himself with casting furtive and by no means loving glances at Sam, who was too busy conversing with Don Rafael to notice him.

By this time, twilight had faded into darkness; not a star was to be seen in the heavens, which seemed to be covered with a thick veil of murky clouds; so intense was the darkness, that we could scarcely distinguish objects in camp only a few feet distant. Upon going to the spot where Mr. Stewart was sitting, I found him in a state of the greatest excitement, with his head inclined forward as if to catch the first sound that should indicate the coming of the Indians. The nature of the man seemed entirely changed by the prospect of an opportunity to avenge the horrible massacre of his family. He seemed to have forgotten everything save a desire for revenge; and the only reply I could obtain to my questions was, "Let 'em come, I'm waiting for 'em."

Every precaution had been taken to give the Indians a fitting reception: our animals were securely fastened to the wagon, from which the cover had been removed lest its white surface should betray our position; our rifles had been carefully examined, revolvers reloaded, belts filled with cartridges, and there seemed to be nothing now to do but await their approach.

The deathlike stillness which prevailed was unbroken save by the murmur of the little stream as it peacefully meandered through its bed of lava, or by the uneasy tramp of our animals; when suddenly Mr. Stewart, who had been peering out into the darkness, raised his rifle to his shoulder and fired. Before the smoke had cleared away from the muzzle, he dropped the breech to the ground, exclaiming, "There's one devil gone, any way."

"What do you mean, you old fool, you, shooting like that? If you don't care a dern for your old scalp, there may be men here as does for ther'n," said the scout, who with Don Rafael, as the click of the lock fell upon their ears, sprang forward in a vain endeavor to prevent the old man from firing.

"I killed him," said Mr. Stewart, curtly.

"Killed who? What do you mean?" asked the scout.

"The Indian there."

"There warn't no Injun there; and if there had have been, it stands to reason you couldn't have seen him, it's so all-fired dark."

"But I did see him, and shot him," said Mr. Stewart. "Come with me, and see." And the two disappeared in the darkness.

They returned in a few moments, Mr. Stewart bringing with him the fresh, bleeding scalp of an Indian, which, after presenting it for our examination, he coolly proceeded to fasten to his belt.

"He hed a bead on that feller, sure," said Sam. "Thunder, but his eyes are keen, though. Why, I couldn't see nothin' out there, and Sam Bean's eyes hain't no slouch nother, on the plains. The old man went straight to the spot, not more'n thirty feet off, and, borrerin' my knife, afore

I knowed what he was a doin' on he had the red devil's scalp a holdin' it up in my face; tain't no Christian way o' fightin', though I don't blame the old man, for he's had troubles enuf with them infernal cusses to provoke a saint! That feller was a scout, I reckon, and he'd got pretty close to head-quarters, tew; we'd better be on the lookout, for the sound of that rifle'll bring 'em down on us like wolves on a carcass, and no knowin' how close they may be now."

Scarcely had the words been spoken when a yell as though from a thousand demons filled the air, and a shower of arrows fell around us; fortunately, however, doing no harm. We returned their fire with a volley from five good rifles, but in the almost Stygian darkness which prevailed, we could not tell whether our shots were effective or otherwise. Another shower of arrows, a confused trampling of horses' feet mingled with yells and shouts, a volley from our revolvers, and then a moment's quiet. I hastily cast my eyes around, and saw all of our party save Mr. Stewart and Jimmy. Another volley of arrows, and again the fearful war-whoop resounded in our ears.

"All right, they fired too much up," said Don Rafael, just as the quick, sharp ring of a rifle far in advance of us was heard, followed by one, two, three shots from a revolver.

"It's the old man and the Irishman gone right in among 'em, by thunder!" said the scout. Again their yells and shouts of defiance filled the air, accompanied by a shower of arrows, immediately followed by answering shots from our revolvers, together with the braying of mules and the neighing of horses, who seemed to have combined together in their frantic efforts to break loose. Indeed, they succeeded in dragging the wagon some little distance, which had the effect of causing most lusty cries for "Hilp! Hilp!" to proceed from the confused mass of legs that surrounded it. Again a voice which we recognized as Jimmy's, was heard calling, "Hilp, in thi name ov thi Blissed Vargin, hilp, for the mules are a-kickin' me to dith."

The scout, turning towards him, said, in a low voice, "Sarves yer right, yer blasted fool; yer ought to be kicked to death by mules; an' ef yer so much ez peep once more, I'll blow yer through, sure's my name's Sam Bean."

Again the ring of a rifle far in advance sounded clear and sharp on the night air, followed by a shriek, which plainly told that it had not been fired in vain; a solitary shot from a revolver, and then all was silent. Even Jimmy and the mules were quiet, and after a while we ventured to converse in low tones, wondering if the Indians had gone, or were only gathering fresh courage to make a more determined and desperate attack.

Thus the long and weary hours of the night passed. No sleep; no rest; nothing but anxiety and suspense. How impatiently we waited for the morning light; how many times we asked one another, what it would reveal! Were the Indians also waiting for the dawn before again venturing to attack us, or were they gone?

Reader, God grant that you may never know the horrors of a suspense like ours that night. Morning came at last, and with it Mr. Stewart, quite as feeble, and looking much older than we had ever seen him before. His step was the tottering step of age; his eye no longer flashed with suppressed fire; he came slowly towards us, as though he had no longer object or aim in life; in one hand he carried his rifle, and from the other dangled five ghastly, bleeding scalps, the result of his endeavors to avenge his wrongs. Seating himself upon the ground, in weak and trembling tones, he said: "That's all I could get; take care of 'em for me;" nor did we ever obtain further information relative to his experience that night.

An examination revealed the fact that two of our animals had been slightly wounded by arrows, while in the brush around our camp we found seven dead bodies and three horses.

Breakfast over, Sam took his departure for Zuni, wishing us "Good luck," as carelessly as though there had been no Indians within a hundred miles of him, and none the worse for the adventures of the night.

His departure was regretted by us all save Jimmy, who, shaking his head in a most significant manner as Sam disappeared in the distance, remarked, "It is a good thing the mon lift as he did, fur I was detarmined to hev a sittlemint wid him fur the disrespictful manner he spoke ter me in yisterday night."

An hour later we broke camp, and started once again upon the road. After five days of tedious and uneventful journeying we at last reached the high swell of land that marks the descent to the valley of the Rio Bravo del Norte.* Arriving upon the summit, we beheld spread out at our very feet the beautiful and fertile valley of the Bravo, with its broad and placid river rolling on and rolling ever, until it finds its final resting-place in the bosom of the vast Atlantic; its southerly course was plainly traceable for a score or more of miles, by the magnificent growth of verdure that skirted its banks, occasionally relieved by the sight of some of the many towns or villages peeping out from among the green foliage, until the whole finally melted away in the indistinguishable purple haze which veiled the dim distance.

Way to the other side of the river rose the lofty peaks of the Sierra Blanca, partially concealed by fleecy clouds, while far to the north were to be seen the twin peaks of the Santa Fé range, their tall white heads towering towards heaven, as though striving to pierce the blue canopy which

*North of the 34th parallel N. Lat., the Rio Grande is called by all donizens of New Mexico the Rio Bravo del Norte, or, Brave River of the North.

covered them. Involuntarily we paused and gazed with rapturous delight upon the glorious sight before us, while we uttered a prayer of thankfulness at being once more permitted to view traces of civilization. Even Mr. Stewart's face lighted up with an expression of satisfaction, such as I had never seen upon it before, while Jimmy in his mad capers seemed almost wild with joy, as he boxed his patient mule's ears most soundly in his frantic efforts to make him appreciate the fact that it was the "States that wuz a lyin' before him, be gorra!"

A ride of ten miles is before us ere we shall reach the river's bank, and the sun is tinging with its crimson beauty the neat white houses, purple vineyards, and waving green corn-fields of Isletta by the time we reach our old camping-ground near the town.

Some time after the dim shades of twilight had settled over the vine-covered hills and peach-orchards of the town, the doctor and I discovered Jimmy, who had wandered some distance below the camp, standing upon the river's bank and engaged in shaking his brawny fists at its placid bosom, while he thus apostrophized its yellow, sandy waters: "Cawl that wather, will yez? It's nothin' but a strake ov saft mud that's pinethratin' thi landscape; dhirty mud, too, fit only for thim corn-aitin' Injuns wid their dirthy bazaque, to dhrink! I hain't afeared ov yez any more; yez scart me onct—"

Just at this moment, as we were effectually concealed from Jimmy's sight by the thick growth of willows which covered the river-bottom, the doctor permitted a long, low, wailing moan to escape his lips, as nearly as he could imitate the sound which Jimmy had once called my attention to, when encamped near the Carizo Spring. With a look of intense horror upon his face, and a yell that would have done credit to an Apache, he gave a tremendous leap, and with a "Howly murther, what the divil's that!" he disappeared very suddenly in the direction of camp, where I arrived in time to hear him caution poor old Mr. Stewart against "wandherin' away frum thi camp, ez there wuz painters in thim woods," pointing to the little copse of willows not more than five or six feet in height where we had been concealed, and at the same time informing him that "whin avenin' come," he "wuz goin' to take his goon and go a-hoontin'." I noticed, however, that Jimmy did not venture out of camp during the evening, and when he spread his blankets, it was beneath the wagon, a precaution which he said was taken for "protiction frum the avenin' air."

The next morning the doctor called my attention to the growing weakness and gradual decline of Mr. Stewart, remarking that if it were possible he would like to have the opinion of Dr. Cooper — the army surgeon stationed at Fort Craig, about eighty-five miles below us — upon his case. We determined therefore to follow the western bank of the Rio

Grande down to that place where we knew that a good ford existed, which would enable us to cross the river should we desire to do so.

It was at this place that Don Rafael was to leave us to return to his home in Albuquerque, and we parted from him with many regrets, and thoroughly convinced that Judge Baird's warm encomiums upon his honesty and ability had been richly deserved, for we had found him an intelligent, faithful, as well as honest guide, a *rara avis* in that country.

Our trip down the river was a most tedious one, as we were obliged to travel very slowly, accommodating our movements to Mr. Stewart's enfeebled condition; and not until the afternoon of the third day did we behold the welcome sight of the stars and stripes as they floated on the breeze from the staff in the parade-ground of the fort.

Here our hearts were saddened by hearing the opinion pronounced by Dr. Cooper, whose quick eye detected at a glance that Mr. Stewart was slowly dying, and that it would be extremely doubtful if he ever reached Mesilla alive.

Five days later, ere we had made ourselves comfortable at home, calmly and as peacefully as a child, the old man drew his last breath, happy in the thought and belief that he should cross the dark waters in safety, and join the loved ones on the other shore, whose loss he had so truly and faithfully mourned, and who had so recently preceded him to that brighter and better land "eternal in the heavens."

We buried him just outside the town, beneath the spreading branches of a beautiful American elm, and there his body rests to-day, as quietly as though we had been permitted to place it in consecrated ground.

The last sad offices performed, I wrote to the post-master at Los Angeles, requesting him to send me the address of one Parley Stewart, Jr., if he was to be found in that city or vicinity; and three weeks from the day that we buried Mr. Stewart, senior, upon the banks of the Rio Grande, I received a letter stating that his son had been living on, and was the owner of, a fine ranche about three miles from the city, but about two months before he had been brutally murdered by a couple of his Mexican herders with whom it was supposed he had had some difficulty, and to revenge either a real or fancied wrong, they had shot him in his own house. The letter further stated that he had left a handsome property, awaiting the claim of his relatives.

But where were they? The last one of Parley Stewart's family had undoubtedly passed away, for although every inquiry was made by me, as well as by the military authorities stationed in the Territory, we failed to obtain the slightest trace of the two girls who had so mysteriously disappeared at the time of the massacre. They either wandered away and died from exposure and starvation, or were captured by the Indians, and after being obliged to endure the most fiendish and brutal treatment, as well as terrible indignities, were cruelly and barbarously tortured to death. In either event, death must have been a most welcome relief from their sufferings.

Let us hope that this unfortunate family, whose history I have related in these chapters, have all crossed the deep waters in safety, and are, at last, reunited on that "shining shore," where partings are unknown, where the "wicked cease from troubling, and the weary are at rest."

But little more than two years after the incidents narrated in this work occurred, Mangus Colorado, the chief of all the Apaches, was invited to visit Fort McLane, a United States military post, near the head waters of the Rio Mimbres, for the purpose of making a treaty and receiving presents. He came with four sub-chiefs in all the pomp of savage royalty; gayly decorated with eagles' feathers and brass ornaments, and gaudily painted in vermilion and ochre.

Upon reaching the fort, the party were treacherously seized and imprisoned in the guard-house; during the night the sentry purposely unfastened their prison door, and as the chief and his companions were endeavoring to avail themselves of the means of escape thus voluntarily offered, they were deliberately shot down by the soldiers in the fort, who had been stationed for that purpose.

The base and treacherous cruelty of this act roused the whole Apache tribe to vengeance. My old friend and guide, Cochise, was elected principal chief, which position he held until his death in 1874.

It has been asserted, that, before accepting the mantle of Mangus Colorado, he was required to take an Indian oath, that, for every Apache so despicably murdered in Fort McLane, a hundred white men should die, — an oath which has been most religiously kept.

Acting under his directions, the Apaches immediately separated into small bands, rendezvousing in the most inaccessible portions of the almost impenetrable mountain fastnesses so peculiar to this portion of the country. From these "lairs" they swooped down upon travellers, or raided upon the settlers, killing, burning, and destroying, seemingly actuated by one motive, viz., the destruction of the entire white race.

It is a somewhat singular coincidence, that not alone Mangus Colorado, but his immediate predecessor, should have met his death through treachery on the part of Americans. Such is nevertheless the fact, and serves to account in some manner for the terrible revenge taken by the tribe subsequent to the cowardly murder at Fort McLane.

The circumstances were these: In the year 1837, the government of Chihuahua, in order to put a stop to Apache depredations in that state, issued what was called a *Proyecto de Guerra*,* fixing a scale of prices to be paid by the government for Apache scalps, also declaring that any booty taken

* Proclamation of war.

from the savages should become the property of the captors. As the Apaches at that time were supposed to possess large quantities of gold and silver, as well as spoils taken from the Mexicans, the proclamation excited the cupidity of several Americans residing in the State, who organized a company of some thirty persons, officered by and composed largely of their own nationality, who set out for the Apache country.

A few days after their departure, they came upon a *ranch-eria* of some fifty warriors, among whom was the famous old head chief, Juan José. Upon seeing the party approaching, Juan rode out to meet them, announcing, that, if they came with hostile intent, he and his warriors were ready to fight them. The leader of the party disclaimed any such intention, declaring that their object was a peaceful one, for purposes of trade only. Upon receiving this declaration, a friendly greeting was extended, and the warriors visited the Americans' camp, who had concealed in one of their wagons a small field-piece, loaded almost to the muzzle with chain and canister shot. After some time spent in talk, they brought forth a couple of bags of flour, which were placed within range of the cannon, and the Indians invited to help themselves.

While engaged in dividing the present, the gun was discharged, and a number of them killed. Before they could recover from the surprise occasioned by the attack, the Americans fell upon the remainder, and succeeded in massacring nearly the entire party, including Juan José.

The death of Mangus Colorado (the second head chief murdered by American treachery) seemed to concentrate upon the white race all the hatred in the Apaches' nature; and, although Cochise profited largely by the foul deed, all his former friendship became changed to the bitterest enmity, as though by the touch of an enchanter's wand, betraying until his death a hatred far surpassing any thing ever portrayed in fiction, fighting with a desperation and bravery, and torturing his victims with a vindictive cruelty, hitherto unknown in history.

Women whom he made captives were subjected to a fate worse than death; little children were spitted upon spears, and roasted over slow fires; men were hung by the heels, fires kindled beneath their heads, and pierced with arrows, gashed with knives, or the flesh cut from their bones while still living.

Cochise himself signalized his accession to office by one of the most daring and brutal murders ever committed before the eyes of United-States soldiers.

Information having reached Tucson, that he was encamped, with a small party of warriors, about forty miles below that place, an officer with thirty-five soldiers, an interpreter named Englehart, and the Indian agent, were sent out to visit the encampment, with instructions to ascertain, if possible, his destination and intentions.

It is said, that, before starting, Englehart observed that he "felt as though he was going to pay an old grudge for some one, and didn't half like the job."

No one thought any thing of the remark, however; and the meeting between the soldiers and the Indians was friendly, and lasted several hours. Cochise conversed affably through the interpreter, and made a most excellent impression upon all.

The interview being over, the parties mounted their horses, and shook hands in token of amity. As they were about to separate, Cochise suddenly leaned over in his saddle, seized Englehart by the collar, and pulled him off from the horse he was riding, over and across his own; and, with a yell of hatred and defiance, dashed furiously off toward the mountains, followed by his entire band. So unexpected was the attack, and so quickly had the movement been executed, that before the soldiers realized the situation, or the commanding officer had sufficiently recovered his presence of mind to order a charge, the fugitive had gained some distance. Englehart had been taken at a great disadvantage, but, determined to sell his life as dearly as possible, he made a desperate attempt to draw his revolver, and had almost succeeded in doing it, when Cochise, by main strength, drew him up in front of him in such a manner, that, in spite of the most determined resistance, he was able to stab him several times in the neck and back; then, although his horse was running over a broken and rocky country, he deliberately scalped his victim, and throwing the bleeding, mutilated body to the ground, flaunted the ghastly trophy he had secured in the very face of his pursuers, and with a shout of triumph and derision disappeared in one of the mountain defiles without the loss of a man.

A large reward was immediately offered for the capture of the murderer dead or alive; and a small army of frontiersmen, actuated as much by a desire for revenge as by a hope of obtaining the promised guerdon, took the field in pursuit of the daring murderer.

Cochise found no difficulty in evading their cleverly-laid schemes for his capture, continuing his work of rapine and murder so successfully, that the superstitious began to believe him protected by the foul fiend himself. The most expert marksmen, men whose rifles had never been known to miss before, shot wide of the mark when aimed point blank at Cochise; and some of the best scouts in the country did not hesitate to assert that "nothing but a silver bullet would ever kill him."

Most frontiersmen are advocates of the doctrine of destiny; and so generally was this assertion believed, that it was no unusual thing for "good marksmen" to refuse to fire at him.

Aware of the fact that our Government was engaged in a struggle for its own existence, and realizing that it must of necessity permit its frontiers to remain in a measure unprotected, he seized his advantage with a comprehension that was indeed surprising to all.

Shortly after the close of our Civil War, Brig.-Gen. George Crook was appointed to the command of the military department in Arizona, and immediately took the field in person against this most redoubtable chief, whose desperate daring, shrewd cunning, and diabolical cruelty, have fairly and honestly earned for him the reputation of being the bravest as well as most sagacious and barbarous Indian chief that has lived upon American soil within the past two centuries.

Although an experienced Indian fighter, Gen. Crook found it impossible to properly garrison, with the small force at his command, the vast extent of country over which the Apaches roamed; while the arid and barren nature of the soil, together with its peculiar configuration, enabled his wary adversary to render futile every aggressive movement against him. Gen. Crook persevered, however, in the face of the greatest difficulties, for years, resorting to every means in his power to rid the country of the scourge which for so many centuries had devastated its thriving settlements, ruined its industries, and depleted its population.

Cochise ever refused to entertain any proposition looking toward a cessation of hostilities; and it was only after long continued ill health and old age incapacitated him from longer leading his warriors in person, that he reluctantly assented to a peace, and, with the remnant of his band, submitted to be removed to a reservation selected for them in the southern portion of the Territory, where they remain to the present time, subdued but not conquered, a constant source of trouble to the Government, requiring the greatest vigilance to prevent them from forsaking their reservation, and continuing their raids in force, upon the people of the Territory as well as upon those of the Mexican States of Chihuahua and Sonora, that for so many years have been the scene of their frequent and successful forays.

It was in June, 1874, that Cochise died. He did not meet death upon the battlefield where he had so often sought it, surrounded by his trusty warriors, in the full possession of savage pride and barbarous authority; nor was the last sound that fell upon his ears the ringing war-whoop that had so often carried consternation and death to the hated white race; but shorn of strength and power, humiliated by defeat, crippled by old age, and racked by the torments of inflammatory rheumatism, he lay for months upon his couch of bear-skins, unable to move hand or foot; a prey to torture more acute than even his devilish ingenuity had ever devised for the scores of victims who had perished by his hand, and who he imagined, in his last moments, were standing beside him, and inflicting upon him the agonizing tortures he suffered.

Thus died, at the age of nearly seventy years, one of the most remarkable characters of modern times, whose name will be remembered with execrations in Arizona for the next century.

In bravery he had no equal, in strategy no superior; while in vindictiveness, barbarity, and cruelty his name will ever stand prominent among the long list of Indian chieftains whose bloody deeds blot the fair page of American history.

Well-authenticated documents in the possession of the War Department show the number of victims known to have perished by his individual hand, at the almost incredible number of a hundred and eight; of whom more than seventy were white persons, twenty-six Mexicans and half-breeds, and the remainder members of his own tribe.

The history of the Apache has for centuries been the same undeviating record of cruelty, rapine, and bloodshed, coupled with treachery, crafty dealing, and duplicity.

Our own government can affirm the truth of the words of the old Spanish historian, Miguel Venegas, who, in 1758, said of them, "These Apaches make treaties, but only for the amusement of breaking them when it suits their convenience."

Baron Humboldt in his "Essays of New Spain," published in 1803, also adds his testimony regarding them in these words: "Neither the soldiers stationed in the presidios, nor the monks posted in the neighboring missions, have been hitherto able to make the conquest over them."

Indeed, experience appears to have demonstrated that the

Apaches can neither be Christianized nor civilized. They are the only tribe who refused to receive the proffered cross from the hands of good old Father Kino in 1670, nor have they accepted it since that time; and I am confident their history will warrant the assertion, that, until they are completely exterminated, the fertile valleys of Arizona will never wave with golden grain, her beautiful uplands be covered with herds of lowing cattle, her vast alkali plains be utilized, her lofty mountain-peaks echo the hoarse whistle of the silver-smelting furnace, or the smoke ascend from the hearthstones of a happy, prosperous people.

Never, until then, will the great mineral wealth of the Territory be properly developed, her rocky fastnesses thoroughly explored, her rich gold-placers worked, and the precious stones that now lie unsought among the rough pebbles of her mountain streams be brought to yield their lustrous beauty for the adornment of her fair daughters.

When this has been accomplished, I have no doubt but Arizona will be found to be the very treasure-house of this great Republic.

After repeated failures, the friends of Arizona, in February, 1863, succeeded in securing the passage of a bill by Congress, separating it from New Mexico, and creating for it a distinct government. (See Appendix A.)

The following month President Lincoln appointed territorial officers; and on Dec. 29 of the same year the officials reached the Territory, and formally inaugurated the government at Navajoe Springs, forty miles west of the ancient pueblo of Zuni. (See Appendix B for list of officers.)

In July, 1864, an election was held for a delegate to Congress, and members of the Legislature; and, on the 26th of September following, that body convened at Prescott, a town just laid out at a point one hundred and fifty-five miles due east from the Colorado River.

The new Territory, embracing an area of 120,912 square miles (or 77,383,680 acres), was divided into four counties, which were named after the friendly tribes of Indians who resided within their respective limits; viz., Pimo, Yuna, Mohave, and Yavapai.

The preliminary steps having been taken, courts were organized, public buildings erected, schools established, and all the machinery of government put into successful operation.

Under the able direction of Gen. Crook, military posts for the protection of the inhabitants were judiciously located; and after a few years the greater portion of the Indians were collected upon reservations under government surveillance, thereby affording opportunity for exploration, and far greater advantages for ascertaining and developing the varied resources of the country than had heretofore been enjoyed.

Thus far, the explorations have been limited, revealing little that is new, although tending to show, by the most conclusive evidence, that nearly the whole area of the Territory was formerly settled by a vast population far advanced in civilization, who, like the early dwellers in New Mexico, have entirely disappeared, leaving behind them no written history.

Within the past few months, extensive ruins have been discovered in the Ancha Mountains, which are in a far better state of preservation than any previously known in the Territory; and the remains of several large arastras, found in their immediate vicinity, would seem to indicate that the inhabitants must have been familiar with the science of reducing silver ore.

Articles of painted pottery, knives of tempered copper, pipes, &c., have been found at a depth of more than a hundred and fifty feet beneath the surface of the earth; and upon the Rio Verde are immense rooms, excavated high up in its perpendicular banks of sandstone; in other portions of the Territory, rocks have been found covered with hieroglyphics, which have as yet been undeciphered.

It is to be hoped, that, when these vast ruins can be properly excavated, discoveries will be made that will throw more light upon their early history; and it would seem eminently proper that these explorations should be undertaken by the general Government, with a view to ascertaining the real facts concerning the early settlement of this portion of our country, which bears the most irrefragable proof of having been made more than a thousand years ago.

Should the reader ask upon what evidence we venture to make this assertion, we have only to carry him to the Moqui towns mentioned in a previous chapter, and bid him examine for himself the paths between the villages, worn deep into the solid rock by the moccasined feet of the inhabitants; then let him tell us, if he can, how many centuries have elapsed since these stony ways were first trodden by the foot of man.

Since the organization of the Territory, every year is adding valuable evidence relative to the immense mineral wealth of Arizona, and proving that the deposits of gold, silver, copper, and lead within her borders are unsurpassed in extent and richness by any in the known world. Post roads have been located, towns are springing up, new mines being discovered, and old ones re-opened. But the distance from any available market, together with the frequency of Indian outrages, tends in a great measure to check the flow of emigration to the Territory; thus the broad and fertile bottoms of the rivers, which, decades of years since, were under successful cultivation, are at the present time untilled; and lands that might be made to yield two crops of cereals in a year, or, if properly cultivated, bring forth fine crops of cotton, rice, and sugar-cane, are now barren plains, covered only with the suwarrow,* the amole,† the maguay,‡ or the mesquite.§

* Cerus Grande. † Soap-plant.

‡ American Aloe. § Gum-arabic tree.

This is particularly noticeable in the valleys of the Verde and Colorado Chiquito in Central Arizona, where tracts of valuable land are open to settlement at the present time (1876) under the homestead or pre-emption laws of the United States, offer rare opportunities for thousands of our citizens to secure homes in a territory where the climate, soil, mineral resources, and facilities for stock-raising cannot be surpassed by any other section of our country.

These lands are within a comparatively short distance of the seat of government, which has recently been located at Phœnix, a thriving town upon the Saline River, about twenty-five miles above its confluence with the Gila. Most of the supplies destined for use in the territory are obtained in eastern cities, and shipped to the terminus of the Kansas Pacific Railroad, thence by wagons, *via* Albuquerque, New Mexico.

Two transcontinental charters exist for railroads through the Territory; and it is confidently asserted that within the next five years, iron rails will span the territory from its eastern to its western boundary; until then the inhabitants must of necessity suffer the inconveniences and privations invariably attending all settlements in a new country. When Arizona can enjoy the benefits resulting from railroad facilities she will astonish the world by the variety and value of her productions.

And now, if the reader will pardon the digression, we will return to our old friend Jimmy, who, before we had been in Mesilla a week after our return from the "Bravo," appeared hat in hand at my door, and looking very foolish, asked for a "saycret interview." It was readily accorded, when he informed me that he was about to marry "a swate little gurrl he hed mit the day before, and sittle down permanently."

I ventured to suggest that a longer acquaintance might be desirable; but he answered my remonstrances by exclaiming, "Wait a while ago, and I'll bring her till yez see her fur yezsilf."

As in duty bound, I waited, and in a few minutes he returned, bringing with him as pretty a little black-eyed *señorita* as ever saw the dawn of her sixteenth summer; and then he asked, with a sly wink, "If yez was in moi place, would yez wait a while?" What should I have answered, gentle reader? To be sure, Juanita couldn't pronounce a word of English, nor could Jimmy speak an intelligible sentence of Spanish; but he thought "he cud do the motions powerful will," he said. So he married her that day, and immediately took up his abode in her mother's *jacal* upon the banks of the Acequia Madre, in close proximity to my own residence; and when I was leaving the country, a few months later, Jimmy informed me that he'd "always been moighty glad he spaked az he did, because you see, ef I'd hed ennybody forninst me, she tould me wid her own tongue, that she'd niver a thought o' the likes o' misilf." Five years later, as I was passing down Broadway, N.Y., one pleasant September morning, I met Jimmy face to face.

He was evidently delighted to see me, for he fairly whooped and danced with delight; his gyrations strongly resembling those indulged in by a band of Apache warriors, previous to seating themselves for a feast of mule-meat.

When I ventured to remind him that he was in the great city of Gotham, and that his actions were attracting the attention of the passers-by, he looked at the curious crowd that had gathered aronnd us, and said, "Will, ef it isn't custhomery to be glad to sae a mon, I'll be ez aisy ez I kin."

As soon as he would answer my questions, I learned that he expected to sail the following day for his old home in Ireland. I inquired for his wife, pretty little Juanita, and learned — Well, it was the old story of man's perfidy and woman's fickleness.

The next day I saw Jimmy on board the steamer, as happy as a boy could be, at the thought of returning to "ould Ireland;" and if any of my readers should ever chance to visit that "green isle of the sea," and pass through the parish of Bandon in the County of Cork, let them inquire for Jimmy Hurly, an honest blacksmith's son, and, my word for it, they will receive as warm a welcome as ever greeted stranger "on a foreign shore."

When the news of the firing on Sumter reached the quiet Valley of La Mesilla, Dr. Parker and myself decided to turn our faces eastward. Securing seats in one of Butterfield's overland coaches, a little more than two weeks saw us in the busy city of St. Louis in Missouri; and a few days later the doctor and myself parted, he going to his home in old Virginia, and I to mine among the sterile hills of New England.

I never saw him after we bade one another adieu at the old "Planters."

He had scarcely reached his home ere he was tendered an appointment as surgeon in the Confederate army, and three years later he met his fate during an engagement with our forces in Louisiana.

I learned of his death with sincere regret; for he was an honest man, a genial and pleasant companion, and a true friend. Would there were more like him!

And now, gentle reader, you and I will part.

If these pages have served to entertain as well as inform you, it is possible that we may some time meet again: if otherwise, I take you by the hand, with a HAIL AND FAREWELL.

THE END.

APPENDIX.

A.

THE ORGANIC ACT.

AN ACT to provide a Temporary Government for the Territory of Arizona, and for other Purposes.

Be it enacted by the Senate and House of Representatives of the United States of America, in Congress assembled: That all that part of the present Territory of New Mexico situate west of a line running due south from the point where the south-west corner of the Territory of Colorado joins the northern boundary of the Territory of New Mexico to the southern boundary line of said Territory of New Mexico, be, and the same is hereby, erected into a temporary government by the name of the Territory of Arizona: Provided, that nothing contained in the provisions of this act shall be construed to prohibit the Congress of the United States from dividing said Territory, or changing its boundaries in such manner, and at such time, as it may deem proper: Provided further, that said government shall be maintained and continued until such time as the people residing in said Territory shall, with the consent of Congress, form a State government, republican in form, as prescribed in the Constitution of the United

States, and apply for and obtain admission into the Union as a State, on an equal footing with the original States.

Section 2. And be it further enacted, that the government hereby authorized shall consist of an executive, legislative, and judicial power. The executive power shall be vested in a governor. The legislative power shall consist of a council of nine members, and a house of representatives of eighteen. The judicial power shall be vested in a supreme court, to consist of three judges, and such inferior courts as the legislative council may by law prescribe; there shall also be a secretary, a marshal, a district-attorney, and a surveyor-general for said Territory, who, together with the governor, and judges of the supreme court, shall be appointed by the president, by and with the advice and consent of the Senate; and the term of office for each, the manner of their appointment, and the powers, duties, and the compensation of the governor, legislative assembly, judges of the supreme court, secretary, marshal, district-attorney, and surveyor-general aforesaid, with their clerks, draughtsman, deputies, and sergeant-at-arms, shall be such as are conferred upon the same officers by the Act organizing the territorial government of New Mexico, which subordinate officers shall be appointed in the same manner, and not exceed in number those created by said act; and acts amendatory thereto, together with all legislative enactments of the Territory of New Mexico not inconsistent with the provisions of this act, are hereby extended to and continued in force in the said Territory of Arizona, until repealed or amended by future legislation: Provided, that no salary shall be due or paid the officers created by this act, until they have entered upon the duties of their respective offices within the said Territory.

Sect. 3. And be it further enacted, that there shall neither be slavery nor involuntary servitude in the said Territory, otherwise than in the punishment of crimes whereof the parties shall have been duly convicted ; and all acts and parts of acts, either of Congress, or of the Territory of New Mexico, establishing, regulating, or in any way recognizing the relation of master and slave in said Territory, are hereby repealed.

APPROVED Feb. 24, 1863.

B.

THE FIRST OFFICERS OF THE TERRITORY.

1863.

POSITION.	NAME.	WHERE FROM.	LOCATION.
Governor	JOHN N. GOODWIN........	Maine	Prescott.
Secretary..........	RICHARD C. MCCORMICK*.	New York...	"
Chief-Justice	WILLIAM F. TURNER	Iowa	"
Associate Justice....	WILLIAM T. HOWELL.....	Michigan	Tucson.
" "	JOSEPH P. ALLYN........	Connecticut..	La Paz.
District Attorney ...	ALMON GAGE............	New York ...	Prescott.
Surveyor-General ...	LEVI BASHFORD..........	Wisconsin ...	Tucson.
Marshal............	MILTON B. DUFFIELD.....	California ...	"
Supt. Indian Affairs.	CHARLES D. POSTON †	Kentucky ...	"

* Delegate representing Arizona in Congress at the present time.

† First Delegate to Congress, elected May 26, 1864.

By the Author of "Abroad Again."

OVER THE OCEAN;

OR, SIGHTS AND SCENES IN FOREIGN LANDS.

By CURTIS GUILD,

Author of "Abroad Again," and Editor of the *Boston Commercial Bulletin.*

ONE VOL., CROWN 8VO. PAPER, —; CLOTH, $2.50.

This book has not only become a favorite among the reading public, but is now generally accepted as one of the best guides to Europe ever published. "Whether describing Westminster Abbey, or York Minster, Stratford-upon-Avon, or the streets of London; the wonders of the Louvre, or the gayeties and glitter of Paris; the grandeur of the Alpine passes; the quaintness of old continental cities; experiences of post travel; the romantic beauties of the Italian lakes; the underground wonders of Adelsburg, or the aqueous highways of Venice; — the author aims to give many minute particulars, which foreign letter-writers deem of too little importance to mention, but which, nevertheless, are of great interest to the reader."

"A Close Observer of the Manners and Customs."

"The utmost that any European tourist can hope to do is to tell the old story in a somewhat fresh way, and Mr. Guild has succeeded, at many points of his book, in doing this. He goes over the beaten track of Ireland, Scotland, England, France, Germany, Austria, and Switzerland, with a visit to Venice and Florence, a close observer of the manners and customs of the natives, and with a Yankee capacity for learning their ways and tricks. 'Over the Ocean' will be a pleasant refresher to those who have gone before, and a valuable guide-book to those who are to come after. Many of Mr. Guild's descriptions of scenery and sights are extremely graphic, and his hints to travellers are frequently very practical." — *Evening Bulletin, Phila., Pa.*

"The Most Perfect Pen-Pictures of Sights and Scenes."

"This is certainly a collection of some of the most perfect pen-pictures of sights and scenes in foreign lands we have ever read. The author carries the reader in imagination to the very scenes he himself has witnessed, conveying as vivid an idea of the places seen as could be conveyed to one who has never visited Europe. Many minute particulars are also given, such as foreign letter-writers deem of too little importance to be mentioned, yet which are of great interest to the general reader." — *Sentinel, Eastport, Me.*

"The Most Complete Book of Foreign Travel."

"There is no end to the books on European travel that have from time to time appeared, and they pretty much all go over the same ground, but in following Mr. Guild's narrative, one almost forgets that he ever read of the countries beyond the seas before, for the subject is presented in such a graphic and lively manner that the reader almost fancies that he is actually witnessing the scenes and experiencing the emotions portrayed and expressed by the writer. The volume is so minute in detail that it serves as a guide-book of travel, as well as one of entertainment. Valuable hints and information are given about the best hotels, and the names of shops in London and Paris are mentioned where Americans can find reasonable prices, &c. It is the most complete book of foreign travel that has ever appeared." — *Union, Springfield, Mass.*

"He has given Us a Life-like Picture."

"The habits of observation acquired by the author of this charming book, during many years' constant occupation as a Journalist, have proved so far a second nature to him, that upon whatever 'sight or scene' his facile pen was turned, he has given us a life-like picture. Europe 'is done' in a style that must serve as an invaluable guide to those who intend to go 'over the ocean,' as well as furnish every one with an agreeable book for a half-hour's entertainment." — *Citizen, Halifax, N. S.*

☞ *Sold by all Booksellers and Newsdealers.*

LEE & SHEPARD, PUBLISHERS, BOSTON.

PRACTICAL TALKS.

EVERYBODY WANTS

THE TELEPHONE.

An account of the Phenomena of Electricity, Magnetism, and Sound, as involved in its action; with directions for making a Speaking Telephone. By Prof. A. E. DOLBEAR, of Tufts College. 16mo, illustrated. 75 cents.

"An interesting little book upon this most fascinating subject, which is treated in a very clear and methodical way. First, we have a thorough review of the discoveries in electricity, then of magnetism, then of those in the study of sound — pitch, velocity, timbre, tone, resonance, sympathetic vibrations, &c. From these the telephone is reached, and by them in a measure explained." — *Hartford Courant.*

THE ART OF PROJECTING.

A manual of Experimentation, Physics, Chemistry, and Natural History, with the Porte-Lumiere and Magic Lantern. By Prof. A. E. DOLBEAR. 12mo, cloth, illustrated. Price, $1.50.

"This book supplies a place no former treatise has filled. For several years we have made frequent use of the oxyhydrogen light and porte-lumiere for class-room illustration, but we find here many things we had never thought of before. The book abounds in descriptions of practical and easily tried experiments, any ingenious teacher can easily try with little expense. It is not an addition to the existing number of scientific treatises, but an exceedingly useful help to all, alike valuable for the beginner and college professor." — *National Teachers' Monthly.*

PRIMER OF DESIGN.

By CHARLES A. BARRY, late Supervisor of Drawing, Boston Public Schools. 75 illustrations. Net, 75 cents. By mail, 90 cents.

"The primary aim of this beautifully illustrated primer is to give aid to drawing-teachers. The principles are illustrated in a way to make them intelligible and useful to every one teaching design." — *New-England Journal of Education.*

"Mr. Barry is an artist of eminent ability, excelling especially as a draughtsman; and his experience as a teacher is made available in presenting with force, precision, and clearness, the principles and laws which he undertakes to inculcate. As a text-book it will prove very serviceable, and we should be very glad to see its value recognized in our public schools." — *Epitome of Literature, Philadelphia.*

ELEMENTS OF DESIGN.

For the use of Teachers and Parents. By Dr. WILLIAM RIMMER, Boston Art School (Museum of Fine Arts). 48 full-page illustrations. Cloth. Net, $2.00. By mail, $2.25.

Dr. Rimmer's manual exemplifies a method of teaching drawing founded on the idea that it does not signify merely an imitation of forms, but that it aims mainly to reproduce expression. It is a bold and attractive Drawing-Guide, which, taking the human form as a model, gradually unfolds from the simplest lines to the full anatomical subject, the elements of figure-drawing, in all their variety of limb, feature, muscle, and form, rendering easy of comprehension every intervening step. It is a work invaluable to the student and the artist.

For sale by all booksellers and newsdealers, and sent by mail, postpaid, on receipt of price.

LEE & SHEPARD, Publishers . . . . Boston.
C. T. DILLINGHAM . . . . New York.

www.ingramcontent.com/pod-product-compliance
Lightning Source LLC
LaVergne TN
LVHW021218110826
845150LV00002B/194

* 9 7 8 1 4 2 5 5 6 4 7 4 2 *